Mind *and* Body:
PSYCHOSOMATIC MEDICINE

Mind *and* Body:
PSYCHOSOMATIC
MEDICINE

By Flanders Dunbar, M. D.

[NEW ENLARGED EDITION]

Random House: New York

To the

PATIENTS WHO CONTRIBUTED
TO THIS BOOK

Introduction
to the Revised Edition

OLD QUESTIONS are answered little by little as new discoveries are made, but each new discovery raises more questions than it answers. As a result of the medical research during the last decade we are confronted with a new and imposing fence of interrogation points.

Since this book was first published, knowledge has been acquired which permits more positive statements about the concomitants of emotional and physical disorders. Much has been learned about "ailments" which a few years ago were labeled "cause unknown." Now some of the question marks can be removed by simple declarative sentences.

For most people answers are more important than questions, and therefore this book was revised in order to include some of the discoveries which have turned guesses into answers. The changes made are in the nature of additions rather than deletions or alterations. The advances achieved by physicians and scientists who study the psychological and physical aspects of health and sickness have strengthened and expanded, not altered, the earlier conclusions.

In fact, the whole history of psychosomatic medicine is simply the correction of a mistake to which leaders like Socrates, Hippocrates and Plato called attention centuries before our present system of counting centuries began. They said in effect: The greatest error in the treatment of sickness is that there are physicians for the body and physicians for the soul, and yet body and soul are one and indivisible.

From century to century ancient hypotheses have been verified. There is no longer any doubt that emotional and physiological changes are inextricably intertwined. Until recently disease was thought of as one or more defects in the body machinery or chemistry which could be probed, dosed or cut out. But it has been learned that such procedures are relatively ineffective in coping with illness "cause unknown." What is more important, some people react poorly to procedures usually effective for a particular kind of trouble because something in their "makeup" makes them react paradoxically to the treatment recommended.

An attempt has been made to incorporate in this book the essence of the contributions to the science and art of healing which points only too conclusively to the fact that the mind and body must be treated as one. On the basis of such observations as these, more and more attention is being given to the troubled person who has an ailment. Physicians are taking ailments "cause unknown" more seriously because they know that in so doing they stand a better chance of preventing serious illness.

As a result of an increased interest in preventing illness, much has been learned about child-parent relationships. It is possible to say on the basis of evidence and experiment that these play a determining role in any individual's relative susceptibility or immunity to most disorders. Ideas about hereditary disease are changing. Many illnesses once thought to be hereditary occur in patients with no heredity adequate to explain them, and have been proved easily alterable by newer techniques. Hence it seemed advisable to add a section on this subject.

Another subject about which much has been learned in recent years is overweight. One out of every five Americans has to struggle with this problem. A section has been added on this subject and another on problems of the reproduction of the race, which of course concern everyone in one way or another.

Question marks are being removed even about cancer, and one

of the other mysteries—why so many people lose so many teeth so soon. In addition there have been marked changes in surgery based on greater knowledge about the ways in which a patient's emotions may affect the outcome of an operation despite his surgeon's skill.

Another field in which research has provided new answers is that of chronic illness, and such all too frequent diseases as gastric ulcer, high blood pressure and arthritis. It is interesting that clues have been obtained about such illnesses, once called iatrogenic, a term which meant "cause unknown." The term iatrogenic has almost disappeared from the literature because we know now where to look. Physicians no longer attempt to diagnose and treat suffering from these illnesses according to the rules they learned in medical school. They are learning that listening to a patient gives as many clues about his real trouble as does a careful physical examination and gradually patients are learning to talk with their physicians.

These are some of the changes in medical thinking and in physician-patient relationships which led to the publication of the revised edition of *Mind and Body*. As physicians and patients become partners in the conquest of disease, each will find himself in a better position to prevent disease among the potential patients in his community.

F. D.

New York
September, 1954

Foreword

THIS IS a book about how people become patients. It is also a book about how they may get over being patients—and even how they can keep from becoming patients again or at all. A wise man once said that if Ponce de Leon had stopped running around the world in search of youth he might have found it in himself. That is the place to look for health, too.

Illness does not transform a human being into something less. The patient does not become a cardiac or a fracture, an ulcer or a psychopath. He remains as much a person as his healthy brother —more so, if anything. The Romans, masters at juggling words into immortal combinations, bequeathed to us an ideal of vigor and good living in the proverb, "a sound mind in a sound body."

Psychosomatic medicine is a projection of this truism into actual practice. It derives its name from "psyche," which has been translated as mind or spirit or soul, but which actually includes all of them, and "soma," which means body. Hardly anyone needs to be told that in this world mind and body are inseparable. But we do not always act as if we knew that, whether we are patients or physicians.

It is obvious that when a man is well, he is well in mind and body. When he is sick, he is more than likely to be sick in mind and body, too. The physician experienced in the psychosomatic approach, therefore, sets out to treat patients as complete human beings.

"Psychosomatic" is a relatively new term to professionals and a very new one to most laymen. But its novelty lies not so much in principle as in methods, techniques, tools which enable the thoroughly trained and experienced physician to apply, with some scientific exactitude, treatments which used to be arrived at by guesswork or accident.

The belief that the patient should be treated as a whole goes back beyond anything most of us would consider as medicine at all. The witch doctor of our primitive ancestors was both physician and priest. He worked on the patient's psychic trouble as on his bodily symptoms, for he never knew there was any real difference between them. In fact, the witch doctor's cures were probably due as much to his treatment of the emotions as to his herbs or bloodletting.

As the functions of priest and doctor became separated, the physician had to overcome a great deal of religious opposition in order to establish his dominion over bodily ailments. Vestiges of such opposition to vaccination and surgery still remain. Concerned with establishing his right to treat patients as his slowly developing science dictated, the physician was content to leave psychic phenomena, which he frankly did not understand, to those who claimed the spirit and the soul as their field.

Less than a hundred years ago, the notion that religion and science were incompatible was widely held. In fact, the subject was a favorite topic of academic debate until very recently. Meantime, about the middle of the nineteenth century, a French physician with imagination, Claude Bernard, began to speak of the mind's share in ailments which manifested themselves in the body. He has been acclaimed as one of the first of his profession to understand something of this fact and to make use of his knowledge in treatment.

Since his day, the advance of medicine in this field has been just as significant as the advances in diagnosis, drugs or surgery. At the same time, our knowledge has far outstripped our ability to train people to apply it. In this country there are only 4,500 qualified psychiatrists, 2,000 certified in their specialty. Recent medical and industrial studies, including army records, indicate that about 80% of our population needs their services, so one psychiatrist would have to take care of about 30,000 people. Since this is impossible, is it any wonder that we have 25,000 *full-time* "psychoquacks" (as Norman and Amelia Lobsenz report in *This Week* for Oct. 19, 1947) trying to fill in and often doing more harm than good.

If this is the situation among medical specialists, it would be surprising if laymen were very clear in their own minds as to the nature and possibilities of psychosomatic research and the techniques which can result. Yet a sound understanding of the subject by the patient means almost as much in successful treatment as proper qualifications in the physician.

This book seeks to contribute to that understanding. It will not tell you how to treat yourself, your family or your friends. It is not an attempt to make a psychiatrist out of every reader. In fact, it will probably leave you with the idea that the practice of psychosomatic techniques and the application of psychosomatic research to the problems of your family and friends require as much skill and training as any other medical specialty. If it does leave you with that idea, it will have achieved much of its purpose.

Finally, I should like to express my gratitude to those patients who, in becoming well, have been willing to share their experience with others. Some stories here recorded are correct, with the consent and cooperation of the person who told the story. Others are disguised because it happens often that several patients consult a physician telling almost the same story at the same time, so that a merging of their stories does not interfere with the presentation of the fundamental principles involved. If you happen to have a friend whose experiences were similar to those described here, do not assume that the story is his or hers. It probably is not. Or, if it is, it is so probably only in part.

Readers should avoid the error made by many first year medical students, that is the idea that if they have some symptoms such as those here recorded, they will probably have all of them. Everyone living has some of the symptoms and personality traits described.

F. D.

Contents

We are not ourselves
When nature, being oppress'd, commands the mind
To suffer with the body.

SHAKESPEARE, *King Lear*, Act II, Scene 4

Mind *and* Body:
PSYCHOSOMATIC MEDICINE

[CHAPTER I]

The Child You Were

§ 1

MEMORIES of childhood crop out at the oddest moments. At least they seem the oddest moments when they occur, although on analysis the chain of cause and effect may be quite obvious. These flashbacks to the past often appear to be singularly impressive, and so they should, for they and the memories which are buried beyond wilful recall have left traces which are the foundations of health and of illness. "What put *that* into my mind?" we often wonder as the long-forgotten incident forces itself into consciousness. Sometimes the reason is part of an illness.

Patience and skill will often dredge to the surface some of the buried memories, and in the treatment of disease through psychosomatic techniques, the dredging process is invaluable. This has been recognized ever since Freud noted that the neurotic suffers from reminiscences. Such suffering is a part of many a disease, and a real understanding of the reminiscence is essential to treatment, no matter how far back it must be traced.

The creation of a sound mind begins at the same time as the creation of a sound body. Of course there are hereditary factors which go back perhaps as far as mankind, but these are a little outside our scope. Almost from the moment of conception, and in a way even before that, the factors in which psychosomatic medicine has a special interest are present.

As yet no one knows very much about the effect upon the child of the mother's mental and emotional experiences during pregnancy. There used to be an imposing volume of legend which attributed to these experiences all sorts of peculiarities, from fear of mice to musical virtuosity. Exaggeration caused a healthy reaction, but we are swinging back now to a realization that there is such a thing as prenatal influence and we must set ourselves the task of finding out what it is.

Enough is known now to prove that both physical and mental characteristics depend to some degree upon experiences in the prenatal period. For instance, the embryo is sensitive to sound. Loud, unexpected noises cause the unborn heart to beat faster, and it is even possible to set up a conditioned reflex based on a particular kind of racket. Repeated disturbances of this kind use up energy which might go into building body and nerve tissue.

There is also good reason to believe that if the mother is subjected to severe emotional strain during pregnancy, it may have an effect upon the unborn child. This may be in part because of a change of nourishment due to chemical reaction; it may be in the transmission of more subtle influences between mother and child.

However, pending a good deal more research in the whole field of human reproduction, we may take it that birth is where a beginning should be made in building a sound mind and sound body. We may assume that the basic material has emerged from the vicissitudes of heredity and pregnancy.

The human infant is a singularly helpless creature. In our civilization, he is confronted from birth with problems which neither his parents nor anyone else has been able to solve satisfactorily.

First of all comes adjustment to the strange universe around him. Because adults find it a very restricted universe, parents easily fall into the error of thinking it must seem the same to a baby whose reactions are, to say the least, primitive. Yet from the child's earliest moments he has a depth and degree of sensitivity which should not be overlooked merely because powers of lucid expression are not developed.

A sound body does not carry with it the assurance of a sound "psyche." Just as neglect of the child's physical needs can damage his body and his mind, so neglect of his psychic needs can have equally serious consequences, although the result may be somewhat longer in manifesting itself.

Furthermore, the psychic needs are less readily apparent. The importance of food, warmth, cleanliness and so on is easily understood by most parents. Not so widely appreciated is the value of affection, placidity, understanding and an emotional atmosphere of harmony and confidence. Particularly unfortunate is the infant who was conceived in the common but sadly mistaken parental belief that the patter of little feet and the cooing of a childish voice will resolve a maladjustment where the intelligence and good will of a pair of adults have failed. The baby, not yet articulate enough to take part in a family quarrel or even understand a single word of it, may become the principal victim.

§ 2

Emotional Contagion

THERE is such a thing as emotional contagion. The youngest infant can be infected with fear or anger or disgust or horror even more easily than with the measles. Any discerning parent can see the symptoms. They appear in little, homely ways long before they develop into major tragedies. By the same token the child can "catch" love and trust and respect.

Emotional contagion is usually brought about as simply as it was in the case of a four-month-old girl who suddenly was reported unable to tolerate liver soup after eating it with obvious enjoyment for a month. Before this developed into a settled habit which would probably have been attributed to some hereditary or constitutional peculiarity, the real reason was discovered.

The baby's mother, at work during the day, had asked her aunt to give the child her noon feeding once a week. Returning early soon after hearing of her daughter's new aversion to liver, she saw the child making faces and spitting out the soup while her great-aunt, in the manner of baby-feeders from time immemorial, murmured soothingly but helplessly:

"Now, Mary, just one more spoonful of that nice liver."

It was all very commonplace, but the mother thought her relative's expression was one of disgust, not so much with the baby's behavior as with the baby's food.

"Won't you stay and have lunch here?" she urged the aunt. "We're having liver and bacon."

The visitor refused with some vehemence.

"I think it's disgusting to eat the insides of animals," she explained.

Her sentiments had been transferred, simply by emotional contagion, to the baby, whose fondness for liver soup was quickly restored by the simple expedient of ordering something else for her on the days when she was fed by her great-aunt. But soon that lady reported that egg yolk, hitherto another favorite dish, seemed to disagree with Mary.

"Don't you like eggs?" inquired the mother, made wise by the liver incident.

"Yes, of course. But not all dried up, the way you feed them to that poor baby," was the reply.

The solution in this case was to let the great-aunt prepare the egg yolks her way, with milk and butter. Mary ate them happily, and was equally satisfied when her father or mother offered yolks in the old dry and (to the great-aunt) unappetizing manner.

Now emotional contagion confined to a distaste for liver or egg yolks would not be a very great danger, except for the possibility of setting up an allergic pattern. But contagion does not limit itself so conveniently. Just as an infant is sensitive to his elders' likes and dislikes in food, even when concealed, so he reacts to like or dislike of himself. No amount of dramatic acting can prevent the unwanted child from getting a pretty good idea of his real place in the family affections. Sometimes the acting is good enough to deceive the parents themselves or their physician, but the contagion spreads to the infant just the same. It may emerge years later in the form of loneliness or a crushed spirit or rebellion, or it may be repressed and covered over with other experiences, but it will remain a menace to health and happiness.

It soon ceases to be surprising to the psychiatrist how frequently his patients turn out to have been children who were consciously or unconsciously rejected by their parents. Nor is this confined to mental patients. The pattern of a good many bodily ailments contains the thread of the unwanted child.

§ 3

The Mind's Revenge

A SECOND danger to the development of a sound mind in a sound body is exposure to intense adult emotions. A child's temper is his own, and of itself will not be harmful to him, however much it may upset the rest of the family. But an outburst of rage in older persons, especially parents and particularly during the first year of life, is a shock which may not be apparent to anyone at the time, yet may well be the seed of a psychic maladjustment which will grow with the child.

This will be especially true if the adult expression of wrath is the child's first experience of anger other than his own. It need not be directed at him; indeed, he probably will not be able to tell in his earliest months whether he is the object or not.

Of course no one can go through life without meeting temper—usually sooner rather than later—but it is far less of a shock to a child if he is introduced to it by a playmate of his own age. The rage of our equals is always easier to support than the fury of a more powerful being. After experiencing the blast of contemporary anger, it will be easier for the child to bear the notion that his parents do not always maintain an Olympian calm. Even the inhabitants of Olympus abandoned it on occasion without losing all of their godlike character.

As with anger, so it is with other emotions. Expressions of excessive fear, of irritability, of exaggerated sensitivity leave their imprint upon the child who is exposed to them. They easily create feelings of insecurity, uncertainty and fear. The resulting unhappiness is usually plain to any observer; the actual end product by way of disease may be much longer delayed and not so obviously related, but the chain leading from emotional shock to bodily ailment will be there, although some of the links may be concealed.

One of the most miserable mortals I ever met was the product of just such an upbringing. Agnes, when I first saw her, was an unattractive spinster of fifty who had been in and out of hospitals for a couple of years because of a heart disease which baffled the attending physicians sufficiently to cause them to write on her chart "cause unknown." Her harsh, bitter manner had led them to the conclusion that she was "unco-operative," and it was plain that she had carried that attitude almost incessantly through her whole life.

From a strictly physiological viewpoint, there seemed no reason why she should be so sick. But emotionally she had never been well. Her parents were stern New Englanders whose traditional saving graces and qualities were eclipsed by some of the unpleasant mannerisms of the breed. Agnes's mother had never wanted a child, and made no effort to conceal the fact from her daughter. She displayed little more affection for her husband, and their frequent quarrels were punctuated by hysterical outbursts, during which the wife turned blue with rage (holding her breath like a baby in a tantrum) and sometimes ended up by fainting.

"The first thing I ever heard my mother say," Agnes recalled, "was when I was wheeled in a baby carriage into the room where she was fighting with my father. She screamed: 'Take that brat away. I hate it! I hate it!'"

Obviously Agnes never recovered from the shock of that moment. One good reason was that she was never exposed to a more soothing environment. The memory of maternal hate was kept green by repeated evidences of it. After more than forty years, the burning resentment against her mother was as fresh and much more vociferously proclaimed than any child could have expressed it.

"I can't tell you how I resent having been born," she said to me on more than one occasion. She wished she could die on the anniversary of the day she was born, and she added that she was always sick in the Fall around the date of her mother's birthday because it made her think of her own birth. "She might have spared me that," said Agnes, overlooking the fact that her mother certainly had not done it on purpose.

Although her family were Protestants, Agnes was sent to a convent school where "the Sisters were strict and stupid, and often beat me," so that there was no chance for emotional recuperation. "Mother wanted to get rid of me," was Agnes's own explanation.

Finally her father left home because of the constant scenes with his wife. Agnes had hoped to go with him to keep house for him, but he had another woman. The daughter's natural bitterness against her parents was shown in two rather striking ways. The first time she was admitted to the hospital, while giving her family history, she invented deaths for both of them, although both were still alive. And she dreamed of seeing her mother in hell's fiery furnace while she herself shoveled in the coal.

Agnes grew up, as one might expect, a bony woman with sharp features and a sharper tongue. A nervous breakdown just as she was finishing college deprived her of her degree, and after four years in an art school she began drifting from one job to another—selling, teaching, mechanical drawing, designing—quarreling with her employers, no matter what the work. She lived in a cheap boarding house, wore black invariably because she said she had nothing to be happy about, and railed against the world and her parents because she felt someone somewhere owed her a great deal in life.

By the time Agnes was sent to the psychiatric clinic because she was "unco-operative," the organic damage to her heart had progressed so far, even though the cause was called "unknown," that there was little to be done for her. She could not have survived the strain which would have been imposed upon her by any real attempt to help her get at the bottom of her emotional maladjustment and understand it. The cardiac condition was too far advanced for that. Her last stay in the hospital was a protracted one and just when she was giving the physicians hope by improving markedly for a couple of days, she took an inexplicable turn for the worse and died suddenly. It was her birthday, and she had always wanted to show her resentment at being born by dying on that day.

Agnes's history, exposed in all its emotional tragedy, sounds a little abnormal, but it is not very unusual in its essential details. Thousands repeat the commonplace story—quarreling parents who did not want a child even after it was born, early exposure to violent quarrels, a childhood spent with irritable, unpredictable, fearful people, a growing sense of insecurity and defeat. The wasted, unhappy life which is bound to follow—unless the individual's psychic make-up can be altered by timely treatment—can only end with the outraged emotional system taking its revenge upon the body in the form of a disease which physicians will be able to recognize but not cure.

§ 4

Stimulants in Moderation

AT THE other extreme apparently—but only apparently—is the baby who is so thoroughly protected from every possible shock that he never learns anything by experience. Over-protection is one of the commonest forms of what some parents think is mother love. Whether they realize it or not, this too-ardent attention is more likely to be a disguise for the real feeling that the child was unwelcome.

An infant needs to be alone just as much as he needs affection; he needs to find out about the world for himself as much as he needs to be reassured by a parent when he is frightened.

The Child You Were

It is impossible for children to be constantly in the presence of adults without getting more stimulation than is good for them. Their emotional systems are not sufficiently complex as yet to absorb constant grown-up companionship. Babies do not need to be amused all the time. They are as likely as drama critics to become bored by over-exposure to entertainment. And, like drama critics, only the rarest and luckiest individuals will be able to retain any sense of discrimination, any balance, after a surfeit of attention.

Too much training is as bad as too much entertainment. Behavior patterns easily become fixed, and there can be much future illness lurking in the complexities of these patterns. The similarity between humanity and sheep has often stirred the wrath or scorn of philosophers, but it has been of some value to scientists. Dr. H. S. Liddell, for example, raised a small flock of neurotic sheep whose experience should be a lesson to every parent, teacher and children's nurse.

Dr. Liddell's sheep were made comfortable in a barnyard laboratory where the only distracting feature was a metronome. Fifty strokes to the minute was the usual speed, but when the animals were fed, it was stepped up to 120, so that they soon opened their feed box whenever they heard the faster beat. So far that resembles a great many experiments on conditioned reflexes. But Dr. Liddell went a step further. The usual rate of the metronome was increased to 80 and then to 100 a minute. The poor sheep were unable to distinguish between that and 120 and therefore could never tell when it was time to eat. They fell rapidly into what in human beings would probably be described as a pitiable state of nerves. Actually their hearts beat faster and irregularly; other bodily functions became upset. Before long the sheep could not even discriminate between the 50 and the 120 rate of the metronome. By this time little barnyard disturbances, previously unnoticed, bothered them a great deal. They bickered with their fellows, or sulked alone and refused to eat. They could not relax at night, even when they were lying down.

Dr. Liddell put them out to grass with other sheep and gradually they recovered. It took a year or more, and even then the recovery was contingent upon continued peace. If they were brought back to the laboratory, the beat of the metronome set them to trembling. They suffered palpitations, and old worries obviously crowded back upon them. Some of the sheep did not even have to hear the metronome; the laboratory with its year-old associations was enough to rouse the symptoms of collapse.

Any notion that babies are tougher than sheep should be dispelled at once. Infants can be easily over-trained, especially if the training takes the familiar form of attempting to mold the child into the kind of a person the parents think they would have liked to become themselves.

A more than usually horrible example, perhaps, was the college professor's son whose father made of him a prodigy rather famous in his day. The boy took the equivalent of a college education by the time he was eleven and at thirteen had done all the work necessary for a doctorate. His teachers and newspaper-feature writers predicted a brilliant future for him. Where, they asked rhetorically, would he be at forty? Well, at forty he died—an obscure, unhappy clerk in Wall Street, working at the same job he had taken when he was seventeen. Once in the interval he had been interviewed, and had expressed only the most bitter animosity toward his parents. They had forced him as a child to conform to their notions of an outstanding success. The only revenge he could devise was to spend the rest of his life achieving what they would regard as hopeless failure.

So far little has been said of the place of sex in a child's life. The reason is that sex, as grown people understand it, does not have a very large place. Frequently, of course, it is exaggerated beyond its real importance through the taboos, fears and prejudices of the adults who surround the child. Almost from birth, infants express sexual tension, but that need not be a cause for alarm. After all, normal people invariably belong to one sex or the other. It should not be surprising, therefore, that normal babies are the same.

[12]

The Child You Were

§ 5

Unexposed Film

IT IS not easy for parents to understand that rather delicate but by no means mechanically efficient being which is a new-born infant. Often the phenomenon becomes no more comprehensible with the passage of time. Furthermore, the situation is or can be complicated somewhat by the fact that, while the human infant is among the most helpless of animal young, the human mother in what we call civilization is in many ways more poorly equipped for her job than are other mammals. This combination of circumstances makes rearing a child far more of an experience, both pleasant and otherwise, than lower animals enjoy.

The new baby has a mind far more susceptible to outside impressions than one might suppose from his inability to speak, to focus very well on tangible objects, to move with a very high degree of co-ordination or to understand the strange things that are going on around him. At a slightly later stage of development, the childish mind is by no means as capable of reason and even of ordinary reception (from an adult point of view) as the fond parents suppose from their offspring's hypothetical resemblance to one of themselves, his ability to smile or his prompt, unmistakable reactions to certain basic stimuli such as hunger or pain.

In the beginning, it is probably a safe rule for the parent to behave as though the infant were as sensitive as an unexposed photographic plate—and just about as capable of discrimination. Aside from the rather obvious needs of food, cleanliness and sleep, the principal requirements for the start of a sound mind are feelings of security, harmony and affection.

As the child grows older, old enough to talk, he reaches the first stage of his existence which distinguishes the human from other animals. He begins to be able to incorporate the experience of others into his own body of knowledge, a feat which apparently (except perhaps in a few elementary ways) is beyond the powers of brutes. But it is not an easy process at first, and unless parents and teachers co-operate on the child's own terms rather than theirs, it can be made difficult indeed.

The mind of the child at this stage has its own peculiar set of realities. It is not by any means a miniature or an oversimplification of an adult mind. It is a different kind of mind.

Last night's dream or bedtime story may be as real as the furniture in the bedroom and far more real than last week's visiting relatives. Furthermore the dream and the furniture have the same kind of reality for the child, and it is only gradually that he will come to distinguish between them. This confusion—which is confusing only to the adult, never to the child—may be carried to the point where the young dreamer identifies himself with the figures of his dreams or just with figments of his imagination. His fantasies should not be mistaken for evidence of a false nature nor as evidence of creative genius. They are simply evidence that he is still a child.

Much of the mystery of childhood is simply lack of experience and information, which will be corrected with time. The child who believes he may melt like a lump of ice does not, because of that belief, have a different mental process from his elders. Only information about the nature of ice and about himself, coupled with prolonged experience of not melting, have given the adult his own genuine assurance that he is not going to suffer the fate of ice in the sun.

One big difference between the child's mind and that of his elders is the way in which both react to the unknown. In our society, the area of the child's unknown is far greater, but fortunately does not normally prove so disturbing. The childish mind is saved by the fact that it does not become baffled merely because it does not understand. The mind accepts the unusual without questioning it as an adult would, and therefore the child refers to the subjects of his dreams in the same matter-of-fact way as he refers to real people. After all, the antics of dream characters or heroes of fairy tales are no more wonderful than the rush of water from a tap, fire from a match, voices from a box on the table.

Any adult confronted for the first time by modern plumbing or the radio—Rousseau's natural man, for example—would find them as magical as anything in Grimm or Hans Christian Andersen. The difference between child and savage is that the child's mind will accept magic and reality as equally natural, while the adult mind (savage or civilized) will deny that anything incomprehensible can possibly be natural.

The child does, however, resemble the savage in many of his fears (but not for the same reasons) and will even add a few of his own. They will go beyond the common, usually accepted terrors of thunder or dark or pain or discomfort. Often these fears are the result of training or experience, and need not happen. But children also manage to identify themselves with all sorts of objects, harmless in themselves but which can become distorted in the childish mind into quite convincing perils. Werner Wolff illustrates this in *The Personality of the Pre-School Child* when he writes:

"Adults in general cannot imagine all the dangers with which a child reckons. For instance, if a match is burning and becomes smaller and smaller, the child may believe that the match feels this painfully and that a corresponding thing might happen to himself. In the child's imagination, a twisted string feels that it is twisted, and a nail in the wall that it cannot move."

The child's mind sometimes puzzles and even infuriates adults through the quality that prompts perpetual, frequently unanswerable questions. "But why?" is the beginning from which all except the most saintly or most understanding parents and teachers quail. "Why do birds fly; why is night dark; why don't cats bark; why is up?" may be annoying interruptions to adult occupations, but the mind that prompts these questions should be cherished, for it is going after the information, the synthetic experience which will enable it to cope with the world.

This stage follows and is related to an earlier inquisitiveness before the child can talk. Then he reaches out to touch objects, puts them in his mouth, for, as Wolff says:

"This child's world is not mapped; the whole world around him is unknown; all seems to be possible because the child has not be-

gun to make his explorations. It is quite natural that the exploration of the world begins with the exploration of the nearest surroundings, and the nearest is, for the child, his own body. It seems
not to be necessary to follow psychoanalysis, which explains the
child's interest in his own bodily functions with the assumption
of early sexual trends."

Now exploration has always been a dangerous business. The
intrepid adventurer sailing into unknown worlds has been ship-
wrecked quite as frequently as he has returned with new knowledge of the nature of the world. Every child embarks constantly
on adventures as bold as that of Columbus or Balboa, and the
principal shoals on which he is likely to founder are adult mis-
understanding, carelessness and ignorance of the nature of the
youthful explorer's mind.

§ 6

The Parents' World

YOUNG PARENTS may have some exploring to do, too. If they
have struggled through adolescence to find a world of their own,
they may be surprised and perhaps rudely shocked to discover
that they have acquired along with the right and privilege of
voting the responsibility for supporting themselves. Absorbed in
adventures of discovery of a new world and of each other, they
may have little time to remember what the universe looked like
to them when they were as small as their young children. During
the time such parents are absorbed in their own exploration, the
little one feels lost and lonely and, if it takes them too long to
be able to take him into their world, he may feel lost and lonely
almost forever.

The child's mind is full of "quirks and fantasies." He has only
the vaguest idea of what is real. If his parents don't listen and
help, he will invent myths to explain the sun and the moon and
animals and people—good myths too, like old legends—but the
parents, who are busy being practical, are only too likely to
laugh them off or accuse the child of lying, depending on their

attitude to the child at the moment. Later when the child says, "My parents wouldn't listen, they rejected me and my ideas," no one could be more surprised than the busy parents who thought they were doing "everything a parent could do." They remember the weary hours when their plans had been interfered with because they had to take care of the baby. They remember their disappointment when the child failed to get their point. Few parents expect the child's muscles to be developed like Father's, but they sometimes act as if they supposed his mind reacted in the same way as Father's.

Even worse, with their idealistic and somewhat tired enthusiasm, they begin to think that the child they have produced will make up to his four grandparents for all the defects of their own offspring. This illusion can be encouraged by a tendency of grandparents to regard a brand-new grandchild as just about "perfect." They often say, "You're much prettier than your mother was and your father never had muscles like that when he was four years old." Most grandparents don't realize that these half humorous compliments are confusing to the youngster who is trying his best to respect his father and mother and is learning his life depends on them.

Parents and grandparents too often think of their children as "beings" who can be moulded into anything they want. Unfortunately they are half right in their conviction. Little ones can be moulded, but when too much moulded they never grow into their own stature. Parents who can blame the child's defects on someone else may accept the inevitable a little more easily. The "moulding" usually leads to disappointment, it is safe to say.

So children are "disappointing," and parents, grandparents and the community have to try to redeem "the little monster." You look into its religious training, you look into its forebears and its genealogy, and you find someone somewhere to tell it how to be a nice boy or girl. But the little monster gets to be a bigger monster. It would take so much less time to remember it is a child, not a "monster," and to listen to the boy or girl who wants to talk to you.

Any adult who has never called a child a little monster or a little nuisance or a little devil is an exception—or just never had much to do with children. The adult may forget such outbursts, but the child at whom the name-calling is directed is likely to remember for a *long* time. The memory may well cause him trouble, sometimes serious trouble, when he tries to find out what he is supposed to be, and a very bad time in getting a sense of himself as a person. When parents adjust themselves to bringing up the child they have, instead of the child they thought they wanted, parents and child are healthier. When, like Pygmalion, they try to make something beautiful that would satisfy the ancestors and attract the admiration of the community, they find when they try to love it that it is just marble.

Parents who have moulded or carved their children after this pattern always want help and pity. Sometimes they ask advice from a psychiatrist and get their feelings hurt when the doctor says, "I could have helped you had you come sooner, but all I can do now is send your child to a mental hospital."

Many children for whom no such happy adjustment was made end up in a doctor's office complaining of skin troubles or colitis or both. The fact that these ailments go together was recognized long before much was known about the emotional factor in either. Doctors noticed that if they "cured" a patient's skin disease, he often developed colitis, and the other way round. People have skins—outside skins and inside skins. Emotional tension creates disturbances in both skins, sometimes simultaneously, sometimes in alternation. The outer skin, which separates every individual from his surroundings, and at the same time represents almost his first communication with his mother, reacts very much like that inner skin in which each vital organ is wrapped, which represented an earlier communication with his mother. It is usually possible to get rid of disturbances in both skins by helping the little one or the sick one—and the sick one always feels little—to understand what hurt him and how, now that he is older, he can keep from being hurt again.

This was the case with Hugo, a shy and lonely young man

with the sort of woebegone countenance which some people
find an invitation to kick and others to kiss. He had gone through
an attack of colitis only to have his chest and arms break out
into a rash when he thought he was cured. Hardly had the rash
been conquered than the colitis returned. He was then encouraged to talk about his youth in an effort to bring to light
the emotional basis for his disturbance.

"I was an awful child," he remembered.

"What does that mean exactly?" the doctor asked.

"My parents just couldn't get along with me," he explained,
and then after a pause, "I was so bad they had to go to a
psychiatrist."

"What did you do that was so awful?"

Hugo mentioned nothing specific but rambled off at a revealing tangent.

"Well, they just couldn't understand me, and had to get somebody to explain me to them. I guess I'm just no good."

"Could you understand them?"

"No, and that's why I felt so guilty. I never wanted to be with
other kids, and my parents kept after me for getting off in a
corner by myself all the time."

This last habit had persisted as Hugo spent his time trying to
avoid reminders that made him feel guilty, although it was not
until he had spent several long sessions with the doctor exploring his own mind that he grasped the fact. The realization was
the first step in getting rid of both rash and colitis.

During the last five years it has become more and more clear
that many other diseases—heart ailments, diabetes, asthma,
hay fever and so on—may be traced to the relationship between
children and parents. Any disease may seem to be hereditary
because the father or mother suffered from it too. Probably no
more than one in a thousand illnesses is really inherited. Others
seem to be because the child unconsciously imitates the symptoms which impress him. It is the family illness pattern which is
catching rather than the illness, and it is catching often enough
to give rise to the term "pseudo-heredity."

People who are "sticklers," or who like to ascribe everything to heredity, are often puzzled by the fact that the children of the same parents, "brought up in exactly the same way," seem often as different "as day from night." But it is even more puzzling to discover that adopted children sooner or later adopt the diseases and often even the appearance and expressions of one or the other side of the adopting family. It is still more puzzling to find two boys, one brought up in Grosse Point, the other in Greenwich, both only sons, born between two girls, appear and behave more like brothers than do two brothers in a given family.

One year three men consulted me, all aged thirty, plus or minus three years, born and reared in different parts of the country but really difficult to tell apart. All were tall and attractive, of about the same weight, all drank too much, all were excessively promiscuous, all were excellent linguists. Yet all had difficulty in communication. They did better business in foreign countries and in foreign languages. They found it impossible to make love to anyone who could speak their native tongue. Each one said he couldn't pour out his soul in English to anyone. Each one asked to reveal himself in French or German or Spanish. As it turned out, all had had poor communication with their families, which included an older and a younger sister and all had escaped from the family as soon as possible. All had won fellowships for foreign studies in their junior year at college; all had married and divorced a foreign wife. They differed only in that they had gone to different universities, and one had married a Russian, the other a Frenchwoman, and the third a Spanish South American. Even a complete outsider seeing them together would have had the impression they were brothers according to the popular conception of what it means to be brothers. They could even have been considered triplets. They had the same mannerisms, the same neurotic patterns of behavior—compulsive character traits—"A desire to write," each said, "because Father is a businessman and I want to get as far away as possible from businessmen." They came from different stocks. They all made fun of their ancestry. They were tired of hearing about the *Mayflower* and the "flowers of the Confederacy." One had a Scottish background before his early arrival in this country and was brought up a Presbyterian. Another was of Belgian ancestry and had been reared a Lutheran. The third, who was of Spanish stock, had been raised as a Catholic. Each had given up his religion along with his family and ancestors. In addition to personality difficulties, all three had physiological complaints. Two had been treated unsuccessfully for hypertensive cardiovascular disease; the third had been treated, also unsuccessfully, for neurocirculatory asthenia—a thoroughly psychologic ailment. The trouble with the third one was that his doctor had said, "A great big strong man like you! Snap out of it!"

It appears that the attitudes of parents rather than the genes make for similarities and dissimilarities.

Most parents change so much from year to year that they really are not the same people at all in relation to a second child that they were to their first. They may be quite unable to treat the newcomer in the same way as they did an older brother or sister, no matter how much they assert: "I love them both equally."

This phenomenon was well illustrated by one good-looking, healthy young mother who was perfectly furious when she found she was pregnant with her second child although she had rejoiced during her first pregnancy. She hadn't wanted another child for several years, she said. It was inconvenient, a nuisance both to her and her husband, she complained. She went so far as to ask her doctor if he could not find some good medical reason for "getting rid of it."

This was the same woman—but not the same mother—who had gone through her first pregnancy with great good humor. She had taken excellent care of herself then, and had displayed great tenderness for the unborn baby in word and gesture. Now she indulged in violent exercise in the hope of dislodging what she kept referring to bitterly as "the thing." Although she probably will insist later on that she cares for both her children equally and may even try to prove it, the chances of her doing so are slim.

There are other reasons why the order of birth may have an important effect on child development. The boy sandwiched between two girls usually has a more unfortunate experience than most. Too often his older sister will try to take over for his mother, while the younger will be a constant source of annoyance to him if he is expected to take care of her. The girl sandwiched between two boys is in quite a different situation. Her older brother will not want to be a father to her at all, and her chief hope for the younger probably will be that he grow up big and handsome and take her dancing and introduce her to his friends. Of course such attitudes are conditioned by the prevailing culture. Cultures differ and create different problems in different places or in the same place at different times.

Many parents find it especially difficult to treat the child according to his age. In pride or folly they demand too much of a baby, child or adolescent. They expose him to too much adult emotion or call upon him for responses beyond his psychological or physiological capacity.

Such expectations lead to too early training, all the way from bathrooms to arithmetic and courtesy. A mother whose arms are trembling, or whose attention is diverted from her child's needs by a quarrel with her husband or the milkman, is not likely to give her children a sense of security. Children who have been dropped, shaken or fed or un-fed, changed or unchanged under these circumstances, are likely to develop a sense of insecurity in trying to cope with the outer earthquakes which result in inner earthquakes. They invent explanations. There are only some kinds of foods they can eat—pretty surely foods they have not been fed by the worried mother. Perhaps they can't eat, perhaps they have to stuff themselves with the forbidden. The bathroom acquires an esoteric dirtiness, and too often no one can be trusted unless perhaps an animal or someone from Afghanistan or South Africa who couldn't possibly talk to the parents.

The Child You Were

Babies cannot stop or start anything as rapidly as five-year-olds or twenty-five-year-olds. They cannot control their bodies and their tempers as readily as they will in a few years. Their sensitivity to a quarrel is intensified by their very helplessness. They may understand an angry "Stop it!" but cannot for the life of them obey instantly. They just are not equipped for that kind of control.

Parents who learn to give the child a chance to respond save themselves many a headache. They may find it easier to understand the infant's emotional inertia if they watch the physical law of inertia operating next time they are in an elevator. The car does not stop instantly at the pressure of a button, so elevator operators learn to push the button a little before they expect the elevator to stop at the desired floor. Anyone who has trained a dog has made the same observation. If you tell a barking puppy to quit, he has to give one more bark. If when you hear the one more bark, you say "Quit it" again, there will be the next one more bark and the next, and pretty soon he will be completely unable to stop his barking, and you will be so angry you'll be likely to do something to him that later you'll wish you hadn't done. But let him have his one bark, or the child his one more minute of play before going to bed and if you keep your mouth shut it usually will be only one more. If it is three more, speak again and wait. This is almost sure to work unless the animal or the child is angry with you for other reasons.

Too great expectations from a child, whose equipment does not allow him to respond even half way, gives the child a feeling of helplessness and rage, which may turn into hate which will leave you feeling helpless, frustrated and almost ready to kill "the little beast."

We see the first sign of the trouble sometimes in a display of genuine hatred directed against the mother by a baby who has not yet begun to talk. Mother is the object because the child knows her well enough. Father at this stage in most families is a more remote being, and it takes constant companionship to arouse the hostility of which babies are capable. This emotion, of course, is unpleasant for the mother to contemplate, but it can be more serious than that for the child. Long after it seems to have been forgotten, the young sufferer may explode into illness like a bursting boiler because he has not developed a safety valve or at least not an adequate safety valve for his pent-up hostility.

The child allowed to take his own pace in venturing into the unknown does not get into these troubles. Those who can best handle the explosions of the atomic age are the ones who were not put in a cast before they learned to walk nor constantly shushed before they learned to talk.

[CHAPTER II]

Delayed-Action Mines of Childhood

§ 1

DISASTER to the exploring childish mind may not come with an immediate crash. It is far more likely to be unnoticed—or at least disregarded—at the time. But the harvest of childhood's experiences may be reaped years later and turn out to be the fundamental or contributing cause of an illness which has no surface connection with the patient's past.

These are the delayed-action mines of childhood, planted either in the shock of some single incident or in the steady friction of a conflict between mind and environment. Once these mines have been planted, they may become covered over with a thick, hard crust of oblivion, but they never cease to be dangerous unless the fuses can be drawn.

One of the advantages of the psychosomatic approach to medicine is that a capable physician can locate these mines before their final, disastrous explosion. His questions and tests are the delicate finders with which he sweeps the ground, groping for the buried danger. His knowledge of human behavior is the instrument which tells him when he has struck the right spot. His professional skill determines whether he can draw the fuse without damage. As in any other medical case, the wrong treatment can frequently be worse than no treatment at all, setting off the very explosions which the physician has sought to avert.

The procedure, or course of treatment, has to be all the more delicate, since in the present state of our medical practice there usually has to be some kind of a blast before anyone—patient or doctor—even begins to think of looking for the cause. Most medical practitioners are far too busy with the sick to devote much attention to the healthy. When preventive medicine really comes into its own, we may find time to examine patients while they still regard themselves as well. Then we may be able to render a great many delayed-action mines harmless even before the first charge has been exploded.

Meanwhile we have learned a great deal about these factors in illness in recent years. We know more than our predecessors about how they relate to the whole patient—both his personality and his bodily ailments.

A colleague of mine recently found that a twenty-one-year-old youth, who was supposed to be convalescing quite well from pneumonia, was having a rather mysterious setback. His discharge from the hospital was delayed by severe headaches and nausea. The physician could not account for these symptoms by anything in the young man's physical condition, and he began delving into the past. This is what he found:

Many years before, when the patient could not have been over five or six years old, his father was in an accident and for fifteen years thereafter had been afflicted with painful headaches and acute attacks of nausea. All through his childhood, the son had been profoundly moved by his parent's anguish. Then at the age of eighteen he had suffered a head injury, but only mild headaches had followed. Now, with time in the hospital hanging heavy and with ample leisure to brood, he was worrying himself into a state of terror that he might be repeating his father's painful history. The symptoms followed hard upon the heels of the fears.

The physician explained to him that his brain was quite undamaged, that the headaches were due to his anxiety. At the same time he was urged to take his mind off his fears by reading and trying to learn some new skill requiring manual dexterity. In a week both headaches and nausea left him. The holdover from childhood had been routed.

§ 2

History vs. Heredity

ONE OF the common experiences of the physician who diagnoses mental along with bodily symptoms is that his patients have developed their particular physical troubles after exposure to certain diseases not usually regarded as "catching." Under sufficiently provocative circumstances, such exposure can actually be more dangerous than a history of the disease in parents or grandparents. If it takes place in childhood, it may become a delayed-action mine with a very slow-burning fuse. The child grows up with the fear and the memory of the disease until in adult life he gives every appearance of thinking himself into acquiring it.

The mechanism is a little more complicated than that because thinking does not go on in a vacuum altogether isolated from the rest of human activity. It is tied directly into emotional and bodily functions too. But it can lose control of the system, and very often does. That is when the dangers of our buried mines become acute, for they are more automatic than thoughtful.

Especially in infancy and early childhood, physical changes are brought about by the workings of the involuntary nervous system. This network, operating independently of any conscious will, transmits the nervous impulses which put into motion the activities of many of the vital organs. Thanks to this system of communication within the body, the heart pumps faster or slower, the pupils of the eyes dilate and contract, the digestive tract secretes more or less of its juices, and so on. These nerves can be stimulated by emotion, and when their owner loses control, they may run wild. In turn, the organs whose operations they govern may be altered through over-stimulation. That is the basis of a gradual change which can blossom finally into full-blown illness.

Such emotions are frequently the result of exposure in childhood to the suffering of a well-loved person or of someone with whom the child identifies himself closely. This sort of emotional contagion is more subtle, less obvious in its reactions than that which prompts a distaste of liver soup, for example. The incubation period may be years long, and may require some later emotional or bodily disturbance to bring it to the point of actually causing illness.

Heart diseases, greatest single cause of death in the United States today, illustrate this point. I once had occasion to make a study of patients admitted to a general hospital over a period of several years. I found that almost half (actually 49%) of those suffering from heart disease had a history of such ailments in their parents, brothers or sisters. But more than 98% of them had been exposed to a serious illness of this kind in someone who was very dear to them, whether relative or not. Half of these cases had seen the loved one die suddenly while the patient of later years was still quite young. The shock of that death was a more important factor in the disease, nurtured as it was through many years within the patient's mind, than any cardiac heredity.

The shock of sudden death, depriving the child of someone who has become an important part of his emotional life, may be unavoidable. But that is far from true of a great many other delayed-action mines. One type is illustrated by the case of a young woman of twenty-nine who was brought to the hospital suffering from diabetes. Her physician seemed to think that she behaved like a spoiled child, and the hospital social worker noted on her chart:

"Patient is of Spanish parentage, and has quite an accent, although she is American born. She particularly dreaded the cold, and as a child was not very strong. For this reason she has been coddled a good part of her life."

At first glance the delayed-action mine in this case would seem to have been the "coddling," which can be quite as dangerous as more traditional forms of mistreatment, especially as this young woman was an only child. But psychiatric contact revealed a somewhat different story.

As far back as she could remember, the girl had been told by her father that her birth had driven her mother crazy. With an unfortunately common parental logic, he conveyed to his offspring that he considered this tragedy her fault rather than his. The explosive charge in the mine was further built up by the fact that the mother, although insane, was cared for in the home until she tried to poison her daughter, then eight years old, and herself. The child, with commendable presence of mind, ran to the nurse; a stomach pump was used on both victims, and they recovered. The father still wanted to keep his wife at home, but when the daughter began having convulsions, the older woman was sent to an institution for mental cases. The daughter, however, continued to have convulsions whenever she was taken to see her mother, until the physician forbade further visits.

To augment the peril of that mine, the guardian who was appointed to take the mother's place treated the girl so unkindly that she ran away from home as soon as she was old enough to get a job, first in a night club, then in an office. She became a sales girl and worked up to become buyer in a hotel gift shop. The effects of a more normal life were rapidly putting layers of oblivion on top of the experiences of childhood, burying the mine deeply in the mind.

When she was twenty-four, the young woman married, but continued to work because her husband did not earn enough to support them both. Apparently she had continued in good health since the age of seventeen, when she had ceased to see her mother.

Then, after twelve years, she decided to visit the institution, probably from a sense of duty, and within a short time she was in the hospital with diabetes. The attitude of the doctor and the nurses, who regarded her as a spoiled child, subjected her to additional emotional strain, and her special delayed-action mine exploded. She developed a tendency to go into shock after insulin treatment.

Significantly enough, a relatively superficial psychiatric treatment, which brought out the reality of her early experiences and completely altered the picture of the temperamental, coddled Spanish girl of the social worker's imagination, had a beneficial

influence on her tendency to go into shock. The damage done by
the exploded mine could be repaired.

§ 3

The Stages of Childhood

NATURALLY not every child is susceptible to the same experiences. Nor will experiences which can be dangerous at one stage
of development do any harm at another. Generally speaking, the
child passes through five stages before reaching complete maturity. These are: (1) the period before he begins to talk, (2) the
years between acquisition of the ability to communicate verbally
and entrance into the first grade at school, (3) school life, (4)
adolescence and (5) the period when the almost mature individual is preoccupied with the first job and marriage problems.

Each of these stages has its own special mental dangers, just as
each has its own set of special bodily diseases. The understanding
of this fact will help parents and teachers to avert some of the
perils.

In the first period, the emotions which are felt more keenly by
the unwanted child than most people realize are typical dangers.
Others even less obvious are the puzzling adventures of the baby
whose first explorations are conducted in the midst of quarreling
or confused parents whose own lives are in a mess.

Richard, a youth of twenty whose trouble was rheumatic heart
disease, had the seed of his illness planted in earliest infancy.
The third child in a family of five, he was exposed from birth to
parents who quarreled bitterly, were frequently ill from digestive
disorders, jaundice, a nervous breakdown. Richard seemed to be
a normal, healthy baby but soon became a feeding problem. He
could retain almost no food, and became so frail that his mother
carried him around on a pillow. This constant care led his mother
to prefer him above her other children, and he enjoyed the ability
to get her on his side in any family fracas. (All the other children
seemed to have copied the quarrelsome tactics of the parents.)
By the time he had developed rheumatic heart disease, Richard

showed clearly the effects of the anxiety which had hardly ever left him.

The first things the child understands or thinks he understands come before him at the second and equally impressionable stage of his development. I remember a Puerto Rican girl who had suffered from rheumatic fever for five years. She, too, was one of five children in a quarreling, strict family. She finally escaped by coming to New York at fourteen with an older sister, but after a few years her mother came to live with her, and she became ill. Then, for fear of losing her job and being unable to support herself, she married. While a good many of her emotional difficulties stemmed from her dislike of the married state—she had always wanted to be a man and play a man's part in the world—the more deeply buried delayed-action mine was revealed when she told of her early childhood and concluded by crying out against her mother:

"She is cross with my child. I can't do anything about it. It makes me crazy. I don't want my daughter to be frightened the way I was when I was a child."

At school age, both mind and body seem a little tougher, but the mines can be laid for future explosion just the same. Johnny, for instance, was a pretty healthy little boy, but his personality was poisoned by a home atmosphere which was more subtly upsetting than outright quarreling would have been. His mother brought him up to look upon the head of the house with contempt, so that at eighteen, when a serious complication of ailments brought him to the hospital, he said:

"Father is a washout and makes Mother and me mad because he keeps putting on airs. She's very nervous and always sore at Father, but I get on pretty well with her."

It was plain that the emotional upsets of the home had twisted the boy's personality so that he had trouble with authority at school and afterward. He developed a tendency to have accidents along with sharp vacillations in his attitude toward work, a career and his friends.

An equally clear case of the delayed-action mine was Harold, who at twenty-two, seemed to be settling down to chronic invalidism, saying:

"All my life I've always been angry with Mother because she lives her children's lives. She stuffs them with food and acts grieved and imposed on if they show any opposition. I used to vomit on purpose to even the score, and now I can't help it."

Molly, an acute cardiac at nineteen, might have been a healthier girl if her adolescence had not been complicated by ignorance and the conflicts which arose in her mind when her mother chose that time to remarry. Molly had been something of a tomboy, fond of swimming and basketball, proud of her ability to fight the strongest boy in her class. Her mother had never told her anything about the facts of adolescence, and menstruation both surprised and angered her. Then in rapid succession her mother remarried, she moved away from her friends, was ordered not to have anything to do with boys, because "Mother says they are no good as friends," and finally her very dearly beloved grandmother died of a heart attack. The disturbance which such a train of events can set up in the adolescent emotional system seemed designed for illness. Molly's arrival at the hospital might have been predicted if anyone with an understanding of the physical effects of such emotions had been attending her. In that case, the illness itself might have been prevented.

Delayed-action mines are nearly always planted long before the last of the dangerous ages of youth, the age of dawning maturity. But new and powerful charges of explosive may easily be added at this time of emotional difficulties in adjustment to jobs and worries over possible marriage. Such a situation obviously contributed to the illness of Betty, a young woman attended in hospital some years ago. At twenty-three she had developed a palpitation of the heart and choking attacks in which she could hardly breathe.

There was no history of any related disease in the family; the girl had been quite healthy with a record showing no more serious illness than colds and digestive upsets. Until she was seventeen she had been reared by her grandmother, although her own parents lived next door. The girl had done very well in high school, graduating at sixteen. She then went to work as a secretary, but took little interest in her work. Certainly she was not a career girl. So far as could be found her only really deep concern was with clothes and her own appearance. She and her better-looking younger sister were keen rivals in dress.

"I am always wondering whether people like me or not," she said. "I think the trouble is my nose. If I could get a doctor to make it shorter, I would be more attractive, like my sister. . . . As soon as I feel someone likes me, I'm walking on air. But I can't be satisfied with just one person."

For seven years Betty had been "going with" a young man, and during the last year had begun to have intercourse with him although she did not like it and was very much afraid of becoming pregnant. She would have preferred just to hold hands. She was determined never to marry because the prospect of pain and childbirth frightened her.

Betty's childhood experiences had obviously planted some of the mines of fear and doubt. But her progress from adolescence to maturity had added to them. She wavered between a desire to attract and a desire to withdraw into solitary contemplation of her own perfection. She felt herself unable to live without love but could not enter into any human relationship that was more than superficial. The pull and haul of such conflicting emotions was bound to have some effect upon the body unless they could be checked. Yet several doctors had told her there was nothing wrong with her. From a strictly physiological point of view that was true. The delayed-action mines of childhood were the cause of her illness.

[CHAPTER III]

The Beloved Symptom

§ 1

"THEY ASKED for it," a disapproving teacher remarked of several pupils who came down with chills and fever after disobeying her injunctions about rubbers, hats and warm mufflers. She sounded a little unfeeling, but she was describing the case of a great many sick people. They have asked for it, and in the hidden recesses of their minds have even made a blueprint of the disease they want. They select symptoms in much the same way that healthy people select clothes, choosing carefully for style, fit and the effect upon others. Yet many do not know they have done it.

The selection is done quite independently of the individual's will. It is the work of emotional conflicts which have continued long enough and sharply enough to have a physical effect. The exact form of the bodily ailment is chosen by an emotional system which is groping for some benefit. It is seeking to save something from its own wreckage.

Tim Healy, that mid-Victorian radical who grew up to be His Excellency Timothy Michael Healy, the first Governor General of the Irish Free State, used to say that Gladstone invented the "diplomatic cold." As a young and somewhat obstreperous Member of Parliament, Mr. Healy noticed that the great Prime

Minister's conspicuously robust health suddenly broke down into these mild indispositions at the most convenient moments. It happened, for instance, when he was scheduled to speak at meetings where a politically embarrassing subject might arise. The address would be cancelled with regret. Mr. Gladstone always seemed to be much better the next day.

Statesmen before and since have found that a slight illness is a far lesser evil than a conference for which they are not prepared. They prefer a cold to the necessity for action when they disapprove of action. A mild laryngitis is a good way to cancel an appointment with an important but inopportune personage.

Jests have been made about the health of statesmen under these circumstances. The surprising thing, however, is not that our leaders should have made the diplomatic almost as well known as the common cold, but that so often they actually do come down with real sniffles and genuine sneezes.

Mr. Gladstone probably would neither recognize nor enjoy the close resemblance (psychosomatically speaking) between his diplomatic cold and the welts I once saw on the body of a young woman whose chief ailment was a clandestine love affair with a man who beat her. But just the same, both were enjoying the doubtful relief which can sometimes come from a "beloved symptom."

The girl, known in the anonymity of hospital records as Case No. S 1, developed the welts shortly after taking aspirin, so it was supposed at first that she had the comparatively rare allergy to that drug. All skin tests, however, were negative; the welts just should not have been there, but they persisted for three weeks. At the end of that time a psychiatric consultation was requested.

During this consultation, the existence of the sadistic lover was revealed. On the same day that the patient had taken aspirin, she had received the man in an apartment to which she had just moved. When, as was his custom after intercourse, her lover began to whip her, she suffered a new humiliation in the thought that the walls of her new home were very thin and far from sound proof. She knew none of the other tenants, but she was greatly distressed by fear of what they would think of her if they overheard.

"He hit me harder than ever before," she explained to the psychiatrist. "I decided I just couldn't put up with it any more. I was sure the people in the house could hear the sounds of the belt. I was awfully upset and told him he could never do this again. He is so funny; he won't stop till he sees welts on my body. He always says he loves to see the welts."

In Miss S 1, being whipped in a room where she might be heard by the new neighbors roused the same fears, the same sort of psychic conflict which disturbed the eminently correct Mr. Gladstone when he was faced with the prospect of an undesired audience. The statesman developed a cold, and didn't have to go to the meeting. The girl developed welts without benefit of the strap, and didn't have to be whipped.

Miss S 1 could no more escape her dilemma by giving up her lover than Mr. Gladstone could escape his by giving up politics.

"I get humiliated by this," she admitted, "and yet he has threatened to leave me unless he can beat me. Besides, I like him and he is so nice in other ways."

Obviously the welts were a welcome symptom, and the girl clung to them with relief, just as the Prime Minister doubtless attributed his cold to the wondrous workings of a divine providence which it was easy for him to believe had a tender concern for the political career of William Ewart Gladstone.

"He hasn't beaten me since because of this awful rash," was the way Miss S 1 put it. "I am all covered with welts anyway. He likes to see them. And I haven't had to give him up."

Perhaps it was unfortunate for the young woman that the welts disappeared as soon as it became clear to her in the course of the psychiatric consultation that they were the result of the inner conflict by which she sought at once to keep her lover and avoid noisy beatings. For, failing either successful treatment of the lover or further work on the extreme passive masochistic personality structure of the girl, she was not much better off than before.

In fact, she might easily have been suffering more. The welts from a strap were as painful as self-induced welts; the humiliation was greater, and soon another ailment would probably take the place of a symptom which was so essential to her peace of mind.

A skin specialist knowing nothing of the history of the case might be satisfied with the perfect cure of the rash. A physician trained in psychosomatic methods would be satisfied with nothing less than the removal of the cause of the symptom. This does not mean necessarily removal of the lover either, but of the personality problem of each of them.

§ 2

Sweet Fruits of Illness

THE PATIENT who cherishes his ailment because it is a means of avoiding an evil which he regards as even greater has one type of "beloved symptom." There is another type, which has to be handled more gently. These are patients who have grown fond of a symptom because it brings them the love and attention which has been denied to them—or at least that is their hope.

I remember in this connection—because he was so much the sort of man who would not be suspected of such tender susceptibilities at first glance—a very tough young fellow who had been successively a carpenter's helper, mechanic, third-rate pugilist and truck driver. He was in the hospital for treatment of a badly knit left arm which he had broken five times in the course of his career. He had been in nine other hospitals in New York and New Jersey, and remarked:

"Maybe it's lucky that this has ended my career as a fighter. I never was as good as I wanted to be. What made it worse was I got my brother started and he turned out better than me."

This young Polish-American obviously had no desire to have his arm heal. He cherished his brittle bone in the first place because he knew that at twenty-eight his best fighting days had passed, but with a "bum wing" he need never admit it. He could always blame the end of his career on the arm. In the second place, he liked the attention he got in the hospital. In his case history appears this sentence:

"After this the patient spent most of his time in one hospital or another and showed little interest in recovering or going to work."

His revelation of the facts of his life did not come as a surprise. He was the second of eighteen children, seventeen of them boys. His father, his mother and his stepmother had been extremely strict without much beneficial effect, for the young man admitted to a long childhood record of lying, stealing and truancy, for which he was punished regularly both at home and at school.

"At nineteen my father licked me for taking a straw ride," the patient recalled. "He said to stay away from girls until I was twenty-five or thirty; that was the time he got married himself. After that I left home because I wouldn't take orders any more. It was the same way in the parochial school. I was always getting licked. I would take my licking and holler and then go out and do it anyway."

Except for the brother he had started on a pugilistic career, the young fellow had kept in touch with none of his numerous family. His opinion of home life was evident in his remark that his father had died "from alcoholism" and that "till I was eighteen I couldn't sit on my behind because I was beaten so much."

Besides getting him a great deal of badly missed attention in various hospitals, the patient's unhealed arm proved useful to him in other ways. His wife (he had ignored his father's advice and example, and married at twenty-one) haled him into court several times on charges of non-support, but he was always able to convince the judge that his pet symptom made it impossible for him to do any better.

Over and over again, we find hospital cases who take comfort from the feeling that illness or accident has entitled them to the ministrations of doctors and nurses. These dispensers of personal attentions take the place, in the minds of those starved for early affection, of the good parents they may never have had.

The pattern is the same for the most diverse people. In the early history of the truck driver with the broken arm were just the sort of emotional complications which under other circumstances started off the greatest literary romance of all time, the Barrett-Browning love affair. There is little outward resemblance between the ex-pugilist and the world's picture of Elizabeth Barrett. But the "inside stories" of the two have interesting similarities.

As the eldest of eleven children fathered by a domestic tyrant and brought rapidly into the world by a frail and harassed mother, the future poetess received little attention except by way of discipline. Her mother died soon after the youngest child was born, leaving all eleven to the far from tender mercies of a martinet who, as a gentleman of means and leisure, had plenty of time to devote to keeping them in line.

His eldest daughter, obviously sensitive and longing for affection, tried hard to adore her father, but got little return for her love. He was, one of his future son-in-law's articulate friends reported, "one of those tyrannical, arbitrary, puritanical rascals who go sleekly about the world canting Calvinism abroad and acting despotism at home." He had indicated his opinion of girls when he ran out of names for his two youngest—both boys. Ignoring the existence of his three daughters, he named his sons Septimus and Octavius. From such a man there was little hope of the kind of love children seek.

When she was fifteen, Elizabeth Barrett injured her spine falling off a pony. She recovered from that successfully, but remained an invalid for more than twenty years. The doctors of the time called it consumption, and in the 1830s this was considered an "interesting" disease for a young woman to acquire, particularly one with literary aspirations. There was pain, but there were compensations. She was spared exposure to most of the paternal rages, and these were frequent and furious. She was spared the competition for family affection among the swarm of brothers and sisters. She got a good deal of thoughtful care for the first time in her life. She had what was a great boon in a family of that size—a room of her own.

So, secure behind the ramparts of her illness, Miss Barrett lay on a sofa and wrote, read, received selected visitors and looked forward to death. The little comforts and attentions, after all, were hardly a substitute for a father's love and the gentleness she craved. Neither was his habit of stopping in her room every night for a stern puritanical prayer. The pride which the whole family began to take in her literary reputation was pleasant, but not worth the pain of further isolation from them. For she knew they had drawn further from her than ever, admiring but uncomprehending, thinking in their hearts that a writer in the family was not quite human.

Under the circumstances, there was nothing for the poor woman to do except cling to her symptoms, her nightly prayer meetings with her father and the fluttering attentions of her sisters. Like the truck driver 100 years later, her emotional system had been unequal to the strain put upon it by her environment. The body succumbed, but in so doing selected a set of symptoms which would give some relief to the emotions.

Of course Miss Barrett was luckier than the truck driver. Her cure is as instructive as her disease for the student of psychosomatic disorders. It (the cure) entered her life one afternoon at three, so he noted in his pocketbook, when she was nearly forty years old. He answered to the name of Robert Browning. He was handsome and healthy and a genius himself. He was six years her junior, popular in Society, the idol of his father, mother and sister. And he fell so violently in love with the pale, middle-aged lady on the sofa that he rushed home from their first meeting, this proper conventional Victorian, and penned a madly impassioned letter proposing marriage in the ardent terms befitting one great poet who makes a play for another.

We know now that her speedy recovery was "in the bag" from that moment. What sick emotion would be able to resist the homage of a man who could write *The Ring and the Book*? Married at forty, Elizabeth Barrett Browning shocked the sensibilities of some of her prim acquaintances by getting well enough to scramble over low mountains at forty-one and bear a perfectly healthy child at forty-three. She didn't need her symptoms any longer.

§ 3

The Perils of Pity

BY NO MEANS all of these patients are seeking compensation for the neglect or severity they may have suffered in childhood. A great many of them have been "spoiled brats" who find in the sickbed the only substitute available at their age for the pampering which they enjoyed as children. They have resented the necessity of earning their own living; they have never untied themselves from mother's apron strings; they have shrunk from the task of establishing themselves as independent human beings in a world of equals.

Typical is the sheltered individual who has been known all his life as a "mother's boy" and never recovers from the desire for over-protection which is the result of his upbringing. Smugly their parents have bragged of lavishing "everything" on their children.

One such patient was admitted to the hospital after several years of marriage which had been made unhappy for him—and doubtless for his wife—because she did not take as good care of him as his mother had done. Obviously he had never reconciled himself to the idea that his wife might have wanted to marry a man rather than a baby, and he longed for the good old days. His injured back, which kept him in the hospital, was plainly a welcome incident in his marital career.

"She'll have to take care of me now," he said hopefully. "I guess it serves her right."

Related to this attitude but far more poignant are the many cases of children who hope by their suffering to earn the affection of the callous or neglectful parents. They usually hope in vain, too, despite the story books. This was the experience of a seventeen-year-old high-school girl whose mother had made it plain for years that the youngster was a highly unwelcome adjunct. She had never wanted a child in the first place. After she had divorced her daughter's father, she could not bear the girl's presence because she both acted and looked like the discarded husband.

Furthermore, the mother was contemplating a second marriage, which the propinquity of a seventeen-year-old daughter seemed to threaten. Therefore, she was proposing to send the girl away to school, and it was at this point that the daughter succeeded in injuring her knee while at play. She welcomed this injury with pathetic optimism, and in the hospital she was preoccupied chiefly with her chances of remaining at home. Almost the only thing she ever asked was for reassurance that her mother would now be sorry for her and allow her to stay.

"She can't possibly send me away now when I'm so sick and may be crippled for life," was the burden of the girl's hopes.

§ 4

The Mind's Eye

WHETHER this clinging to symptoms is caused by too much affection or too little, it is a last resort for those who have never found a secure place for themselves. Men, women and children turn to pain or discomfort only because of the inadequacy of their own (or their parents' personalities). Their inability to cope with the environment in which they find themselves sets up an emotional disturbance which translates itself into a physical disorder, and the tortured system thriftily selects an ailment which may have compensating features. The sufferers lose their symptoms when their personality difficulties are remedied, that is, when they are helped to become the kind of people they have the capacity to be.

Despite their appearance of welcoming illness or injury, they do not deliberately set out to become nuisances. No one really wants to be sick. But these misfits may want something else so badly that sickness is brought upon them. If it helps achieve the desired end, it is welcome for what it brings, not for what it is. If it fails, as it so often does, it becomes a double tragedy. It should be remembered that the personality inadequacy of these patients results from parents and circumstance rather than from innate weaknesses in themselves.

It should not be surprising that the most common form of this release is accident. Accidents happen quickly, and the damage is usually obvious to those whom the victim wishes to impress. But while the supposed need for a symptom ranks high among the reasons for accidents, it is a factor in many bodily disorders.

It is especially pronounced in some of the diseases which afflict our special senses—sight, hearing, touch, taste and smell. In a great many cases, the first symptoms make their appearance at a moment of considerable emotional upset, although usually the victim has forgotten that. More heartening for the sufferers, the removal of the emotional disturbance frequently takes the disease away, too.

The psychic factors in eye trouble give a good idea of how other senses can be affected. Experience during the war reinforced the opinion that a little treatment of anxiety or a man's emotional problems—psychotherapy—may be better than a prescription for glasses. Under various sorts of military strain, men came to the clinics complaining about their sight. Many of them were suffering from fear, anxiety or anger rather than eye afflictions.

One clinician in a large hospital was swamped on two different occasions by ammunition handlers from a single depot. Nearly all of them had acquired a species of temporary "dimming out" or even complete momentary blindness which the oculists call *amaurosis fugax*. None of them had suffered any damage to the eye or optic nerve. All of them, however, showed evidence of having been under severe nervous strain. Furthermore, each time they came rushing to the clinic, the doctor discovered that there had been a minor accident in their depot the day before.

Any kind of accident in an ammunition dump is a more than ordinarily frightening experience. Some of the emotional systems which could not stand it any longer selected the eye as the scapegoat. The oculist discovered that others had turned up at the psychiatric clinic, having selected quite different sets of symptoms. All in all, the emotional strain following the minor accidents had actually trebled the sick call on those two days.

This same oculist attributed several cases of eye trouble to the anxiety which followed rapid promotion in the Navy. Some of the young officers worried themselves into states of partial blindness over their new responsibilities. A clue was provided when several naval aviators, grounded because of sudden attacks of temporary dimness or loss of sight, complained that their symptoms were much like those they had suffered when pulling out of a power dive. As the plane pulls out, the pilot "blacks out" because the sudden turn drains blood out of the brain. The tissues are deprived of oxygen which they receive from the blood, and the blackout results.

The anxieties of some of these young officers affected the nerves in much the same way as a power dive. The result was a lack of oxygen for the retina, and a failure of vision. Readjustments in their assignments to give them relief from their current anxiety restored the sight of every one of them to normal.

The mind's relation to the special senses of the body is not confined to the military. Civilians are people, too. There is apparently some connection between the senses and the emotion which stems from the fact that all experience is gained through the senses. This connection is a factor in the selection of one of the senses when a bodily disorder seems necessary for the relief of the mind.

The same relationship leads many sufferers to attribute all sorts of pains and aches to the senses, usually to the eyes. Very wonderful apparent cures of diseases, ranging from migraine to paralysis have been credited to relief from eye strain. In reality, the fitting of glasses seems to have relieved emotional strain in many such cases. There is the case of a ten-year-old boy whose severe headaches were believed due to astigmatism. He was fitted with glasses and the headaches disappeared. It was not until three years later when the boy, still free from headaches, was tested for new glasses that the truth came out. His lenses had been made so far off the prescription that he actually saw better without them than with them. What had happened to the headaches? Obviously they had been removed by suggestion. The cause of the headaches was in the mind, not the eye, and the suggestion that they were going to be relieved worked so far as the symptom was concerned. But a permanent cure would have depended upon getting at the cause as well.

The existence of psychic factors in such apparently physical eye trouble as near-sightedness has been indicated, too. The reason for myopia is a more than normally convex lens in the eyeball. But there are people in whom temporary or even permanent near-sightedness can be brought on by the workings of the mind. This psychic factor is especially plain in those whose vision is normal at times but lapses into myopia at others. Mere prescription of glasses will give some relief perhaps, but many also fix the condition forever. Treatment of the victim as a person rather than as a lens may reveal the basic emotional factor, the reason why the body is selecting an ailment which tends to shut out everything except the immediate surroundings. The chain of reactions which, starting with this emotional factor, causes the involuntary muscles to twist the eyeball out of shape, falls apart from mere exposure.

§ 5

The Roots of Evil

THERE can be a good deal of danger in treating only the symptom at any time. This is particularly true of the "beloved symptom." Superficially it is enough for the victim of eye trouble to get glasses and see again. But he has little cause for rejoicing if unnecessary spectacles are forced upon him for life or if the emotional conflict turns itself into new bodily channels. There is no great medical victory in curing Miss S 1's welts if the young woman's psychic disturbance is going to drive her from a relatively minor ailment into, say, a serious heart disease. The physician must go to the root of the trouble, and his triumph is not complete until the root has been hacked out completely. Every gardener knows that it is much easier to mow weeds than to uproot them. But every gardener knows which is the sensible course in the long run.

"Let's see what made you do it?" is an approach to discovering the roots of the trouble so that the trained physician will be enabled to get his psychic grub hook on them.

The patient who prefers his illness to making a mistake in business or in the home (diplomatic-cold type) can be handled more directly, treated more roughly than the patient whose symptoms are cherished in the hope of inspiring affection or in revenge for missing it. But even for the first, a direct injunction to go back to work or relax in the home is no solution. It is important for him to know why he was afraid of making a mistake or was uncomfortable in these two powerful life adjustments.

Often the patient is not conscious of the family environment against which he is reacting, or he will have covered the unpleasant facts with a fantasy of harmonious relationships which it is necessary to penetrate. It is not unusual to have a patient start off with a story of kindly parents, only to have a picture of stern discipline (keenly resented by the patient) emerge from later remarks.

One boy of seventeen at first described his mother as an easygoing person. But as he grew more interested in explaining himself to the physician, he told with unconcealed annoyance of her domestic tyranny. She kept him away from his favorite sports if he got poor marks or failed to come home at the exact hour she had set for his return. He complained of her harshness, lack of understanding, unreasonable punishments. Only quite a bit later did he remark:

"Did I say Mother was easygoing? I'm not quite sure that was quite the right word after all."

With these patients more circumspection and careful evaluation of the recited history is needed in getting at the basic cause of the "beloved symptom." Usually the unmasking of well-established but unfounded fantasies surprises the patient a good deal more than it does the physician. The patient easily mistakes the sham for the reality, while the well-trained physician knows there is something there all the time.

But the something may be missed in the routine handling of an apparently prosaic case. That was what happened to a man who was brought to a Connecticut hospital with a broken leg. He said he had fallen off a train. There seemed nothing unusual either in him or in his broken bone until just before his discharge a young physician, animated by curiosity and an interest in the psychic aspects of all illness, engaged him in conversation. Only after the man had been drawn into a discussion of himself and his problems did he confess that he had not fallen; he had jumped. The complexities of life, to his mind, could be solved not by a mere illness but only by suicide.

To the young doctor, this suicidal tendency seemed to call for treatment, for it is as much a disease as pneumonia. But when it was suggested to the chief of the hospital, that gentleman pooh-poohed the idea.

"We've done our job," he said. "The man's leg is healed. That is what we're here for. The rest is not our problem."

Now this hospital head was not a stupid bungler. He had a deserved reputation in his own field, but he resembled a good many medical men whose training has not brought them an appreciation of emotional factors in illness and whose imaginations are unequal to a flight into the unfamiliar. The patient was discharged as cured. A week later a small item in the local papers chronicled the fact that he had been killed in New York. He "jumped or fell," as the journalistic phrase has it, from one of Manhattan's better-known skyscrapers.

§ 6

Styles in Sickness

ONE OF the human traits which preserves color in life is individual taste. Fortunately not all women wear the same hats and gowns; not all men choose the same pattern in neckties and shirts. The reasons for any individual's tastes are a mysterious part of his personality, modified by training.

Similarly, given the psychic or even physical necessity for an illness, there is a stubborn individuality in the selection of a disease. Even when the disease itself is settled, the part of the body to be affected may still be governed by unconscious choice. Why, for instance, does a gonorrheal infection settle in the joints of one person, in the tubes of another? Why, granted a tendency to blood clots, do they afflict one man in the legs, another in the heart, another in the brain?

The answer appears to lie partly in the physical make-up of the individual and partly in his behavior pattern. Faced with the inevitability of conflict in his own mind, first with his parents and then with his partner in marriage, he is likely to get diabetes. The irresponsible, relatively unstable character with a cavalier attitude toward family and sex and an impulse to be always up and doing tends under the same circumstances to have an accident. The devotee of hard work and self-discipline in all phases of life develops heart trouble.

But there are other factors which govern the choice of a symptom. One is style. There is a tendency to acquire a disease which is fashionable or at least respectable. Hysteria, for example, was once a rather common phenomenon, especially among women. Charcot, a famous French physician of the last century, was the founder of a whole school of specialists in it, and gave his name to the disease. It is seen no more. It fell from favor because hysteria has lost not only its claim to being a mark of sensibility, but even its badge of respectability. Nice girls just don't get fits of hysterics any more.

Another element in the selection of a symptom is emotional contagion. Too often to be dismissed lightly as coincidence, the victim of his own emotional need to acquire an ailment comes down with a disease from which he has seen others suffer. The man who has seen close relatives and friends stricken with heart disease, and has been frightened of it ever since, will have all the symptoms of it himself, although there may be no organic damage to his heart at all. In selecting his symptoms he has responded to his fears and the shocks of earlier experience. Of course, if he is allowed to continue with the symptoms of his choice, the organic damage is likely to come along later.

The Beloved Symptom

A physician with whom I once worked offered a fine example of how and why a symptom can be selected. He had a woman patient suffering from pains which were suggestive of appendicitis, but there were good psychological reasons why she should have just such symptoms without having anything the matter with her appendix. The doctor was attempting to get at the cause of the trouble by psychoanalysis, but he could not get out of his mind the case of a colleague who once had a patient die of a ruptured appendix while undergoing the same treatment. Finally he decided to break the rules of psychotherapy, which dictate hands off the patient during these discussions, and tapped the patient's abdomen. Her reaction was such that he decided not to wait for a blood count but to rush her to the hospital. There she was operated upon immediately, but even so it was a "near miss," for they had got her just in time.

The patient was saved, but the doctor was not out of danger. The incident took place during the Christmas holidays, and while it was still fresh in his mind, he had a long talk with his mother before proceeding to a family party, the first such holiday gathering since his father had died. It was the anniversary of his death, too. His mother's memory dwelt upon a narrow escape her husband had had when he almost died of appendicitis. All in all, the doctor was not looking forward to the party with pleasure.

In this state of mind he met another physician, whom he had invited to the party, at Grand Central Station. Suddenly he was stricken with such severe abdominal pains that he could not conceal them from his friend. The description was just like appendicitis, and the friend recommended an immediate operation. But the doctor hesitated. He began to think of what might have caused his pains, and being a thoroughly experienced man in his field he realized these three points:

First, that worry over the narrow escape with his patient had given him the idea of appendicitis. Second, that his talk with his mother and the anniversary of his father's death had strengthened the idea. Third, that his desire to avoid the family party altogether had led to his unconscious wish to spend Christmas Day in the hospital.

As soon as he had reasoned this out thoroughly, the pains left him. The two friends proceeded to the party as scheduled, and the doctor felt fine the whole time. When he returned to the city, he was examined by another physician who confirmed his self-diagnosis that there was nothing wrong with his appendix. This man, thanks to his own experience in psychosomatic methods, had been able to remove his need of an illness just as the symptoms began to appear.

The mind which selects an illness is not at all related to that fortunately rare state of emotional upheaval which leads the victim to mutilate himself. The chooser of symptoms does not set out to get sick with malice aforethought. There must be a real emotional need for illness first. Then on the borderline between the known and the forgotten, the choice of symptom will be made.

Before it does permanent damage to the body, the emotional need for the illness must be removed. It can be done only if the victim first understands just what has roused the need and faces up to the situation. Self-understanding is not always the most pleasant thing in the world for anyone. But it may be worth the price. It may help to remove the cause along with the symptom.

[CHAPTER IV]

The Doctor Looks at the Patient

§ 1

WHEN THE young physician emerges from his years of training to embark upon the practice of his profession in America, he finds that science has played him a rather shabby trick. For science has driven into rather rare holes and corners exactly those very diseases which science has taught the young physician how to cure most readily.

He has a very sound, imposing body of knowledge about typhoid, scarlet fever and small pox. He is ready to diagnose them in a flash, and cure them almost as quickly. The catch is that actual cases of typhoid, scarlet fever and small pox are not likely to enter his life very often. Instead, he will be called upon to deal with heart diseases and arthritis, about which he knows very little because those who have taught him know very little themselves.

Actually this state of affairs, discouraging as it may seem to the young physician on practical grounds, represents a major medical victory. The fact that his predecessors in medicine have banished those causes of death which took the biggest toll only half a century ago is a triumph of which the profession is justly proud. But (like world wars) the conquests of science do not solve all our problems. Having mastered typhoid, we find that we have spared our patients only to have them fall victim to arthritis, heart disease or cancer. We may be sure that when we finally achieve enough knowledge of these illnesses to make that knowledge virtually useless to a new practitioner, mankind will fall heir to some other ailment.

The resiliency of the medical profession as a whole is evidenced by the fact that most physicians accept cheerfully the fact that very few people contract the diseases they know all about, while very many manage somehow to acquire those about which scientific information is most scanty.

The young physician does not meet the same kind of people, much less the same kind of diseases, that his elders encountered. The young physician meets people who are a great deal older, for one thing. Today almost 80 per cent of any general practitioner's patients are more than fifty years old. In 1900 more than half would have been under forty.

This change in the make-up of what may be called the patient population has been a long process, greatly accentuated in recent decades. When Shakespeare was a boy, the life expectancy of a new-born infant was four years. By 1900 it had become, in the United States at least, fifty-five for men and sixty for women. By 1940 a male child could expect to live sixty-five years and a female child sixty-eight and one-half years.

Naturally the whole population had become older. One hundred years ago, there were six times as many children under five as there were adults over sixty-five. Today the two groups are about equal. One hundred years ago more than half the population was under twenty. Today only one-third are that young.

This wholesome change has been brought about entirely by applying medical knowledge to the work of treating and protecting people. But this achievement carries with it the responsibility for continuing the advance of medical progress so that the diseases which now baffle us will yield to treatment and prevention as have the dread plagues of our ancestors.

The combination of older patients and patients suffering from chronic diseases calls upon the physician for new techniques. For some years, the chronically ill have taken up about half the time of all doctors in hospitals, and three-fourths of the time of their nurses. Now these are what might be called the psychosomatic illnesses. They have to be treated with the best laboratory techniques and the best psychological techniques if any progress is to be made in reducing the enormous wastage in human suffering represented by invalidism. While relatively little is known about these illnesses, it is certain that emotional factors play an important, often a determining role.

Even this much knowledge has been gained against substantial inertia within the medical profession. Middle-aged doctors can remember when most of their colleagues believed that a bodily ailment might well cause a state of hysteria so acute as to lead to suicide. But they doubted that there was any reciprocity; they did not think that an emotional disturbance might cause a bodily disorder or be another manifestation of the same "real" ailment.

In 1930, F. G. Crookshank, in an aptly titled article, "Organ-Jargon," poked a little fun at these men who clung to their views although as students they broke into a profuse perspiration before important examinations, or as young soldiers had actual experience of that looseness of the bowels which accompanies fear in battle.

"I often wonder," he added, "that some hard-boiled and orthodox clinician does not describe emotional weeping as a 'new disease,' calling it paroxysmal lachrymation, and suggesting treatment by belladonna, astringent local application, avoidance of sexual excess, tea, tobacco and alcohol, and a salt-free diet with restriction of fluid intake; proceeding, in the event of failure, to early removal of the tear-glands. This sounds, of course, ludicrous. But a good deal of contemporary medicine and surgery seems to me to be on much the same level."

§ 2

Patients Are People

SINCE Crookshank wrote those lines, an increasingly large number of medical men have taken the attitude that when they see a patient, they are looking at a human being. But the very humanity of the patient can be confusing to the doctor. This shows itself in cases of men and women who often are regarded in hospitals as "model patients." They give no trouble, but they do not recover their health. They are the ones who are most likely to die or return later in a more serious phase of their illness. By the standards of many overworked attendants in these institutions, the model patient is this sort of a character:

1. Keeps quiet and minds his own business, thereby offering no disturbance to doctor, nurse or other patients.
2. Carries out the physician's instructions to the letter and without embarrassing questions.
3. Refrains from asking for extra attentions.
4. Sleeps, or at least remains quiet, all through the night.

The doctor does well to take another look at such patients. With the best intentions in the world, they may be hiding something and never be aware of the fact.

One of these supposedly well-adjusted patients was a woman of thirty-five who since she was ten years old had been a "model" sufferer from heart disease. She had been in the hospital thirteen times for cardiac breaks, and her reaction to treatment had earned her medical praise, "In view of the extent of cardiac damage, amazingly untroubled by her condition, co-operative, free from nervousness and worry."

Actually it turned out that her life experience—both physical and emotional—had been such that the only place she felt safe was in the hospital. She, therefore, fell into the rather familiar class of patients who welcome the illness which brings them to their favorite refuge.

The poor woman was by no means as free from nervousness and worry as her meek manner indicated. A number of circumstances, especially the facts that she was an orphan and a girl, had combined to make her feel all her life that she was a useless and inferior creature. An older brother, who fostered this sentiment by bullying her, still had the power to terrify her simply by paying a visit to her bedside. In fact, she herself attributed the first attack of her illness twenty-five years before to a fright for which he was responsible. With this history, it was hardly surprising that she had deliberately cut herself off from all association with men, and that her heart did not respond very well to treatment.

She was so badly adjusted, even to the hospital which she liked, that she frequently woke up in the night in a panic, although she would deny having dreamed anything. Furthermore, every afternoon between one and two, her pulse rate and blood pressure rose "unaccountably." At least it was unaccountable until it developed that this untroubled, carefree patient actually went into a near frenzy of fear just before rounds in her ward, which took place at two o'clock. She knew she was being unreasonable, but she couldn't get away from the impression that "all these doctors were going to do something terrible" to her. This she never revealed by word or manner until a physician trained in the psychosomatic approach to illness examined her.

This sort of thing obviously calls for psychiatric treatment, but the doctors had been so beguiled by the apparent placidity of the patient that they had never looked below the surface, except with a large variety of mechanical devices ranging from stethoscope to electric cardiogram. Yet even a superficial psychiatric contact benefited her, while a sound treatment fifteen or twenty years earlier might have made all the difference in the world, both in her illness and her life.

In the course of any practice, a physician will encounter two types of patients who are most discouraging. One is the patient who makes him sick (literally, not in any idiomatic sense of the word) from emotional contagion or irritation. The other is the patient who aggravates the physician's owns ailments by displaying the same symptoms or by confounding medical wisdom by refusing to get well.

The number of doctors who fall victims to their patients psychosomatically is surprisingly large. Every teacher of physicians has seen a great many of them. As medical men, they turn out to be human, and as patients, they are just as much people as anyone else.

In view of this record, it is not surprising that most physicians, contrary to popular impression, do not yearn for the insoluble case, the patient with a mysterious, lingering ailment, a baffling illness with which they can experiment.

§ 3

The Ideal Patient

THE IDEAL patient is not the meek patient, the silent patient or the helpless patient, but the patient who gets well. Furthermore, he is the patient who co-operates with the physician in the process, who behaves like an adult rather than a baby despite the tendency of illness to reduce all of us to children, who has the will to get well.

Every physician has had experience of the patient whose fierce desire to recover has seemed to defeat Death itself. Perhaps even more common are those other patients who succumb to apparently trifling ailments out of what seems sheer laziness.

However, the most memorable of the patients who refuse to co-operate are not necessarily those whose diseases have a fatal outcome. Just as stubborn an example was a mason who at the beginning of the depression was not only unemployed but constipated. I was able to help him, I thought, on both counts. I found him a job with a contractor who was remodeling a building, and I recommended some such light exercise as walking in order to relieve the constipation.

Two days later this patient walked off the job indignantly. He was outraged because the boss had him working on the third floor and provided no elevator service. The fact that walking up and down two flights several times a day would be beneficial to his health was beside the point. He had his rights, and one of them was elevator service to the third floor. Probably another of them was the inalienable privilege of keeping his constipation.

The ideal patient, for himself as well as for his doctor, is the one who can proceed down the road to health on his own two feet—with guidance but without having to be dragged or carried. The physician should not have to do the thinking for his patient. It is true that he must begin by realizing just what it would be like to be such a person. But his role is to help the patient get into condition to think for himself. The patient's job is to do the thinking.

Often we are inclined to credit patients with too little ability to solve their own emotional problems. The fact is that a healthy adult is his own best counsellor in this field. A sick adult is not.

One of the most illuminating cases of this kind was that of a woman who appears in the office records as "Case No. H.P. 3." When she was first referred for psychiatric treatment some years ago, she was thirty-nine years old and had been through eighteen years of invalidism, starting just after her marriage. Stomach and heart troubles had been her constant companions. She complained of pains all over, of nausea, dizziness, palpitations and general weakness. She walked with a cane for fear of falling. Two years of treatment in the hospital had left her with somewhat more startling and painful symptoms than those she had had on arrival. Co-operation from her toward her own recovery was conspicuously absent.

"'Mrs. 3" had come to this country from Russia when she was eleven, and a year later had to find a job in order to help support a sick mother and father. By the time she was sixteen she had worked up from file clerk to private secretary, working hard at night school all the time, but at the cost of a good deal of emotional conflict.

First of all, she was both ambitious and intelligent with a keen desire for a college education. This was denied her; in fact, she had not finished high school, and she harbored hot resentment against an older sister who might have but did not help carry the family responsibility. She also resented her parents for needing her help.

Resentment was not allayed by the girl H.P.'s discovery of romance, for her parents forbade her to marry. The final touches to her inner conflict were furnished by some doubts as to her real love for the man. This led to a good deal of argument with him over their possible marriage as soon as she was old enough to dispense with parental consent.

"If only there had been someone to advise me!" she exclaimed in recalling this period of her life. "I was nearly crazy. I used to cry myself to sleep every night and woke up with nightmares, feeling sure I was going to marry the wrong man, and yet somehow I couldn't help it."

At twenty-one, she made the typical worst choice of the evils which offered themselves to her. She married the man she was not sure she loved, and she cherished a feeling of guilt for having disobeyed and deserted her parents. To make up for it, she decided to go on working for their support.

However, as a girl H.P. had been completely unprepared for marriage. The reality of sexual relationships with a man about whom she had become quite disillusioned anyway was a profoundly shocking experience. At the same time, her father intensified her feeling of guilt by undergoing a stomach operation. Young Mrs. 3 promptly reacted by developing such severe attacks of nausea that she had to give up her job.

The psychosomatic nature of her illness seems plain enough today, but at the time a general physician recommended pregnancy as a likely cure for her indigestion.

By this time, the young wife had decided that her husband was not her social equal. Actually he made fun of her aspirations and her intellectual interests, so that she did not care to entertain her old friends. The marital maladjustment was complete. In this atmosphere, it would have been remarkable if the conception of a child had had any therapeutic value. In fact, Mrs. 3 spent the whole nine months of her pregnancy in bed, generally nauseated, and at the end suffered a difficult labor and instrumental delivery.

"I nearly died," she said, and it is a fact that her attacks of nausea continued after her daughter was born.

A year later Mrs. 3 had an appendectomy, followed shortly by an abortion. Her sentiments concerning the sexual act had not changed, and she had refused contraceptive advice because she thought that if she took it, her husband would have a good excuse to insist upon more frequent relations. After the abortion, the couple avoided intercourse altogether or the husband practiced withdrawal. It is hardly surprising, then, to learn that at this time he began to solace himself with other women. Nor is it surprising that this conduct further angered his wife.

Her years of invalidism passed slowly, varied by successive attempts at relief through Ethical Culture, Christian Science, Theosophy and Yogi. The little family generally was in poor financial shape, their economic crises reaching a peak (along with millions of others) in 1929.

In 1930, when Mrs. 3 was thirty-seven, her father died of the same stomach disorder for which he had been operated at the time of her marriage. Her mother, suffering from hypertension and angina pectoris, then came to live with her, whereupon Mrs. 3 added to her own stomach ulcer symptoms all the appearance of heart disease. The heart symptoms were intensified when the mother died six months before Mrs. 3 was first referred for psychiatric treatment. This event was followed by recurrent nightmares in which she saw her parents jumping out of their graves. At one time, in describing these dreams, she said:

"I felt murderous, as if I could kill them, and I felt all day that if I picked up a knife I might kill."

Now all these years, it is obvious, no one had helped this woman do any clear thinking for herself. On the contrary, her whole life experience was such that thinking was virtually impossible. She had no idea that rage and repressed aggressive tendencies were hidden in her, much less that they had anything to do with her long invalidism. The real meaning of her relationships to her parents was a closed book to her, although it became clear enough to the psychiatrist in the course of treatment that these extended to incest wishes of which she was and remained ignorant.

The treatment consisted of ten periods of talk extending over two months. Naturally the earlier ones were devoted to bringing out the patient's history, but all were directed toward showing her the connection between her psychic and her somatic symptoms. It was during the seventh of these periods that she spoke spontaneously of the practical problems she faced in readjusting her life on a healthy basis, saying:

"Whether or not my marriage eighteen years ago was a mistake, two courses are open to me; divorce and supporting myself and my daughter; or to see what I can do toward working out a satisfactory relationship with my husband. I have realized that all along, but I was too sick to *think* about it."

Here Mrs. 3 put her finger on the point which any doctor must bear in mind whenever he looks at a patient. Illness prevents thought; at least it prevents healthy thought.

During the next few years, Mrs. 3 proceeded to demonstrate that, with healthy thinking abilities restored, the patient is her own best counsellor. Incidentally Mrs. 3 voluntarily sought advice on sexual hygiene. She gave up blaming her husband for all their troubles and set out to help him with his work. Since she was a capable as well as an intelligent person, he got ahead rapidly in business in spite of the depression (it was now 1932), and they were able to send their daughter to college. Her blood pressure, which had returned to normal at the close of treatment, stayed down.

She has had no symptoms of any kind. After eighteen years of invalidism and pain, the application of psychosomatic principles, which revealed the whole individual both to her doctor and to herself, was able to restore her to health and usefulness. She had been able to help herself; she saw her own needs once the physician had torn away the distorting veils of illness. Incidentally, this was done without ever referring to her incest wishes or an Oedipus complex—words which, so far as I know, she has never heard in her life.

Mrs. 3 was really cured and has continued as shock-proof as one would expect of any human being. After five years, her husband suffered some new financial reverses, and as a means of compensation ventured upon a new love affair. But his wife was able to go her way serenely, without any rise of blood pressure or palpitations, and without further psychiatric treatment. She once remarked that if she had been able to have such treatment in her 'teens, she probably would have married a different man. But, she added, she had learned to accept life as it is. As a result, she has now been completely free from symptoms—pain, nausea, palpitations and the rest—for almost as long a time as she had previously suffered from them.

Mrs. 3, in short, has become the ideal patient; she got well.

[CHAPTER V]

The Patient Looks at the Doctor

§ 1

A SICKBED seldom gives the best perspective on any prospect or problem. Most of us have acquired the habit of appraising our fellow-men from an upright position; we are likely to get a rather distorted impression of them if we are lying flat on our backs. When we look at our doctor, therefore, we may see him clearly enough, but from the wrong angle.

It is in the very nature of illness that it impels the individual back toward his childhood, and even beyond. This is especially true of his emotional reactions. He wants to be taken care of, to have the burden of decisions taken from his shoulders, to be protected and cherished and disciplined. In many ways, this is a helpful feeling because the sick are seldom in the best frame of mind to make decisions, and they need the care they crave—or at least some of it.

But with the return to childhood's happy dependence goes a return to other infantile qualities, not all of which are of benefit to his progress toward health. The patient tends to assume the attitude, readily recognizable as a throwback to childish habits, that it is great fun to trick the good doctor or to annoy him with invented symptoms, evasions of medicine or other treatments, the relation of circumstantial but highly fanciful experiences.

The Patient Looks at the Doctor

Adults are a good deal more plausible in these tricks than babies, so they are correspondingly more difficult to detect. Children delight in doing this sort of thing to the best-loved parent or nurse. The triumphs of babyhood consist of the successful perpetration of such mischief. Similar pranks are the triumphs of invalidism, and for somewhat the same reasons. The competent physician may well let the patient appear to "get away" with them, just as the competent parent may not invariably disappoint or punish the child by exposing his tricks. The question in both cases is whether there is danger in permitting the prank to go unnoticed.

Of course stern punitive measures are not necessary. Often, even with a child, a friendly discussion will relieve a great deal of the anxiety which prompts the mischief. The approach may well be some such calm and simple inquiry as:

"Why did you play this joke on me?" or "Why did you do this to yourself?" or "Why did you want to do it?"

In asking this, whether of child or adult, the physician should be careful to eschew the role of judge. Most people find it an easy part to play, but medical practitioners should be careful to keep the temptation behind them. As A. P. Herbert points out in one of his penetrating little essays, "Why Is the Coroner?" they are not well qualified by training or experience for the fine subtleties of the judicial bench. Judges are supposed to presume the innocence of people who appear before them. But a medical man, says Mr. Herbert, "by professional habit, assumes that all those who come before him have something wrong with them." The essayist deplores this habit in a judge, but by the same token there are judicial habits which ill become the physician. A prescription should not be handed down like a sentence in court.

In the sort of case where the patient has been indulging in tricks which should be corrected, he should be his own judge. His verdicts will be quite severe enough. In fact, the physician will find his own share in the proceedings limited to lightening the self-imposed sentences. Only on rare occasions will he wish to administer any kind of rebuke.

However, the physician's temper may frequently be tried quite as much and in the same way as the parent's. For a busy man, perhaps, there is nothing quite so exasperating as the patient who will invent a quite elaborate set of lies apparently for no other reason than to learn if the doctor is bright enough to see through them. There was a Negro patient who went to the trouble of painting one side of his chest with iodine before he went to the clinic, and then complained of a great pain on that side.

"Sam," said the doctor after examining him, "I don't know why you have pain there. The real trouble is on the other side."

"Yes," Sam agreed cheerfully, "I know it, but I wanted to see if you did."

Such tricks may not do serious harm in cases of illness which can be diagnosed readily, but there are patients who die as a result of their lies or come close to dying if no one takes the trouble to elicit the real facts. The lies are not always told in a spirit of mischief or fun by any means. Frequently they are meant in the nature of a test for the physician in all seriousness or because of shame or—in the case of information withheld, which is one of the most insidious forms—because it is considered of no interest.

Mrs. X was a good example of the harm a patient can do to herself by trying to fool the doctor. In giving her medical history on admission to the hospital, she said that both her parents had died of heart trouble. She herself had a cardiac ailment. She failed signally to respond to treatment, and was going rapidly down hill when she happened to have a conversation with a physician who had had training in the psychosomatic approach to such cases. To him she confessed that she had lied because she didn't want the doctors to know about her parents. Both actually were still alive and hearty, but the father was in prison and the mother a constant source of irritation to her daughter. Before Mrs. X could respond to any kind of treatment she had to be relieved of some of her tension, rage and shame about her parents.

Like many other patients she could have saved the staff the extra trouble of ferreting out this information. In fact, patients who indulge in this sort of deception may find that the doctor has not the time nor the training to unravel truth from fiction. The patient who wants to get well is taking unnecessary risks by withholding or distorting facts. Even when he looks upon the doctor as in *loco parentis,* he would do well to avoid filial trickery.

The tendency of patients to create a sort of synthetic parent-child relationship between themselves and the doctor can be of immense help to the physician who knows how to learn from it. When he has that knowledge, he may be praised for an admirable "bedside manner" or he may be "given hell." In either case, he justly counts it as one of the important parts of his equipment for treating people successfully.

§ 2

Bedside Manner

A "BEDSIDE MANNER" was one of the first formulae for effecting cures which mankind was able to learn. Physicians worked wonders with it in bygone ages when it was the only real weapon they had with which to combat disease. Of the actual illness they may have known nothing and guessed fantastically wrong. But their "bedside manner" was of distinct help to their patients. It offset much of the harm they did with prescriptions of pearls ground up in wine or the dried skin of toads or the hair of animals caught at the witching hour of midnight.

In those days, the wonder-worker was more akin to a god than to a parent. But the lesser role suffices today. When an ability to assume the role of parent to the sick and therefore temporarily childish is reinforced by some understanding of the sick person's past life, it is particularly effective. Here lies the advantage of the family doctor, especially the family doctor in a relatively small community.

Such a physician is familiar with the background of his patients, and in intimate detail if they are young enough to have had him in attendance since their birth. He knows why Mary doesn't eat liver and can't digest eggs. He knows that John has an unreasonably strong desire to prove to his mother that he can take better care of her than his father did. He knows that the banker's lady and the porter's wife shared a fear of pregnancy and a distaste for the children they bore. He knows all about the girl whose future was marred by the experience summed up in her mother's petulant cry, "Take that brat away. I hate it! I hate it!"

Knowledge of this sort is essential to medical treatment if the patient is to achieve good health. The family doctor in his daily rounds has absorbed a great deal of it without actually being conscious of it. The same knowledge can emerge only by painstaking and careful work in the clinic or the consulting room where the patient is encountered as a stranger.

At the same time, the family doctor labors under some disadvantages—the defects of his qualities, so to speak. This will appear especially in his contacts with the younger people of the community, for they will tend to be afraid of the very knowledge which should enable him to help them. They are often uncomfortably aware of his omniscience and his friendly relations with their elders. They may well be afraid of him for what he has been told or what he might tell. Whether these fears are groundless or not, the damage lies in their mere existence.

The same individual will often reveal freely and easily to a stranger secrets which would be hidden tenaciously from the most trusted friend—and the family doctor frequently is that trusted friend. If the stranger is a physician trained in the psychosomatic approach to his problem and skilled in the application of his techniques, he will soon find himself in possession of all the information about early experience and environment which the family doctor has accumulated by first-hand observation over the years.

The technique, however, must be learned, and it must be learned largely by experience. The elements of it may be imparted in the classroom, but the application comes with practice, like anything else. There is method in the apparent casualness with which the experienced physician guides the talk with his patient. The passion for exact records, which can be satisfied by nothing less than taking copious notes while the interview proceeds, defeats the purpose of the conversation. The patient, who should feel that he is being treated as a person, begins to feel like a bug pinned down for zoological examination. This feeling will persist even if he is the sort of fellow whose surface mind would be inclined to resent the implied casualness with which his words are treated if the note-taking is omitted. Under the compulsion of the flying pencil, he will react just like the bug, squirming away from the probe. But skilfully handled, he will find himself saying:

"Why, Doctor, I don't know why I told you all this. It must have been on my mind but nobody asked me about it."

When a patient looks at his doctor, he is seeking help in a problem which is more than commonly puzzling to him. He may or may not have his own ideas as to what ails him and what ought to be done about it, but his primary purpose is to get well. This is true of patients who start out by attempting to have themselves kept sick. Therefore, the patient wants to see in his doctor the man or woman who can make him well. Furthermore, he is quite understandably ready to quote Scripture for his own end: "Physician, heal thyself!" Patients rapidly lose confidence in the practitioner who becomes sick himself either emotionally or physically unless the illness makes the doctor easier to exploit for the patient's own purposes.

Patients naturally like the physician who inspires confidence in his ability to cure. However, the bedside manner becomes effective only if it is backed by the ability to understand that particular patient as a human being. It is for better techniques of understanding that the psychosomatic approach to disease is striving.

§ 3

The Ideal Physician

FORTUNATELY for physicians (who also are people), about the only quality patients agree upon as altogether desirable is ability to cure. This enables all sorts of physicians to win and hold a practice. Some patients in describing the ideal doctor put emphasis upon his reputation for skill and knowledge. Others are primarily concerned that he display an absorbing interest in their own particular case. Others will hail him as a great man if he satisfies their demand for protection and loving care. Still others will be most impressed by the weary, care-worn manner of the physician who is giving too much of his strength to his job. And finally there are those patients who consign their health and well-being most confidently to the physician whose air of infallibility makes them feel themselves in the presence of a superior being.

There are indications that certain of these attitudes tend to associate themselves with certain diseases. For example, Dr. Jurgen Ruesch reports that the general population of the country seems to rate highest the physician who gives his patients the truth about their ailments and the physician who impresses them with his authority. On the other hand, says Dr. Ruesch, ulcer patients prefer the physician who satisfies their need for affection and encouragement, or the one who gives an impression of noble benevolence. Such a person tends to soothe the special emotional conflict which is the basis of ulcer formation.

For a good many patients, the search for the ideal doctor may never end. The "Mrs. 3" of the previous chapter had visited some twenty physicians and all the big clinics in New York in the course of her eighteen years of invalidism. Apparently none of them had won her lasting confidence, and certainly she did not start out on her course of psychiatric treatment with any belief that the psychiatrist was the answer to her problem. In fact, the first session was devoted to overcoming her loudly vocal anger at being referred to a psychiatrist at all. She walked up and down, alternately weeping and shouting, her hair in wild disorder. The burden of her tears and her screams was that the doctors must have given her up altogether or were refusing to take her seriously if they had turned her over to psychiatry.

This is a fairly common reaction. The theory of these patients and of many of their relatives (and perhaps of some physicians) is that mental and emotional upsets are trivial outbreaks, largely imaginary and relatively harmless, or else rather shameful and hopeless exhibitions of complete collapse. "Mrs. 3" obviously believed that reference to a psychiatrist was just an excuse to get her out of the hair of more competent and important doctors. She was justifiably indignant when she became convinced that her attendants thought her suffering was imaginary. A pain is a pain, and it hurts just as much whether it be caused by an emotion or a club, a fear or a poison.

In wandering from office to office, from hospital to clinic, always in search of the ideal physician, many patients will withhold the clue which might lead to a cure. They will cherish secretly a considerable contempt for the deluded professional man who fails to understand them, but they will not help him or themselves to achieve understanding.

They will talk at length of their bodily aches and pains, old and new. They will describe physical symptoms with gusto and in detail. They will remember the illnesses of their childhood much further back than they can remember pleasant happenings. They will volunteer all sorts of information about headaches, bellyaches, chills, fevers, palpitations and so on down a long list. But not a word about emotional shocks or fears. And if the physician asks about these matters in too pointed a manner, he is more than likely to reap nothing but a harvest of lies for his pains. They may not be conscious lies, either.

At one of the hospitals where I conducted a series of psychosomatic studies a few years ago, there was a diabetic patient named Rose who had been treated unsuccessfully for seven years. She had developed in the meantime some pains which were diagnosed as diabetic neuritis. She also complained of dizziness, headaches and numbness. So far as the hospital staff could make out from what she had told them, she was a happily married woman of forty-three with three lovely children, an attentive husband and no special worries.

The physician who had most recently failed to help her was a woman who was distinguished by what seemed to Rose to be an extremely motherly attitude. It turned out that Rose had a deep-rooted hatred for her own mother, a complaining and exacting woman. Upon her absent head Rose heaped a good deal of the blame for all her own troubles—from her very name of Rose, which she detested, to the fact that she had been obliged to leave school after her elementary education and had thereby been deprived of realizing her life ambition of becoming a teacher. Rose was intelligent and had a profound respect for intelligence in others. She had reached the conclusion that annoyance, rage and fear caused more sugar in her blood than potatoes, candy and ice cream—hence the impression in the hospital that she was unco-operative.

"But of course I couldn't tell the doctors," she confided to me once confidence had been established, "because they couldn't understand."

They might have understood much better, however, if Rose's reaction to the motherly type of physician had not kept her from explaining some of the facts which she told me later. One of the important ones was that she was not too fond of motherhood herself, especially since her son was disappointing her dream of making a brilliant teacher out of him. Another important but unrevealed fact that was that her husband's desire to be made comfortable and his lack of ambition, which were qualities entirely different from those of her own admired father, angered her constantly. And finally, she admitted, she was not really the kind of woman to be calm in the face of adversity, although she fought to repress her feelings at no matter what cost. But her attitude toward the other physicians had prevented them from knowing all this, or even that she had discovered what she thought to be the futility of her diet. She wanted this concealed from them, saying:

"They are very nice to me and I like to come to see them once in a while just to chat."

The difference between her chats with them and her chats with me was that I fulfilled her particular ideal of a doctor more nearly than the others. For one thing, I was a teacher as well as a physician and she had always wanted to be that. For another, I did not give her orders or treat her as a child the way her mother had done. Toward the end of our first interview, in which she had relieved herself of many pent-up grievances, she was surprised at her own frankness, and told me:

"I ought to be very mad at you, but I guess I feel much better."

"You're much less stiff," I observed, referring to the tenseness which had been so exaggerated that she said she couldn't bear to bend her elbow. "How about the pain?"

"It isn't there any more," she replied in obvious amazement. "I feel as if I could walk better. Perhaps you were really right about its making me stiff."

It was plain at this first interview that Rose was deeply influenced by what she saw in her physicians, as most patients are. The other woman doctor would have had just the right personality for a different type of patient—one who was looking for maternal care in his escape back to childhood—but Rose said of her:

"She was too busy to be interested in me, and she tried to take care of me like a mother instead of talking to me like an equal as you do."

Because of what she saw, or thought she saw, or was persuaded into thinking she saw in me as a psychiatrist, Rose was able to talk freely, to co-operate willingly in treatment, and to improve greatly in health despite the fact that she could not escape from the family environment which had done so much to induce the onset of her disease. But, as has so often been the case, psychosomatic treatment which included an understanding of her emotional and personality difficulties helped her to combat them successfully.

Relatively superficial psychotherapy—twelve interviews in five months—enabled her to understand why her psychic disturbances led to tension, suffering and increasingly severe diabetic symptoms. As a result, her various cardiac pains, her headaches, her sensations of numbness and dizziness disappeared. She lost weight, which had been one of the goals of her other physicians for years, and her diabetes improved markedly.

The case of Rose is far from unique. Patients tend to look for a physician more or less in their own image, at least in what they believe to be their own image. Rose, for example, identified me with the career and personality she had wanted for herself.

This quality in patients can be valuable aid to the physician in making a psychosomatic diagnosis, especially if he has a reasonably dispassionate understanding of his own personality. After some experience of how those people who are patients react to contact with him, he is able to appraise the attitudes of new patients as they are exposed to him. Their variation or likeness to what he has found to be "normal" are guides to treatment. They may look at him and see their ideal or a horrid resemblance to someone they have hated. He looks at them and sees the way to better health for them.

[CHAPTER VI]

The Patient's Dilemma

§ 1

Two MEN lay side by side in the hospital ward, both advanced stages of cardiovascular disease. The seriousness of their condition is typical of hospital cases, since these victims generally do not arrive for anything they or their physicians regard as trivial. They wait until they require major treatment of some kind, and congratulate themselves upon their fortitude in holding out so long. They might have been cured easily at an earlier stage, but would not have showed so much courage. The two lying side by side were rather extreme examples. Each was pathetically eager to get well. Each watched the physician breathlessly during his examination. Each spoke his uppermost thought at the end.

"It's up to you now, Doc," said one.

"I've got to do something to get well," said the other.

These patients were on opposite horns of a common dilemma. They were not quite sure of what their own role should be in working out their restoration to health. They had similar past histories and similar symptoms, which probably resulted in the acquisition of essentially the same disease. The personality of the first, however, was not so well integrated as that of the second. The result was that the response of the first to treatment was to leave it all to the doctor. The response of the other was: what can

I do to get well? The first died, the second recovered, although laboratory tests and clinical examinations failed to show any real difference.

Ordinarily persons with a given disease will respond in a given way. This does not happen because one disease has one effect upon one individual while another disease would have a different effect. It is rather because the individual's emotional experience and constitution are likely to lead to one disease rather than another. Thus in general, patients with coronary disease are attracted by the authoritarian physician and they will adopt a submissive attitude toward him. With relief and gladness, they put themselves in his hands, happy to transfer responsibility to what they believe are broader shoulders.

The typical fracture patient, on the other hand (at least the one who makes a habit of accidents) wants to maintain his own freedom of action. He will resent the domineering approach which the sufferer from heart disease welcomes.

The patient who wants to leave everything to his physician will have in his mind's eye a tall, imposing figure with well-brushed gray hair, a goatee and piercing eyes behind polished lenses of glass. If the actual physician on the case cannot conform to this physical prescription, he need not necessarily resort to a wig and spectacles. He may achieve the same respect if he is known to have a long string of degrees after his name, or is recognized ostentatiously as a notable expert, or can speak in an impressive manner on some of the more technical aspects of the case which are completely beyond the patient's understanding or gives orders with a note of authority. Of course, behind whatever facade he may choose or be able to assume for the occasion in order to meet his patient's need to be impressed, there must lie a solid understanding of the case at hand. There must also be the ability and experience to treat it successfully.

The typical fracture patient does not react very well to this approach. He will be more likely to respond to the physician with an informal manner, colloquial talk and ordinary dress. In making a psychosomatic diagnosis of the case, the physician will find this type of patient more difficult to draw out than his coronary brother. Treatment may not be any more difficult, but it will take longer to establish the background against which the treatment must be prescribed.

Patients who expect the physician to do everything for them frequently handicap themselves by encouraging the removal of their symptoms without any attack being made upon the root of the malady. Patients who want to do the whole job themselves may prevent the physician from giving them the help which only medical training and skill can provide.

Both types are obvious cases for which psychosomatic treatment is indicated. They must be shown how their emotional attitudes affect their bodily ailments before any real disposition of their basic trouble can be made. No matter which horn of the dilemma has impaled them, they are where they are partly because they have never made inner peace with authority. Their emotional conflicts with parents, teachers or employers have been far beyond their own powers of adjustment. They have been unable to establish a strong, healthy, disciplined relationship with whatever the most immediate authority in their lives may be.

In the case of the patient who wants to do the complete job of restoration for himself, this maladjustment manifests itself in a rebellious attitude. This patient wants to go his own way. Often he turns out to have been the product of a stern upbringing in a household where the rule was severe punishments for minor infractions of the family code. He had a tendency to regard the bodily injury or ailment from which he is suffering as a punishment for disobedience. But he remains noticeably lacking in any desire to respect authority after he is cured.

In the case of the patient who puts the whole burden upon his physician, the apparently opposite maladjustment reflects a lifetime habit of yielding to parents, spouse, children and associates. The patient wants to be told what to do and when and how. Why is not so important to him. He may feel that this attitude displays some sort of innate weakness of character, but he will make no effort to overcome that weakness. People who know him well enough will say that he has a weak backbone or that he is a jelly-fish.

To themselves, they frequently make up for their submissive state by being nasty to anyone who helps them. They may wail, or may shock somebody. If they can make their doctor so impatient that they have to go to another one, or if they can get the doctor sick or bored, they feel that they have scored a real triumph. The reason for this is that they themselves are sick and bored, and they want the doctor to feel what they feel. This is an attitude which is found with special frequency among sufferers from ulcer and colitis. When they have the jellyfish personality, it does not mean that they are always perfectly flaccid and harmless, for they are not. The jellyfish that stings is still a jellyfish. And the sting can be mighty painful.

§ 2

Overpowered

ONE OF the common escapes for people who have a deep-seated emotional conflict with authority—any authority—is to try to emulate the person to whose power they submit. Another way is to avoid exposure to authority. Neither method is an escape from illness, however much it may be a trial to the family, boss or friends. Neither emulation nor escape will solve the basic conflict.

Theresa M. tried the first way. The oldest of three children, she was obviously fond of her brother and not very much interested in her sister, attitudes which seemed to be reciprocated. Her father had died when she was five, and she had been reared by her mother, who was strict and positive, and by her grandmother, who was affectionate and comforting. Theresa was fond of athletics, liked the attention of boys, dreamed about having nice clothes and taking trips. She tried to please everybody, and took a good deal of pains to have people like her.

Her home life she described at first as pleasantly happy with her brother devoted to her, her grandmother kind, her mother good but strict. In the middle of Theresa's adolescence, Mrs. M.

had married again, and the girl described her stepfather as "a nice man." She made a face, though, when she said it. She repeated the grimace every time she mentioned him, and finally remarked:

"I really don't mind him at all now. He doesn't bother me. My mother likes him, so I like him."

As the story of her life emerged in more detail, it became apparent that the girl had always tried to do as her mother told her and be what she thought her mother was, regardless of her own character and inclinations. She even tried to be grateful and no doubt thought she was, but she described her relationship to her parent in these words:

"She is good and very strict. But when I see what happens to other girls, the way they're brought up, I guess I should be glad of it. Mother believes you should get up early and work hard."

Theresa did not say, it should be noted, that she really was glad her mother was so strict, nor that she shared Mrs. M.'s passion for early rising and hard work. Further evidence of a very real hostility to her mother was not long in developing, although the girl did not realize it. She accepted her stepfather with obvious reluctance only because her mother liked him. She gave up sports and games to take a job as nursemaid after school because her mother believed in work, and doubtless because the family needed the financial help of her small earnings. During her last year in high school she had grown fond of her studies and of school life, but her mother did not want her to continue her education, so she went to work.

"If I could go back to school, maybe I would make some friends," the girl said on one occasion rather wistfully.

Theresa had even conformed her sex life to her mother's ideas and prejudices. The only information Mrs. M. thought her daughter needed about the facts of menstruation and sex was that she did not need to worry and the important thing was to keep away from boys. When Theresa expressed a desire for children, her mother assured her she would have plenty when she was married and that then she wouldn't want them.

"But I don't believe her," the girl added in one of her few open contradictions of a maternal dictum. "I like children."

Perhaps the most submissive of Theresa's actions, and one which gave rise to much of her strongly repressed hostility, was revealed when she said:

"I had two boy friends, but Mother says they are no good as friends, so I have given up all that stuff. I am always dreaming about pretty clothes, but I guess it's silly. You can make people like you without them."

The constant repetition of "Mother says" and "Mother taught me" and "Mother believes" shows that in finding herself in that common patient dilemma of a conflict with authority, Theresa had chosen the submissive, emulating role. She developed an acute rheumatic heart trouble, and there could be no doubt that it was linked directly to her emotional conflict.

§ 3

No Escape

WHAT IF she had chosen the other horn of the dilemma, the avoidance of authority? Edward D. was an example of what might well have happened to her. He, too, was on the surface devoted to his mother but admitted to constant friction in relation to his father. He had two attacks of rheumatic fever, one when he was eleven and the other when he was seventeen. In between he had been extremely busy avoiding authority.

He admired his mother and wanted to be like her, but had not made Theresa's effort to do so. He dodged authority at school by the simple expedient of quitting when he was sixteen, and then commenced a round of leaving jobs. He left his first as a newspaper boy to go to work on his grandfather's farm, but could not get along with his grandfather. He returned to the city and went to work in a restaurant. A short time later he quit again, saying he was in danger of being fired because he broke so many dishes. He

The Patient's Dilemma

decided to go to a school for dental mechanics but discovered that his failure to finish high school disqualified him. Unable to decide what to do next, he had his second attack of rheumatic fever.

When he was recuperating in the hospital he did a good deal of thinking about himself, and decided he ought to get a "responsible position." His brother-in-law, assistant manager of a cafeteria, seemed to be a desirable person to emulate, and Eddie said of himself later:

"At first I was so sick I thought I was dead, and when I became conscious again and began to get better it seemed as if I was a different person."

His emulation was now of someone in authority, but his effort to remodel himself without help failed miserably. In a year the boy was back in the hospital, his rheumatic heart condition so much worse in that time that the medical note on his case contains the following sentence:

"It is difficult to see how this cardiac lesion could have progressed to the present point since then."

To the psychiatrist who entered the case at this time, Eddie's heart presented no such difficulty. It was obvious that his attempt to shift from his former role of avoidance of authority to one of responsibility was a failure because he did not know what really troubled him. Anxiety over his inability to get along in either role had involved his heart to an extent which surprised the other physicians. Relatively brief psychiatric treatment enabled Eddie to understand what prevented him from assuming responsibilities. Knowledge enabled him to overcome the then relatively slight obstacles to an emotional adjustment, and for several years the young man was in good health. His heart disease disappeared. He got a job as a salesman and held it for three years, when he was appointed a manager and realized one of his youthful ambitions. But after a time the psychiatrist received this letter:

"I was under your care five years ago and due to your talks with me I improved rapidly. About a year ago I began to notice a change in myself which I did not like. . . . I called you about a month ago to arrange for an appointment. I didn't go through with it because I thought I could help myself. I would appreciate seeing you soon."

Eddie's personality conflicts had become more difficult with the years. He had matured a good deal, but he had been unable to break away from his mother because "it would break Mother's heart" if he moved out of her home. At the same time he was going regularly with a girl, but he could not bring himself to marry her and leave his mother. His moral scruples prevented him from having premarital relations, and the emotional disturbance which he was undergoing was carried over into his business, and he had quit his good job.

"I just couldn't stand so much responsibility," he said. "It made me discouraged with myself because I was failing again. Then I thought of going back to dental mechanics, but there's too much competition. The only way I might make a living in that field would be if I could open a laboratory of my own. While I was worrying about all this, I started to be sick again and decided to take it easy. So I haven't worked for a while, but that's no good either."

Eddie apparently had become a different person, as he wanted to do. Even when his emotional problems became too much for him, he did not suffer a return of his old heart disease. This time he developed hypertension! But avoidance of authority had not solved his problem, any more than submission to it had solved Theresa's.

Unfortunately for the young man, the series of studies which had enabled him to get psychiatric treatment at the hospital in the first place had been completed. As is the case in most clinics, there was now inadequate staff time to give him the attention he needed. The psychiatrist was obliged to note:

"His personality conflicts are still too strong for him and the possibilities of adequate adjustment are slight without extensive treatment which at present is impossible for him."

Three months later, Eddie had achieved some relief but no cure by shaking off responsibility. He had taken a job as a salesman, given up his girl and got rid of his hypertension, but he did not feel very well.

"He is not happy about these decisions," the psychiatrist noted, "but feels himself not enough of a man to do anything better."

§ 4

The Better Way

> "It's me, it's me, it's me, Oh Lord,
> Standin' in the need of prayer."

OBVIOUSLY it is the task of medicine to rescue patients like Theresa and Eddie from their dilemma. Psychosomatic techniques, as they become increasingly used, are found to apply to an increasing range of human difficulties. The first successes were achieved with patients who were suffering from diseases which were connected with the functions of the body over which the individual has little conscious control. These were the diseases of the intestinal tract, those connected with respiration and circulation, the skin allergies. But in the last five years it has been found that the same rules apply to the voluntary nervous system, which is affected in such diseases as tuberculosis, cancer and arthritis. It used to be that for some of these ailments, medicine had little more to offer than a slap on the back and a sedative. If that did not work, the doctor might resort to the desperate expedient of smashing the machinery. Such an expedient is the brain operation which involves severing the nerve which connects the frontal lobe with the cortex. The effect, in cases where intense pain is being suffered, is to prevent the impulses deriving from that pain from being sent to the cortex, which is the seat of anxiety. The victim is relieved (if he survives) from a large part of his anxiety but not from pain.

There is a better way of releasing people from their emotional dilemmas. That is to show them the way out; they can be trusted to take it without the benefit of surgery once they see it clearly before them. That is true even when the dilemma has had a chance to get a firm hold on them, for in spite of the amount of illness in the world, human beings are singularly tough, emotionally and physically. It is more surprising to observe how much they can take than how easily they succumb.

Mrs. C., for instance, had survived frustrations which to her were much more punishing than regular severe beatings would have been. After years of it, the only physical effects were headaches, painful menstruation and finally lumps in her breasts. When she consulted a physician, she said that there was nothing much wrong with her but she felt that she needed some help. As is rather a usual feature of such cases, she recited on her first visit a perfunctory story featured by reticence about her married life. A good husband, described as a good provider and good-natured, was just barely mentioned. She skipped lightly over some unpleasant features in her early married life a dozen years ago or more, saying they had been remedied.

Her early treatment consisted in helping her to understand the conditions of her childhood life which had bothered her, and there was a marked improvement in her feeling of stability. But midway in her third year of consultations the lumps in her breast developed, and her local physician had told her that they would have to be removed if they did not respond to X-ray treatments. She was being watched for cancer.

This time, Mrs. C. visited her psychiatrist clutching a series of letters in which she had described to her husband all the tortures of her married life. She had written them with a great deal of feeling and with a display of considerable literary ability, but she had never shown them to him or to anyone else. From them the real nature of her emotional difficulties was easily understood.

The couple had been married after a three-year courtship, during which the man had proposed several times. The girl, very young and not very violently in love, had hesitated because she was not sure of her own feelings, but even more because Mr. C. was a traveling salesman and neither she nor her family believed there could be much happiness in a home from which the nominal head was absent most of the time. She yielded to his pleading when he told her that he was being promoted to a position which would enable him to remain at home.

This did not happen, and in her letters Mrs. C. described bitterly her conviction that he had only been exercising his selling abilities upon her. He would, she accused him, do anything at that time to "close" a deal, and had no compunctions about making her promises which he knew he would not keep. Whether that was true or not, whether he had really thought he would get the promotion or not, Mrs. C.'s belief in his perfidy was firmly rooted. She had good reasons, too, for from the very first her married life was a frustrating one.

"It seemed I was highly desirable to you until the wedding ceremony was read," she wrote. "From the first night it was just one big excuse."

Mrs. C. remembered vividly the unhappiness of a honeymoon which the bridegroom spent mostly in the society of his nearest salesman, while the bride moped around their mountain cabin in solitude. It was a dismal foretaste of her married life. Mr. C. was away most of the time, and his wife suffered the loneliness and the snubs of a deserted woman in the midst of friends who were all paired off. She went out a good deal at first, but when men showed her little attentions, their wives were suspicious and when there were no attentions, Mrs. C. was a wallflower, a role to which she was not at all accustomed.

"Of course," she wrote, "the thing that did the real damage was the sex heartbreak. I think I could have stood the long years of bitter loneliness, the uncouth salesmen, the absolute nothing-else-ness besides your business, if it hadn't been for that. . . .

"I was young and had waited a long time to be a man's wife. Of course I wasn't adept at making love. A bride isn't supposed to be. It's up to her husband to teach and woo her into expertness.

"I'd be eaten up with yearning and desire and loneliness while you were gone. I'd count the days until you'd come home, and when you did you'd pay no more attention to me than as if I'd been your great grandmother. You had enough strength to talk about business, and that was all. I used to snuggle up to you to coax you to make love, but you were too tired. When you did make the supreme sacrifice you never made the slightest effort to try to make it teamwork or enjoyable or anything else. You took the attitude it was extracurricular as far as you were concerned."

Little by little the frustrations of her marriage were piling up on Mrs. C. Each incident in itself was a trifle, but the accumulation was resulting in tortured nights and nerve-wracked days. As she put it:

"When you were gone I was torn apart with desire and loneliness. When you were home it was worse, because there was the potential of what should have been relief. I shall never forget the long hours of ache from head to foot in bed with a man who was just too much absorbed in his own affairs to bother to be my husband. That man, who had cut the corners to sell me this marriage in the first place!"

Mrs. C. consulted a doctor, who told her she was all right and that the trouble was with her husband, who ought to seek medical advice. But when she urged it on him, the corners of his mouth turned down and he muttered: "Aa-a, it's unimportant!" Mrs. C.'s narrative continues:

"That night I had a bad headache and vomited, trying to throw you off. It took two or three days before I could stand the sight of food. You railed at me, saying, how could I expect to get strong if I didn't eat?"

The couple's chief companionship came when she escorted her husband to sales conventions or visited his associates to talk business. They had a child, a daughter, and at first Mrs. C. left her in the care of nurses while she accompanied her husband on some of his travels, but soon the little girl was the lonely one, and the mother gave up her trips. The chief effect upon her marriage was that Mr. C. felt himself abused. He really believed he was sacrificing himself for wife and daughter, but by the time the child was four years old, Mrs. C. had decided to divorce him. She changed her mind on children's day at their church.

"You were 'out of town' as you always were when everything happened," she wrote. "I was forever sitting alone in some church pew or audience or civic function. So there it was, all these angelic little children and flowers—soft organ music in the background playing 'Precious Jewels.' The mothers and daddys were beaming at their darlings and having a wonderful time. Down the aisle came Dollie in that sweet little blue organdie dress with white lace that always did make her look like an angel. Her curls were about shoulder length and she was carrying a bouquet of small flowers. She went onto the rostrum with the other little tots and stood there with that so-wistful look she had at that time. At that moment childhood seemed so fragile and important. The little things must be guarded and protected and saved, above all else. . . I vowed that for her I'd stick it out if it killed me. I'd lie, I'd act, I'd swallow my pride, I'd forfeit my own personality, *anything,* but I'd keep her home intact at least until after she had come into adolescence, which at that time looked like an eternity. I remember whispering to myself—'It's all right, sweetheart. A tragic mistake has been made, but I'll pay for it myself.' "

A feeling of nobility buoyed Mrs. C. up considerably as she put this program into operation, but it did not make home life essentially more satisfactory. And in time the eternity passed and the girl reached adolescence. That was when Mrs. C. consulted the psychiatrist. As she went over the misery of her marriage, she found that she was getting the resentment "off her chest," as she expressed it herself, and the congestion of the breasts cleared up too. She also was able to convince her husband at last—without showing him her letters—that he ought to mend his ways for the child's sake. He was really, she reported, devoted to his daughter, and saw his neglect of his family as an injustice to her.

As for Mrs. C., the condition which had threatened cancer, the headaches and the abdominal pains disappeared. She has found some satisfactory expression of her own energies in helping others, for she thinks that her own years of unhappiness have equipped her for this work. She is still not at all sure whether she wants her marriage to continue, saying:

"It doesn't seem to matter so much any more whether it does or doesn't."

§5

Artistic Realism

MRS. C. had escaped from her dilemma not by throwing herself limply upon the doctor's hands, not by struggling in lonely courage to solve her own problem without help. And if her story sounds like something out of a novel, that is quite understandable, too. Physicians who listen to stories like those of Mrs. C. are often struck by their resemblance to books. There are perhaps two reasons for this. One is the fact that patients read books. They are influenced by them, and unconsciously phrase their own troubles in imitation of a favorite novel. Physicians can learn a good deal about the personality of their patients by paying some attention to their taste in reading.

But the more important reason why psychosomatic case histories frequently sound like plagiarisms from best sellers is that the writers of best sellers, the novelists and the historians who really know their business, know people as part of that business. Their observation of what makes people click is not confined to appearances. They observe emotional reactions, too, and in their delineation of character they take those emotional reactions into account.

Critics say of the writer who has seemed to bring his characters to life that they are made of flesh and blood. They are a great deal more than that. They are made of emotions, too. When they are only flesh and blood, they seem to have no life at all, and the critics say that the writer has created nothing more than a lay figure.

The danger to living people who have become patients is that in the dilemma they will be treated as lay figures, too, with nothing except their bodily symptoms under consideration. When the physician imitates a bad novelist, he may well flounder in a sea of words to the same extent. When the patient imitates the bad novelist, it is less devastating, provided that the physician has some experience in the emotional difficulties of people who are tempted to talk about themselves so stiffly. The story of aches and pains, of blood pressure and blood chemistry, of previous illnesses and operations, of the family history of disease is important, but it is not enough. Patients who are helped out of their dilemmas have to become more realistic than the pot-boiler novelist. They have to talk about themselves as a whole person, not just a physiological specimen. Most dilemmas will fade before such treatment.

The two men in the hospital who provided an excuse for the beginning of this chapter can be extricated by a little firmness and encouragement. When the one says, "It's up to you now, Doc," the physician replies: "And to you, too, my boy." To the other's determined, "I've got to do something to get well," the physician answers: "Good for you; tell me how you got this way." The replies will bring out, under experienced guidance, the real emotional difficulties of both—bringing them out where the patients themselves can see them and understand them and deal with them. For the patient who has reached that point there are no dilemmas. Those are now reserved for the physician.

[CHAPTER VII]

The Doctor's Dilemma

§ 1

EVERYBODY, even physicians, can be thrown off balance a little by flattery in one form or another, and all the more easily if the flattery is sincere. To the medical practitioner it can take no more overpowering form than the attitude of worship which is sometimes induced by his ability to relieve pain.

"Oh, Doctor, you're wonderful!" and "Oh, Doctor, I can't get through the day without you!" are typical expressions of a dependence which may be the symptom of a disease that requires a different bedside manner than has been employed.

The physician attending such a patient has his own dilemma. The easiest course for him to follow, and often the most pleasant, is to live up to the conception of sturdy oak and allow the sickly vine to cling to his strength for support and encouragement. An equally natural reaction is to forswear the godlike role and force the patient to adopt a more independent attitude toward his own illness.

The physician who permits his patient to throw all the burden of cure upon him is a well-loved individual, as a rule. He can have the satisfaction of being welcomed and even sought after with fervent and thoroughly sincere expressions of affection, respect and admiration. He will hear very often in the course of his daily rounds the happy cry:

"I've been feeling so bad, Doctor, but now you're here I'm better already."

This is highly gratifying to a great many medical men as human beings. We like to be appreciated. The only criticism anyone can make of it is that when the admiration is carried to the point of complete dependence upon the great man, the physician may be very pleased, but the patient may not recover. The illness might have yielded to an appropriate treatment which would demand the patient's co-operation. Failing that, it might settle into a state of chronic ill health. The physician, carrying through his oaklike role, will relieve pain and even remove symptoms. But new pains and new symptoms will develop.

A more subtle version of the clinging vine is the patient who says gratefully:

"I feel so well now. I think I can get along without any treatment, but I would like to see you every once in a while."

This sounds reasonable. If the speaker means it only as it would apply within the limits of sound practice, it is reasonable. A few of the good rules for such practice after discharge of a patient are: a check-up once a year or more frequently; an understanding that the patient will return whenever he feels sick; avoidance of the clinging role by both patient and physician. However, there is a big difference between these rules and a rather common fetish of patients who want to make a sort of magic amulet out of their doctor by coming to see him all the time to get reassurance that they are all right. Then if they do not see him for a while, they get sick. They are really seeing him only to get attention, not to get help, and they will not be cured by inventing symptoms as an excuse to get that attention.

In dealing with this type of patient, the doctor must be careful to get a good picture of the facts before jumping to the conclusion that the patient has a germ or a serious illness. On the other hand, the patient should understand small pains and learn to work them out himself. Some of the preliminary study of his condition can be done by the patient, but not too much on his own and not too quickly. After he has had the experience of treatment, he should think about himself before he rushes off to the doctor. Sometimes thinking will clear up the thing that is bothering him, and he will not need to go to the doctor at all. But if he does, he will then approach the physician in this frame of mind:

"I thought it better to come and see you because something might be wrong."

This is better than inventing a symptom, but it has not completely solved the doctor's dilemma of just how far he should go in encouraging or even permitting himself to be used as a prop. But he always bears in mind that when he rejects the role of a sturdy oak, he does not, by so doing, overcome the patient's desire to dodge responsibility for his own health. The physician may cut the tendrils of his clinging patient's dependence either because of a temperamental dislike of the part he is expected to play or because he realizes that it will not do the patient much good in the long run. But mere ruthlessness is not likely to solve the patient's problem of how to get well.

Nor is a wisecrack always safe, although the temptation is sometimes almost irresistible. Dr. Edward Weiss tells of a woman of eighty who came to consult him after leaving one of his colleagues in a huff. In the course of his examination, while taking her blood pressure, he inquired why she had decided to change. She explained readily that her former physician had been using the same apparatus, and she had asked him what doctors called ailments like hers before they had such new-fangled gadgets to play with.

"Bad temper, madam, bad temper," he had replied.

Brusque or severe tactics may do more than lose a patient for the doctor. They may damage the patient, for the already sick individual may not be ready to stand on his own feet. He may lose his confidence in the physician's ability or interest in the case. The path to a real cure may then be blocked.

The safe path between the horns of this familiar physician's dilemma is to concentrate on and help the patient to remove the reasons for his desire to cling to a stronger personality. The physician should always remember that for these patients the role is that of a parent not over-protecting, but also not too much in a hurry. He may need to guide his patients to security step by step, but he must be sure that his attitude as well as that of the patient is focused on this goal. Here, as is so many other cases, most people will know what to do for themselves if they understand just why they are leaning upon the physician instead of standing alone. Together they will be able to cure the disease as well as the symptoms.

§ 2

The Physics of Emotion

IN CASES such as this, the disease and the desire to throw the burden of cure on someone else both stem from the same source. This source lies in the emotions of the individual, and in some obstacle to the efficient operation of those emotions.

Efficiency and emotion may seem a contradiction in terms to some people. But there is a relationship whose exposition was perhaps the greatest work of Sigmund Freud. It may be compared with the more generally understood laws of physics relating to energy.

In the physical world, we know, no energy is ever lost. It may, however, go into other forms than man intended. It may be expressed in terms of heat or light or motion or chemical change. Thus a given unit of energy may become heat which in turn generates steam which runs an engine which operates machinery, and so on to the end of time. If blocked at any point—say at the point of generating steam— the unit of energy will not cease to exist; it will cause an explosion.

In the same way, what we might call emotional energy is never lost. It, too, can express itself in a variety of ways, and in some which man does not intend and may not even perceive. We say that it is operating "normally" when it expresses itself in speech or thought or action not obviously harmful either to the individual or to society.

But, as Freud was the first to point out in explicit terms, if usual channels of emotional discharge are blocked, it will be diverted into others which will turn it into destructive and constricting force. Furthermore, Freud found, the amount of emotional energy, the force of its drive, will remain equal to the strength of the emotional impulse which originated it.

When the normal channels of emotion are blocked, we call it a repression. The emotion, turned from its logical course, will not be expressed, but will operate along new lines within the individual's personality and probably without his knowledge. Freud's great contribution was in explaining this process. He traced the emotion along its hidden paths, showing that if it could be brought to the surface and given an outlet in speech or action, it served its purpose, while if it remained buried but still active in the individual's mind, it could be harmful even to his body. Later investigation shows that it creates an unbalance in the autonomous nervous system.

Since then we have learned that it can be more harmful than most of Freud's early admirers realized, although Freud himself recognized the implications of his discoveries in the physical as well as the emotional aspects of the human organism. The repressed emotional energy may very well transform itself into symptoms of physical illness.

Everyone has experienced in himself the changes of temperature or the rapidly altered operation of the sweat glands which result from a strong emotional stimulus. Most of us do not feel so acutely the chemical changes within ourselves under the same circumstances. Enough of these experiences, however, if they are turned out of their normal channels of action and talk, can add up to an internal physical change of the kind called an illness.

A neglected machine gets to the point where it is no longer an efficient transformer of energy. Such a machine may soon be beyond repair. The human emotional system can lose its efficiency in transforming emotional energy into desirable uses. If neglected or abused for too long, it too can suffer beyond repair.

This brings us back to the sturdy-oak physician and the cling-ing-vine patient. Somewhere along the line emotional energy has been diverted from its proper channel in the patient. The way out of the doctor's dilemma at this point consists in finding the obstacle which blocked adequate expression of the patient's emotions. In so doing, the physician removes the cause of the bodily ailment as well. This, in brief, is the aim and purpose of psychosomatic treatment.

Of course it is easier to say that the source of the inadequate unresolved emotional conflict should be detected and the patient helped to remove the obstacle to its expression than it is to carry out the course. The application of psychiatric methods to treatment of even common diseases is difficult, in part because we are only approaching detailed knowledge of the subject.

Psychiatry has been called the oldest of the medical arts but the newest of the medical sciences. Men and women who can master the techniques of an art are always scarcer than those who can master the application of known scientific principles. As long as we are still learning the facts underlying psychosomatic principles, it is hard to use them effectively.

One of the areas which is still being explored indicates the complexity of the doctor's dilemma. Just as patients can make a physician sick, so the process can be reversed. This may sound rather like an heretical admission for a professional to make in writing for a lay public. But it is a fact which neither physician nor patient can safely ignore.

Perhaps it will sound a little better if the physician in this instance is called a pathogenic agent, which means an agent that produces disease. It does not mean that the physician is incompetent; I am not talking about the doctor who mistakes an abdominal tenderness for appendicitis when the patient has typhoid. The physician who is a pathogenic agent is likely to be just the reverse of a bungler, working veritable miracles with ninety-eight patients only to have a strangely baffling failure with the ninety-ninth.

What can happen is that his personality, reacting upon that of the patient, sets up or intensifies certain emotional conflicts which may block a cure or lead to some brand-new illness after the one for which the physician was called in has apparently been exorcised.

It may happen, for instance, that the physician is a belligerent fellow who has found that he gets excellent results by bullying his patients, standing no nonsense from them, issuing gruff orders in general behaving like the elder Barrett among his fluttering, dutiful offspring in Wimpole Street. But every so often he will get a patient who really had a father like that and never got over it. The result can well be the explosion of one of those delayed-action mines of childhood. Both physician and patient may be dumbfounded by a failure to respond to treatment which has been eminently successful in dozens of apparently similar cases.

In dealing with his dilemma, the physician—and the patient, too, for that matter—should note the remarkable powers for self-therapy of which the human mind is capable. It should not be surprising that the emotional force which can cause a disease ought to be strong enough to cure one, but many who have been willing to concede the importance of the mind in bringing about an ailment will refuse to permit the same medium to help in the cure.

Whether permitted or not, the mind will take part, however. That section of it which possesses consciousness cannot be ignored any more than the "unconscious" which bulks so large in literature, lay and medical. This conscious section is the one which the individual uses to test all reality; it is the reason we can know anything. It is the ego. In treating disease, physicians will have difficulty with inadequately developed egos of two types. The whining-child sort of patient is the obvious one, but just as often quite aggressive characters are equally weak. They find it necessary to call attention to their egos more or less in the same way as one would put a hand to a place that hurts.

§ 3

When the Ego Hurts

THE ENLISTMENT of the patient's mind in his own behalf is part of psychosomatic techniques. It is illustrated in the case of a girl who was in the hospital with an ulcer on her leg. After a surgeon who did not believe in psychiatry had exhausted the possibilities of his science without discovering any physical cause for the ulcer and after grafting skin from the child's stomach failed to help, a psychiatrist who had treated the girl before was called in. The patient improved so rapidly that she was out of the hospital in a few days, greatly to the surprise of the surgeon, who did not believe the mind healed that fast.

The child, Stella, had what the psychiatrist in reporting the case described as "an uncanny, unconscious rapport" with her mother. What the mother seemed to think, Stella did. Until she was four years old, she had always slept in her mother's room. Then a baby brother was born, George, and took her place while she was relegated to her father's room. When she was in the middle of her eighth year her father was inducted into the Army, and Stella felt deserted. She developed colitis, but after a year of psychoanalytic treatment was freed from this symptom. During this time she grew to understand her jealousy of her brother and her resentment of her mother. Two years later, when an emotional strain seemed to indicate colitis, the girl was no longer able to produce that disease but acquired a new symptom, ulcer of the leg. The attending physician sent her to the hospital, since she was a difficult patient and force had to be used before she would allow her leg to be seen and treated.

In the hospital the psychiatrist saw her again. Her conflict was whether to get well and go to school, which would mean leaving her mother, or to remain sick, which would mean not only keeping her mother, but taking her away from George. After this was made clear to her, the ulcer cleared up. Three weeks later, her mother kept her home from school because she had a cold. Furious, Stella declared she'd get even; she'd get sick and make her mother empty bedpans for her. She did stay up all night, keeping the bedpan hopefully beside her, but what she got was ulcer of the leg again.

This time she went back to the hospital under the surgeon's care. She hated it, and when the psychiatrist finally took over, Stella declared that she had felt deserted by even that physician and just hadn't cared. But now she wanted to get out of the hospital. The psychiatrist agreed to get her out if she would promise to help fight her own impulses instead of the doctor's. Stella was so eager to comply that, although the surgeon had thought it would be unwise to let her leave for at least several weeks, her condition improved so that her ulcer was virtually healed and there was no need for medical treatment within a few days.

Treatment, of course, was by no means ended. Stella still had a great many anxieties. One concerned her dog. Usually children who have live pets make much better adjustments to the world than those who have played only with inanimate toys. They become better parents themselves because they have learned a little of what happens in life. They have learned without shock or fear that there are some things Papa can't fix if they go wrong. Stella was anxious about the dog, however, and complained that her mother, who had been reluctant to get it because she disliked animals, would not even let the child take her pet into the yard.

"And what good is a dog if you don't feel it's yours and can't do whatever you want with it?" she asked.

The reaction might have seemed a little excessive. But apparently Stella was not just worrying about the dog. She had been brought up with a great many sexual fears and doubts and misconceptions which were painful to her. She had the impression that all children were born with a penis but that her mother had taken hers away and given it to brother George. She had been warned of terrible nameless things that would happen to her if she yielded to sexual impulses. She was disturbed by fantasies in which impregnation took place by mouth.

During all this time, Stella's mother had been as attentive as the child in her desire for maternal affection could desire. But the poor woman was at the same time deeply anxious about losing the love of her son. She felt that she was neglecting George. Part of Stella's treatment was improvement in her relations with her mother, who said one day:

"I would never have believed that such a change was possible. Or have I changed, too?"

She had, of course, because both she and her daughter had learned to take care of themselves. The mother no longer visited upon the daughter the consequences of her own fear of being unable to control her feelings. The daughter no longer reacted with spite and jealousy to her environment. Stella had learned to stand on her own feet, which took quite a while, both literally and figuratively, since the effects of the ulcer prevented her from using her leg fully for some time. Finally it was with a real sense of triumph that she reported:

"I won a contest in jumping rope today. I can jump rope and skate now as well as any other girl on the block."

Until this time, Stella had resented greatly the fact that she was a girl. The thought of having children had frightened her; her desires were to make herself a man. But one of the benefits the use of her mind in connection with her illness had brought was that she became satisfied with her sex. Her mother reported that one day after coming from the psychiatrist's office, the girl had expressed a confidence that she would not go to the hospital for any recurrence of her ailment.

"You know when I will go to a hospital again?" she asked. "When I have a baby."

A pleasantly innocuous remark, but it proved that Stella's conflicts were resolving themselves and that her emotional system was taking part in the healing of her mind as well as her body.

§ 4

Miracle at Lourdes

MUCH MORE dramatic evidence of this therapeutic quality of the emotions may be seen at Lourdes, and anyone interested in the psychosomatic ideas of illness and health would do well to ponder the curious phenomena which take place in this French shrine of miracles.

Its own citizens, and millions of others, call it "the holy town," and it attracts its pilgrims by hundreds of thousands, while the sick who came seeking cures numbered some 17,000 a year at the time I visited it more than a decade ago.

Perhaps the most striking thing about Lourdes is that there is nothing very striking about it as a town or in its setting. The valley is beautiful, but there are many even more beautiful and many towns more attractive to the eye. The most distinguishing feature is one narrow, winding side street leading down to the church and crowded with shops for tourists, especially for tourists seeking souvenirs of some religious significance. The church itself, rising above the Grotto and the baths which give Lourdes its reason for being, is architecturally ineffectual, even ugly, although its great semicircular ramps outlining an enormous plaza are distinctive. Certainly there is nothing in the beauty of the town or its setting to account for the miracles.

The talk of miracles here is as casual as the talk of fish in Gloucester or automobiles in Detroit or government in Washington. They are the main preoccupation of the people. But you will not find in Gloucester or Detroit or Washington the fervor and devotion so evident in even the casual conversation of the dweller in Lourdes. The common talk is of the cures, and often of the strange ways in which they take place. The stories are in the spirit of some peasant who has lived all his life in a remote valley in close dependence upon the forces of nature which, for all his communion with them, he can never understand.

Why does the lightning strike here or there? Why does the rain fall some seasons and not others? Why did our Lady of Lourdes the other day heal the unknown orphan girl and yet leave the young son of one of her most devoted servants at the Grotto still speechless year after year? These are the mysteries of God and of nature about which the people of Lourdes speak with reverence and faith.

Into this atmosphere pour the hundreds of thousands of pilgrims, according to a fixed schedule which allows each pilgrimage its three or five days. One group will be Dutch, another Italian, then French and Belgians and Poles and Austrians and so on through almost all the nationals of the world. Each pilgrimage has its daily schedule, given out by its priest. There will be so many Masses, so many hours of prayer for the sick at the baths, Stations of the Cross, nursing service and participation in the great processions. Lourdes is a silent town save for the chants and prayers, which can be heard at intervals from the first Mass at 5:30 in the morning until the winding torchlight procession, with its *Ave* to an air of moving simplicity, lends a strange beauty to the evening.

Most people when the place is mentioned think of Lourdes and its priests; some think of the physicians at the Medical Bureau; but strangely enough neither group presents anything particularly out of the ordinary. Nor does either group have the ultimate power where the sick are concerned. This rests with the nurses and stretcher bearers; many of them personages of more or less distinction, more or less incognito, doing all sorts of menial tasks, each one with his story; a miraculous cure of a member of his family for which he is paying, as he will say; or a tragic life history.

The sick were cared for in two hospitals, generally lacking in modern improvements and equipment. Yet they received from 1,000 to 1,500 new patients every three or five days. That fact alone made them something exceptional in terms of hospital administration. The uncomfortable stone buildings had damp rooms in which the patients lay in long rows, bed touching bed, receiving hardly a minimum of care and often suffering acutely.

Yet there was an atmosphere of confidence and contentment which is not found in our more comfortable, better-served hospital wards. These sick and suffering human beings, representing as diverse a group of diseases as can be found anywhere, were happy and uncomplaining. Their tired eyes came back again and again to the figure of our Lady of Lourdes, which was the only break in the bare stone walls around them.

At least once and usually twice a day these sick and dying people, many of whom would be regarded as much too ill to be moved in any other environment, were carried down to the church, to the baths, to the procession of the Blessed Sacrament. Hundreds of them on primitive stretchers or drawn in wheel chairs over rough cobblestones made up the average procession. Patients with broken backs, with tuberculosis in the most extreme stages, with disfiguring skin diseases, draining wounds, all sorts and conditions of ailments were carried slowly along to the accompaniment of constant prayers of their attendants and themselves. Those who died on the way looked only a little more contented than the rest.

Arriving at the Grotto, the patients were—and doubtless still are —allowed to bathe in the miraculous waters, and bathing is continuous except for the noon hour until 4:30 in the afternoon when the sick are carried to the semicircular ramps of the church. Here they will lie for two hours in sun or rain. The procession of the Blessed Sacrament will pass them; other pilgrims will press in around them; finally a priest will bless them one by one while the thousands of pilgrims and onlookers shout in unison prayers of the most moving sort. Each cry rings out again and again as the priest makes his way slowly around the huge semicircles.

It is against this background that the cures which are achieved or the relief which the sick obtain at Lourdes must be assessed. Now and then it will happen that a patient who for months or years has not stirred from his bed will get up and walk in the procession. However, demonstrations of this kind are discouraged, because Lourdes aims to guard against hysteria in many of its forms.

But in the evening in the hospital some patient will begin to eat, then get out of bed and busy himself in caring for the others in his ward. The pilgrimage physician will be called and asked if this patient has been cured. If a large nervous element is suspected, even though there is also an organic disease present, the patient is told to thank God for his cure, but not to visit the Medical Bureau.

This Bureau was established to confirm purely organic cures, and the physicians are not interested in studying psychic forces. Hundreds are turned away because they do not offer any evidence of organic cure, while it is obvious to any observer that only a small number of those whose illnesses have been relieved at Lourdes bother with the Medical Bureau at all. Most of them naturally care more about the fact that they feel themselves cured or benefited than they do about obtaining a doctor's certificate to that effect.

Even if anyone could gather a complete count of those who are cured, it would fall far short of exhausting the significance of Lourdes in relation to health. I once asked a physician from the North of Europe who had been coming to the town as medical director of a pilgrimage for twelve years whether any of his patients had been cured.

"No patient of mine has ever been cured," he replied, "although I often advise them to come. So far as I know, our people never have had a real cure. We are too cold; we do not believe easily enough. The naïve, simple faith of the priests and the people of Lourdes is foreign to us.

"But what is remarkable is that everyone who comes goes away quiet, and that not just for a few days; often it is a quietness lasting a lifetime."

This same factor is stressed by physicians who have had cures among their patients. One of them remarked:

"Whatever may be said as to the value of bringing to Lourdes each year these hundreds of sick on the chance that one or two of them may be cured, the important thing to me is that all of them are in some way changed, and go back with a different attitude toward their illness and able to help others, whether it be only the fretful patient in the next bed in the hospital to which they return to die, or whether they get well and go out into the community."

As for the cured and those who claim to be cured, the nurses and stretcher bearers have their own standards and are usually better judges than the physicians. These attendants have seen real cures and cures which they knew would not last. They stress the deep confidence and quiet in those who really are cured as compared to the hysterical excitement in some of the others.

During my first week at Lourdes, I saw two girls, each with tuberculosis in such an advanced stage that their physicians had advised against their coming, on the ground that they probably could not survive the journey. After the bath at the Grotto, one of them shouted:

"I am cured! Our Lady has cured me!"

The curious thronged about her, and she was immediately the object of much bustle and attention. The second girl merely turned to her nurse and said:

"I wonder if it can be true? I feel as if I were cured."

She said nothing to anyone else, and no one paid much attention to her. I saw both of them the next day. The first girl had collapsed somewhat and was being talked to by the Sister-in-charge about discipline of the spirit. The other stood out from the masses of sick around her by the radiance of her personality. Two days before, I had seen this girl on a stretcher, scarcely able to raise her hand, unable to eat, coughing painfully. Now she was radiant, although emaciated, walking about in the service of her sick companions. The cough had disappeared, and she felt perfectly well.

She interested me so much that I visited her three weeks later in her own little village near Como, and talked with her physician. He said that he had not expected her to return and was astonished, for there had been a complete revolution in her condition.

The attendants had diagnosed the difference between these two girls at once. It is remarkable how accurately these nurses and stretcher bearers are able to distinguish on the basis of their experience the real or the possibly real from the pseudo.

The drama of Lourdes is exciting for anyone. But from the standpoint of those who are interested in the psychosomatic approach to medicine, the important thing about the Lourdes phenomena is that emotional forces without the help of scientific method or many of the tools for healing which science has given us—indeed, in disobedience of many of the principles which mechanistic science has taught us—are making people happier and freer to act.

Yet the present resident physician at Lourdes, Dr. Francois Leuret, was quoted as recently as July, 1947, as saying that the records of his office, dating back to 1888, show fewer than 200 recognized cures. Yet, he also estimates the pilgrims at about a million a year.

Dr. Leuret makes clear that his responsibility is only to report cures that cannot be completely explained in terms of present medical knowledge. The Church then decides whether or not they are miracles. Relief of symptoms on the basis of personality or emotional changes is generally not considered miraculous, although from the point of view of mechanistic medicine it should be. But actually Dr. Leuret looks upon himself as a "devil's advocate" who must pour the cold water of what he considers scientific skepticism upon the ardent claims of miraculous cures. He, therefore, declines to recognize any which he cannot prove by X-ray or laboratory analysis. Yet it is obvious that in the actual results of alleviating human suffering, the record is better than the 200 patients out of the 68,000,000 which Dr. Leuret reports. There have been many more changes in personality which have resulted in improved health for pilgrims who could never satisfy the mechanistic tests of the medical bureau at Lourdes, as the pilgrimage physician from Northern Europe indicated.

If the scientific methods of the psychosomatic techniques could be added at Lourdes to the purely somatic preoccupations of the good resident physician, the record of the "place of miracles" might be better. An understanding of the emotional forces which are released by the experience of the pilgrim would enable the doctors to direct them into more healing channels. There need be no loss of prestige either, for the ability to make a personality whole is surely as wonderful as the healing of a running sore.

Until then, the scientific skeptics who make up the staff of the "devil's advocate" cannot escape from the doctor's dilemma. He cannot deal with the patient's personality, which can give the clue not only to the "miracle" but to the disease.

Seemingly miraculous cures occurred with and without faith, but a physician with a scientific understanding of the psychosomatic approach can effect cures by medical methods which would have been considered miracles a generation ago.

[CHAPTER VIII]

The Accident Habit

§ 1

BROKEN bones and hearts have two things in common. First, they are frequently so misunderstood that one is called an accident and the other an impossibility. Second, psychosomatic studies reveal that both are diseases in which emotional conflicts play an important role. People hurt themselves more often than they are hurt by others or by fate or by the impersonal failure of machines.

The disease of the broken-bone habit has no name in the medical dictionaries, but it might be handy to coin one and call it "accidentitis." It covers a definite personality type whose sound bodies get damaged in mishaps brought on in the course of a state of mind which is far from strong, although not at all what we usually mean by "unsound." At least 80 per cent of the millions of major accidents which happen every year are due to this ailment.

This does not mean that you have it necessarily if you sprain an ankle or burn a finger. Nor is it another way of saying "clumsy." Graceful people are just as susceptible to it as awkward ones. There are a good many incorrigibly inept individuals who cannot hammer a nail in straight but do not smash their fingers, who trip over their own feet but break no bones. They tumble down stairs, fall off docks, bump into stone walls, slip on the ice and scrape the fenders of their cars without damage to themselves or anyone else, although their friends sometimes wonder how they remain in one piece. The fact is that for all their clumsiness they do not have the accident habit. On the other hand, some deft, seemingly well-balanced men and women turn up repeatedly in the accident wards of our hospitals. They think they are the victims of pure bad luck or divine punishment. In reality they have been struck down by their own emotional conflicts.

Safety campaigns and safety devices multiply to deal with this situation, but so do the accidents. Commentators are inclined to blame carelessness and the perversity of human nature in refusing to obey the elementary dictates of caution. The close student of human behavior and human emotions, the psychosomatic student, discovers a pattern in the confusion, and instead of accidents he finds "accidentitis."

Accidents, not being popularly considered a disease, are generally overlooked in considering the factors which enter into public health. Yet they are among the major causes of human pain, suffering and disability. They account, too, for a substantial part of medical practice and therefore of the patients who are in need of medical care.

Each year 740 out of every 10,000 people in this country are injured badly enough to be incapacitated for a full day or more, and twenty-six of them suffer some permanent impairment. More are killed in this way—100,000 in 1946, the National Safety Council estimates—than by any regularly recognized illnesses except heart diseases, cancer and cerebral hemorrhage. Accident is the biggest killer of the young, outranking all others in the age groups from one to twenty-nine, figures of the National Office of Vital Statistics show. Accidents afflict men more than women; they kill more males between the ages of two and thirty-eight than any illness; they kill and disable more young than adults.

The risks of the so-called peaceful world in which we live are shown by the fact that a citizen who falls down by accident in the course of his normal routine at home or at work is six times as likely to be permanently damaged as a soldier wounded in battle. Of the country's workers, less than a third of the total population, some 4,000,000, are killed or injured each year in accidents, and usually not in connection with their work either. The price in human suffering is incalculable. The loss in terms of man-days is a good deal higher than the loss from strikes, even in a year of high industrial dispute. The National Safety Council estimates that the 10,400,000 disabling injuries of 1946 cost $5,600,000,000 which is enough to service the national debt.

Automobile accidents are far from accounting for the major part of this annual waste of human life and strength, although they receive the most attention. Of the 1946 deaths, for instance, 33,500 were caused by motor-vehicle crashes of one kind or another; 34,000 Americans were killed in accidents in their homes; 32,500 died in industrial accidents, airplane crashes, railroad smash-ups and all other accidents. As for the injured who recover, falls alone cause twice as many of these cases as all the automobile accidents put together.

The studies of a good many authorities in recent years have established the conclusion that only about 10 to 20 per cent of all these injuries, fatal or otherwise, are caused by really accidental accidents. The rest are linked to the personality of the victim.

I myself was unaware of the work being done on this subject when, some years ago, I and several associates began a study of all the patients on the general admission rolls of a large hospital in New York. This survey lasted for more than five years and took in a thoroughly representative cross-section of the nation's urban population. At the outset, the special purpose of the study was to gather data on the emotional factors in cardio-vascular disease and diabetes.

One of the first questions which had to be answered for this purpose was just how the personality factors in cardiac and diabetic patients could be considered characteristic of the disease, and just how they differed from those encountered among healthy people. Healthy people are hard to find in hospitals. Furthermore, it is impossible to go outside and obtain a good average sample of the general population willing to submit to the routine needed for these studies. So, acting on the supposition that accidents are accidental and can and do happen to anybody, it was decided to use the fracture patients in the hospital as representing the outside world. These people are generally regarded as the most "normal" lot in any institution.

Most of us were somewhat disconcerted to find as our study progressed that fracture patients as a group are not particularly "normal" at all. The existence of this strange ailment "accidentitis" deprived us of the control group we thought we had found, and we began to look into what other scientific workers had been doing to discover just how its victims get that way.

§ 2

Profile of the Accident-Prone

A GERMAN named Marbe was the first to note publicly the existence of an accident habit. In 1926 he proved statistically that the person who has had one accident is more likely to have another than the individual who has never had any. In 1934 a Viennese, Alexandra Adler, suggested that an unknown factor in the human personality was responsible for the curious repetition of injuries to those who are prone to accidents.

Meanwhile some important contributions were made in this country by engineers and industrial managers who were trying to do something about the increasing number of accidents. For example, one public-utility company which operated a large fleet of trucks and had a good many inspectors traveling about in passenger cars became seriously alarmed at the rate both of its accidents and of insurance. The company's vehicles traveled as much as 2,900,000 miles a year at the time, and the accidents were becoming a serious detriment to profitable operations.

The company managers ordered tests of everything they could think of, from the weather to the reaction time of employees. They tried intensive education of their drivers and they tried imposing severe penalties on those who had accidents and survived. The accident rate went right on rising, and the elaborate series of tests and orders ended in the mildly worded conclusion that "the methods which the psychologists thus far have used cannot be made very effective in predicting a driver's performance."

Baffled by this failure, the company fell back upon the simple expedient of shifting men with bad accident records from the driver's seat to some other work in the plant. In less than four years, by carefully weeding out the principal victims, the company reduced its accident rate per year to about one-fifth of that prevailing in 1928, and they held it down for years.

The efficiency of operations on the road was much increased; the insurance premiums dropped. But after a while it was discovered that the men taken off the trucks still had the accident habit. Instead of smashing up their vehicles, they were injuring themselves in mishaps around the plant or at home. The National Research Council, which made a study of this and three other firms, reported:

"Since that time analysis of the records of more than 2,000 drivers employed by the four companies showed that their automobile accidents and their personal injuries tend to accumulate side by side."

The statistics gathered through our hospital study showed that fracture patients (even including the victims of accidental accidents) had fourteen times greater a tendency to have disabling mishaps than the average of all the other groups of hospital patients studied. The fracture cases had averaged four accidents, even including those with their first; the other groups averaged less than three-tenths of an accident per person. The percentage of injuries among the other patients was in no group more than the 10 to 20 per cent which are believed on the basis of insurance and other statistics to be real accidents, although many of these groups, such as victims of heart disease or diabetes, might be expected to be more accident-prone because of their illness. We found that 80 per cent of our fracture patients had two or more accidents. The highest among the other patients was a group with a certain type of rheumatic fever, who were found to be mildly accident-prone themselves. Of them, 14 per cent had two or more accidents. More

than half the fracture patients had a history of three or more accidents. None of the other patients suffering from a single ailment
had had so many, but a few suffering from two or more overlap-
ping illnesses did.

Certain characteristics are common to the whole group with
"accidentitis." They are generally decisive to the point of giving
an impression of impulsiveness. They concentrate upon daily
pleasures with little interest in long-term goals. They display a
relatively cavalier attitude toward sex and family, but take very
good care of their own health. Their illness rate is well below that
of the general population. Even in their extra-marital sex relationships they maintain enough concern for their own welfare to have
a very low rate of venereal-disease infection or unwanted pregnancies, yet are not bothered by exaggerated fears on either score.
Ten per cent of the women in the hospital group studied had a
high abortion rate, but every one of these was married. Most of
them, furthermore, for religious reasons either refrained from
using contraceptives or had difficulties on this subject.

The frequency with which the patient described his upbringing
as strict was surprising. Later it was learned that in the pattern of
the accident-prone there is usually an extreme resentment of authority, often unconscious, whether that authority is represented
by parents, guardians, relatives, spouse, church or employer. An
unusually large proportion had neurotic traits in childhood. These
expressed themselves for some of the patients in the form of walking or talking in their sleep, in others as persistent lying, stealing
and truancy. Later these tendencies disappeared, apparently replaced by the accident habit.

These traits show themselves in the same ways over and over
again. The decisiveness of the accident-prone is part of a drive for
independence and self-reliance in a situation of the moment rather
than as a part of a planned career or program. In conversation,
these remarks are typical:

"I always like to keep working, and can't stand around doing
nothing." "Adventure and excitement appeal to me." "When I find
a way to do a thing, I always stick to it; but if I don't, I do some-

thing anyway and take a chance." "I like to finish what I'm doing, but sometimes I like to do something else first, so I jump up and do it."

When this personality pattern is set beside those of other groups in the population, it turns out to match very precisely that of the juvenile delinquent and the adult criminal. The behavior characteristic of the persistent breaker of laws is virtually identical with that of the persistent breaker of bones right up to the point where the one commits a crime and the other has an accident. It is a fact that few criminals get sick. They find release from their emotional conflict in what society has chosen to regard as an unsocial act, just as their counterparts in the accident wards of hospitals find their release in the accident habit.

In both, the early history has been one of poor adjustment to a strict authority in home or school, usually accompanied by a story of parental rejection. They have had the same childhood neurotic traits, and in both groups these tend to disappear as the child grows older. Their parallel development diverges when the one carries the early record of lying, stealing and truancy into a broader field and becomes a criminal, while the other begins to hurt himself instead of the community.

There is no hope of a real understanding of the criminal or the accident habit until preconceived moral judgments have been eliminated. One does not necessarily condone holdups by trying to get at the motivating factors in the holdup man any more than cancer is condoned by the researcher into its causes. Yet it is hard for many to strip away from their own minds the habit, which has been induced by all their early environment, of passing moral judgments on the minds of their neighbors. Perhaps it will be easier to do this in a case involving an emotional system which almost no one will demand should conform to his own set of moral standards. This is the case of Nick, the dog, who had a well-developed accident habit and got it just the same way as millions of human beings do.

Nick was observed over a period of ten years, relatively longer in a dog's life than anyone is privileged to study most human beings. He learned rapidly enough, but he was not as friendly or co-operative with his master and other people in the house as other dogs were. He never could reconcile his obvious conflict with authority, so that although he was housebroken he had a tendency to wet the floor when his owner or someone in authority entered the room suddenly. Nick asserted his independence by refusing to come to the family car when called, but he ran to it of his own accord when someone got in or blew the horn. In a child all this would have been called evidence of truancy, disobedience, neurotic behavior.

Nick's accident habit started early. He had a genius for knocking into things, getting under people's feet, bumping into machinery. One year he developed a habit of tangling himself in his chain and hurting himself with it. Several years later, spending the summer at the family's farm, he twice fell into an abandoned privy. Each time he was trapped in it for several hours before his barking brought rescuers. His master and observer, W. Horsley Gantt, records another of Nick's achievements:

"On one occasion at night he followed my car without my knowledge, but as he could not overtake me, I met him on my return homeward. After passing him going in the opposite direction, I turned around and went back, but he again had recognized my car and was again running toward me. I put on the brakes, but he continued running into the car which knocked him down and dragged him along, resulting in two scalp wounds. However, he trotted on home at a rapid pace, so that I did not find him until I had also arrived."

§3

A Need for Pain

OBVIOUSLY there was nothing wicked or shameful in Nick's behavior or emotional responses. The same thing is true of human beings. They are not trying to hurt themselves, because they are possessed by evil spirits nor even because of some perverted masochistic tendencies. They simply have reached a point in their inability to handle an emotional conflict where both body and mind are in a position to have something unpleasant happen to them. In fact, the something unpleasant has become a physical as well as an emotional necessity.

A good example of the sort of person who develops the accident habit was a girl of twenty who was admitted to the hospital for treatment of an old injury to her left arm. It had been broken and mangled in a machine at the factory in which she had been employed. Anne, as we may call her, had returned to the hospital for an operation because the injury had healed badly.

The first thing we learned about her personal life was that she was one of the ten children of a janitor who had always been "good to me" but was fairly strict with all his children, and quick-tempered besides. On the other hand, the mother "is grand and very understanding." Anne was a regular attendant at the Catholic Church—a majority of those who have the accident habit were brought up in a strict religious atmosphere. Her concern for her health was indicated by her use of vitamin tablets and tonics, and by this sample from one of her talks with the psychiatrist:

"I've always taken pretty good care of my health but I always was thin. A few weeks before the accident I was losing weight. . . . I tried to eat as much as I could and I force myself to drink milk. I make sure I get enough sleep; if I've had a strenuous day I go to bed and don't go out. I never stay out very late because I think it would be bad for my health."

In addition, Anne spent a lot of time out of doors and was active in athletics, not only because she liked them but because she supposed they were good for her. She avoided smoking, coffee and alcohol (in this she was not typical) because she thought them harmful.

The girl had many friends, belonged to a club, had a boy friend about whom she was rather reticent. She did say that she planned some day to marry but not this lad. Sociability and popularity also are typical of the "accidentitis" patient. Anne had felt a little lonely since her arm had been hurt, partly because most of her intimate friends had married recently and also because her injured arm kept her out of things.

"The trouble is," she said, "I have to do everything alone and I don't like to be alone. Everybody else is working while I'm playing."

The usual decisive, pseudo-impulsive behavior of the accident habit was revealed when she said:

"I'm pretty fast to make my mind up. Like other people would be scared to undergo an operation and I just made up my mind like that. It's the same way when I go some place."

The concentration on the present at the expense of a broader view was shown by the fact that although she was very ambitious, of average intelligence and bitterly ashamed of the fact that her father was only a janitor and that most of the family worked in factories, she did nothing very decisive to change her lot. In the psychiatric history of her case appears this passage:

"She focused upon immediate values rather than long-range goals. Her strong emotional attachments were to people—her family and friends, and to concrete experiences of the moment—swimming, tennis, horseback riding. She had no intellectual interests."

Anne had been trained for secretarial work. She held a clerical job for a few weeks, but lost it and went to work in a factory, tending a machine, and was secretly ashamed of it. It was not, however, dissatisfaction with the work which contributed directly to the accident. She had been losing weight and as a result of the weakness she had been transferred from the machines to lighter work. Furthermore, she had been promised that in a couple of weeks she would get the stenographic position which she much preferred. She had just returned from a very pleasant week end, and between that and the promise of the more attractive job she was, she said, "in high spirits." That morning another girl fainted at her machine.

"It was very smoky and she couldn't stand the smoke," Anne explained. "It never bothered me. I never faint."

Anne therefore volunteered to take the other girl's place. Before long her glove caught in the machinery and drew her whole forearm in before the mechanism jammed and she could be released.

Most accident victims of this kind have a suppressed guilty feeling about their broken bones. Especially if they are accident-prone, they tend to regard the injury as punishment for sin or rebellion against authority—not as something they have done to themselves. Anne was no exception. She mentioned her sensation of guilt spontaneously, saying:

"I didn't like the work and I was always complaining to my mother. I wanted to rest, and now I've got a good long rest—too long."

Perhaps a more completely "normal" story could not be told, at least normal on the surface. But beneath the surface, this girl's emotional life had engendered some conflict which never before had escaped in action, speech or even very much thought. Her essential conflict with stern authority, as represented by her father and her church, was reduced by her concentration on momentary desires. Achievement of her real ambition would have opened up the gap between her and her family. Her complaints about her own factory job were indirect criticisms of her father, yet when she had the promise of the better job it turned out that she had a deep sense of guilt because she was being raised, as she felt, above her father. Probably carelessness, induced by the feeling of superiority and the feeling of guilt, precipitated the accident.

§ 4

Events Leading Up to the Tragedy

THE ACTUAL circumstances which precede most accidents—and, in the opinion of the patients, cause them—are often the most valuable clue to the hidden conflict which creates emotional forces driving that particular individual into the accident habit. Here are some thoroughly representative examples of what patients in the accident ward of the hospital had been worrying about just before the moment of the accident:

Mr. A. was hurrying—"I am always in a hurry, even if I have plenty of time," he said—to apply for a job. He had just been laid off from work he liked, and was afraid he would not get the new job at once. This fear was due chiefly to the fact that he had not told his wife about being unemployed, and he dreaded the tearful scene to which he would be subjected if he had to admit it to her before he had another job. Brooding on this possibility, he slipped on the ice and broke his leg.

Mrs. B., a young Catholic wife, was on her way to church for confession. She had been using contraceptives (which her church regards as a mortal sin) and was worrying about the fact that she would have to confess and also would have to promise to give them up. Worrying over this, she fell down the front steps.

Mr. C. had been working on Sunday morning, "which made me mad but I couldn't refuse my boss." He was still fuming at the injustice of his employer's request—and at the fact that he had had to get up for 6:30 mass instead of lying luxuriously in bed until 10:30 as he usually did on Sundays—when he succeeded in fracturing a vertebra.

Mr. D. was playing football because he was angry. He had found in the course of his twenty-nine years that he could dissipate rage by this kind of violent exercise. This time he broke a leg.

Miss E. was coming home from a dance where she had enjoyed herself immensely. But she was worried just the same because she had been unable to get the kind of work she wanted and had to help her father in his business, which she hated. She fell and broke her arm.

Mrs. F. was hit by a car while crossing the street on her way home from work. She was just opposite her church—a Roman Catholic institution—and was disturbed because she had been too late to go in that morning as usual. "I should have gone," she said, "it's a comfort; I think about all the members of my family who are dead."

Miss G., aged seventeen, fell off a sled. Her worry at the moment was that she had no business to be out at all because she was disobeying her parents by so doing. Two years earlier she had sprained her ankle under similar circumstances.

At first glance these seem to be wholesome little every-day worries which should not have had anything to do with the accidents except possibly that preoccupation would make the victims a little careless. But on analysis, the worries turn out to be all of one kind; they turn out to be connected with a characteristic typical of the accident-prone, and they turn out to be symptoms of an emotional conflict more fundamental than the specific worry of the moment.

The worries are all of one kind in that they involve the patient's relations with authority. Mr. A. was spared the unpleasant scene with his wife, obviously a woman of whom he stood in some awe. Mrs. B. could put off the evil moment of confessing the sin of contraceptives and yet would not be able to compound that sin by using them for a while. In the case of Mr. C. the conflict involved his employer. With Miss E. it was her parents, with Mrs. F. her church, with Miss G. the parents again. This resentment of authority and failure to do anything very substantial to escape or cope with it is characteristic of the accident-prone. In cases which have been explored more deeply, the specific worry was hardly more than a symptom of the basic conflict.

Mr. D. for example was doing more than blowing off steam for the particular anger of the moment. He was expressing an emotional upset which began in his family. He had been brought up by a very stern father in Germany, then subjected to the domination of older brothers and finally was obliged to abandon a business which had been in the family for thirty-seven years and leave Germany. His emotional life had been a series of repressed emotional conflicts with authority—father, brothers and the State.

Actually the fracture patients who fall into the accident-habit group suffered their injuries almost entirely under one or more of these circumstances: when their strong aggressive hostility was aroused or the pressure from authority became too great, as in the case of those whose self-esteem had been damaged by unemployment and nagging; when they built up too much resentment against their superiors at home or at work, as in the case of those forbidden to use contraceptives or forced to work on Sundays.

The well-defined accident pattern was not a question of the

The Accident Habit

length of time the conflict had been going on, but the severity of its emotional drive. The older patients in this group had no larger number of previous accidents than the younger ones. In fact, they had had fewer. Of those between fifteen and twenty-four years old, 87 per cent had had previous injuries. In the age group twenty-five to thirty-four only 68 per cent had previous injuries and in the thirty-five to fifty-five bracket 66 per cent. This suggests that "accidentitis" is a disease of youth. However, since accidents are such a major cause of death or disability among the young, it may be that the discrepancy is accounted for by the fact that so many of the victims are killed or permanently crippled before they are twenty-five.

There was the seventeen-year-old mentioned on page 38 who was brought into the hospital with a broken ankle, the result of sliding desperately into base during a baseball game. Johnny's chief interest in life was athletics, and he explained that he was perhaps playing harder than usual in anger because his side was losing. However, it developed that he had had seven previous major injuries and countless minor ones. None of the seven had been suffered during an athletic contest, although he had always preferred to play football and basketball with larger, heavier boys—he was a bit undersized—"because those my size don't play roughly enough. I like tough going."

In his first conversation, it was apparent that Johnny had been in trouble with authority, both at home and at school. Of his father he said: "He means business when he speaks at home." He described his mother as relatively easygoing. The family were Methodists, and the boy went to both church and Sunday school every Sunday until he was twelve, when he switched to the YMCA. He was still devout enough to think that he would take up church again sooner or later.

Of an active and sociable nature, like most fracture patients, he had also had the typical nervous troubles of childhood—sucking his thumb until he was nine, walking and talking in his sleep. He was characteristically careful of his health, basing his fondness for sports on the theory that "they build you up." He added:

"I am always in the pink of condition; being in training helps to keep from doing things that are unhealthy."

He had the accident patient's happy-go-lucky but cautious sex life. He had been going with girls since he was ten, but sought a new one every six months or a year. His current girl was one of his worries.

"She has already planned our honeymoon, house and children," he said, "and I haven't the vaguest desire to marry her at all."

Johnny's neglect of the future, not so much in marriage as in school, was also an accident-habit trait. He had planned to go to college and study engineering, but casually overlooked the requirement that he study languages in high school. He thought it hardly worth while to make up for this oversight, and so had settled for a course in aeronautics.

As he talked, it became apparent that his resentment to authority was greater than he knew. It was some time after his first mention of his mother that he spoke feelingly of his real annoyance with the sort of punishment she inflicted upon him. She would make him stay indoors for two weeks at a time if he failed once to come home at the very moment she had dictated. When he broke his ankle, he finally admitted, he was really as angry at the fact that he was playing more poorly than usual because of being kept away from practice as he was because his team was losing.

"Did I say Mother was easygoing?" he remarked at this point. "I am not quite sure that was quite the right word."

Obviously Johnny was largely unaware of his emotional conflicts. He probably would not have had the accident habit if he had known what caused it. On the other hand, if he had known that much, he would not have been a high-school boy of seventeen either.

Treatment for Johnny and the other accident-habit or accident-prone patients involves a deep understanding of all the factors which go into "accidentitis" in a particular individual. Obviously it is not just because they have conflicts with authority. Nearly everyone has them at one time or another in his life, but most people do not get sick at all from them, let alone develop a habit of breaking their bones. The particular type of conflict, the particular kind of family setting have a good deal to do with it. Then the way in which the individual seeks to meet the conflict plays a large part in deciding whether it is going to result in a bodily ailment or injury. The mental and emotional and physical capabilities of the individual as formed and developed by all his past experience must be taken into account.

All these factors add up to enough variations that it is difficult to set down rules which will apply to all cases of "accidentitis," or any other disease for which understanding and treatment demand a psychosomatic approach.* Over the centuries, a chasm has yawned ever wider between the physical and psychic worlds. On one side, the witch doctor, the leech and the physiologist were working. On the other labored the priest and the psychologist. Recently, as time is measured, a start has been made toward building a bridge over the chasm, and that bridge is the psychosomatic approach. When it is completed we may be able to deal with the fundamental causes of "accidentitis" as we now deal with the fundamental causes of malaria, by draining the swamps.

---

* See for example the statement made by Martin Hewitt: "If I were in search of a man of whom I knew nothing but that he squinted, bore a birthmark on his right hand, and limped, and I observed a man who answered to the first peculiarity, so far the clue would be trivial, because thousands of men squint. Now, if that man moved and exhibited a birthmark on his right hand, the value of that squint and that mark would increase at once a hundred or a thousand fold. Apart they are little; together much. The weight of evidence is not doubled merely; it would be only doubled if half the men who squinted had right-hand birthmarks; whereas the proportion, if it could be ascertained, would be, perhaps, more like one in ten thousand. The two trivialities, pointing in the same direction, become very strong evidence. And, when the man is seen to walk with a limp, that limp (another triviality), reinforcing the others, brings the matter to the rank of a practical certainty."

[CHAPTER IX]

The Mind and the Heart

§ 1

MORE WORDS have been spoken and written about the heart than about any other organ of the body. Our literature is full of them, but no one who knew the heart only through the voluminous outpourings of centuries of sentimental authors would ever recognize this important muscle if he saw it on the dissecting table. Yet he would have learned a certain amount of truth from the legends. It makes a great deal of difference, medically speaking, whether a personality is ruled by head or heart. It can make the difference between broken bones and broken hearts—and no breaks at all.

In the bright lexicon of many generations of romantic writers, the heart was the seat of all emotions. It leaped for joy and broke for grief. It palpitated for love and stopped for terror. Fear drove it into the mouth and depression into the boots. It throbbed in sympathy, beat more strongly in courage, fluttered in modesty. It was apostrophised by lovers, heroes and poets. Only to the physiologists, traditionally men of small gift for colorful expression, was the heart merely a delicately contrived mechanism, ingeniously designed for its important function, but no more attractive in appearance than the liver. And they did not discover its primary function—to pump blood—until the seventeenth century.

Neither the romantic nor the physiological approach to affairs of the heart can be ignored in a psychosomatic consideration of the diseases which afflict that organ. Both have important elements of truth, including some which neither proponent would be likely to admit. Either by itself is far from a complete picture. The emotions, on which the one will lavish the language of poetry, and the mechanical functions, which the other will describe in the terms of a highly educated plumber, are equally important to an understanding of the human heart.

Fortunately or otherwise, depending on the point of view, real life in this as in many other instances of mankind's development has caught up with fiction. The heart is subject to almost as many influences as the story tellers and song singers believed.

For example, heartbreak used to be the major cause of death in the romantic novels of our forefathers. It figured in a good deal of soberer but still highly romantic interpretation of history. Unhappy royalty and generals were taken off by heartbreak as by an epidemic. Heroines die more grimly and with better clinical descriptions in contemporary fiction, but real people today are twice as likely to die of heart diseases as of anything else.

By far the largest killer in modern society, heart diseases also account for about 20 per cent of all time lost from work because of illness. These ailments take men away from the job for a total of about a million man years or 250,000,000 man days a year. Only nervous and mental disorders are responsible for more chronic invalids.

Diseases of the heart are not all the same. Neither are the emotional factors which enter into them. But the similarities are as great or greater than in the case of the accident-prone. Furthermore, the heart-disease victim's appearance is strikingly different from that of the fracture patient, for instance. Each type of heart disease has its own type of personality as well. The personality factors and their history are often of more importance than the presence or absence of actual organic damage.

§ 2

Pattern for Heartbreak

AN ILLUMINATING example of this point was provided by two men who were admitted to the hospital at about the same time, suffering from the same symptoms. For purposes of comparison we may call one Joseph, the other Josephus. At first glance they did not seem to resemble each other very much, except that both were Jews. They were entirely different physical types. Joseph was thirty-two and married; Josephus was twenty-four and single. Joseph had an organic heart disease; Josephus was quite free of organic damage. But if the two cases are placed side by side, as they were seen in the hospital, an interesting pattern develops.

Joseph (with organic disease)	*Josephus* (without organic disease)
Joseph was an only child of a more than usually over-solicitous mother. When the boy was three years old his father died, a shock which was intensified for the wife and child by the fact that a year earlier the head of the house had had a sunstroke. The mother nurtured in her son strong feelings on the subject of sunstroke, and the incident had played a considerable part in his emotional life.	Josephus was the only son—he had one sister—of an over-solicitous mother and a father whose emotional make-up was so like his own that a friend said it was impossible for them to get along. The father had suffered a mild sunstroke on a golf course only a little while before Josephus became ill, and his father had always been an important factor in the boy's emotional development.
Always a sickly child, Joseph bit his nails until he was fifteen or sixteen, began to masturbate at thirteen and worried about it a great deal until he started having casual sex relations although never, as he put it, with a "nice girl." He married a few years before his illness, but only because, he said, he "felt obligated" since he had "strung the girl along" and	In childhood, he was a nail biter and had temper tantrums which, he said, were "beaten out of me by my father." A period of masturbation was followed by casual sex relations with a series of girls, and the previous summer a heart specialist had advised him to get married. Two years before, he had been engaged to a wealthy girl whose

she finally asked him. Since his marriage he had had no more inclinations toward casual sex adventures, partly because he was afraid of his wife, a possessive woman of whom he said: "I think of her more as my mother, really, than anything else. She treats me like a little boy, and I like it."

As a young man, Joseph went to work in an insurance office, but finally lost his job (apparently through no fault of his own). He then resorted to odd jobs of various kinds until he settled down to a pleasant job as a gymnasium teacher. He had always been fond of outdoor sports.

A heavy smoker, Joseph did not enjoy it much and often felt a little nauseated as a result, but he stuck to it because it killed his appetite to eat between meals. He had a compulsion to eat which led him to tuck away a heavy meal even if he was not hungry, and this had come to bother him so much that he tried to substitute tobacco.

Joseph, who actually had organic trouble, was quite sure there must be some mistake about it. Even after he left the hospital, he wanted to check up on the diagnosis that had been made there. He said he was confident enough that "the doctors at the hospital were very capable." But he just couldn't believe they were right in his case and he wanted to make sure. He had suffered some pain for four months. During that time

mother had been almost an equal object of his affections until she defrauded him (as he thought) of $3,000 worth of commissions to which he was entitled for handling her investments. She turned her affairs over to someone else, whereupon Josephus parted from her daughter and herself, without any obvious outburst of anger but with considerable inner turmoil, of which he was not fully aware.

Josephus went from school into his father's insurance business. That and the handling of his prospective mother-in-law's affairs had come to an end together, for when he broke off with her daughter, he also gave up working with his father, with whom he "couldn't agree" anyway.

Eating, Josephus thought, was related to his troubles in some way. He was interested in food, and recalled that an earlier heart attack came while he was at a road-side restaurant with his parents. "I remember I was eating a cheese and ham sandwich, and had a glass of beer, something I never drink," he said.

Josephus, who actually had no organic damage, was always sure he did. He had been to a half-dozen physicians after his first attack. The first one told him he had indigestion, the second that he had heart trouble and should see a third, a specialist, who told him his heart was all right, but later "slight irregularities" developed. Some time later, the fourth told Josephus he had a bad murmur.

he had been treated by several doctors for "heart trouble, indigestion or some other disease," but the words of wisdom they had spoken to him had obviously been heard lightly and dismissed easily.

There was no record of any heart disease in the young man's family. However, his mother, who at the time of his illness was sixty, had thought for a long time that she might have heart trouble because she had pains in the chest.

For all his passive acceptance of the dominance of his wife and mother, Joseph regarded himself as a quick-tempered man and so sensitive to pain that he was enraged by the least inconsiderateness. His dreams were full of fights and arguments, but not his waking moments. On one occasion when it seemed he might get involved in a street fight, it was actually his wife who wanted to beat up the other man. Joseph cherished his grudges for a long time and enjoyed revenge on those who had offended him. But he took no straightforward action to satisfy his feelings. Rather he showed his anger in such ways as calling "Simon" or "Kohn" to a man who had changed his name to Stedman Coles, and doing it in the presence of others.

One evening, Joseph had dinner at the home of his mother who inquired most anxiously about his health, as she always did. "I never felt better in my life," he replied. "I feel as muscular and strong as can be." That night he got sick

The fifth and sixth told him his heart condition was functional and mostly nerves, but by this time he was so confused by the conflicting stories that he could not believe anyone, and he continued to be quite positive he had organic trouble.

He had an actual cardiac heredity, an uncle having dropped dead of heart disease just after Josephus experienced his own first symptoms. His mother, at this time forty-eight, complained of pains in her chest which she thought might be heart trouble.

It was typical of Josephus that he never mentioned his anger to his prospective mother-in-law when she cheated him, although he was full of rage. He never gave his feelings toward his father full play. "I would just get burned up inside," he explained. "Shut up and not say anything for days at a time." The link to the childhood temper tantrums which had been beaten out of him was obvious. The many violent conflicts with his father had been repressed for years, and were accentuated by the experience with his mother-in-law-to-be. After that incident, he said, he "got all balled up," but he said nothing to anyone and did not seek relief in action.

One evening Josephus took a girl to the movies after dinner. He had remarked earlier that he never felt better in his life as he had just returned from a vacation taken to recover from his previous attack. While watching the picture, he de-

and was admitted to the hospital with severe pains under the breast-bone, so acute that he had to be quieted with three hypodermics. veloped a slow, stabbing pain in front of the heart, and was doubled up by it when he reached the hospital.

As the treatment of Joseph and Josephus progressed, it was apparent that they were faced with similar conflicts—both had repressed their hostility and anger, both accepted a passive role in the home although Josephus was younger and still fighting a little against it, both felt themselves sexually inadequate and both suffered from premature ejaculation.

Neither obtained as much psychotherapy as the cases would have demanded under ideal conditions. Treatment had to be directed toward the conflicts which were most immediately connected with their bodily ailments. Yet both were able to resume their activities—normal ones in the case of Josephus who in three years had no more bodily symptoms. He had not, however, remained free of what might be called his psychic symptoms. He had to go back to work after eight periods of psychotherapy. While he still had no organic heart disease, the whole background of psychosomatic studies suggests that if he cannot be relieved of his emotional disturbances, he will return to the hospital in later life with organic disease too.

Joseph, whose discharge note described him as "a case of classical coronary thrombosis unusual in such a young man," had seven periods of psychotherapy and was seen at intervals of a few months for nearly two years. He was able to be a little more active than he had been on his discharge from the hospital, and he had had no more attacks.

The fact that Joseph, with no cardiac heredity, was the one who had organic damage was somewhat at variance with a popular notion of heart diseases. But in our hospital studies, we found that exposure to someone with heart disease, or even with the symptoms of heart disease, seems to be more dangerous than the actual heredity. This is particularly true if the exposure has taken place under somewhat dramatic circumstances, or at a time in the patient's life when the incident seems especially tragic or painful.

§3

The Brittleness of Strength

IT IS characteristic of people who suffer from heart disease that they are hard workers, driving themselves without mercy and apparently enjoying it. It is typical of them to say: "I have to keep doing something useful." Now this is very different from the restlessness of the fracture patient, who would put it: "I have to keep doing something, it doesn't matter what."

Time after time, in our hospital studies, we took down the views of our cardiac cases on their work and its conditions. They were proud of the long hours they worked, and incidentally resentful of the little appreciation they got for it. They were not in the usual sense, however, victims of overwork. They were victims of the psychological circumstances which were responsible for their apparent ambition.

These patients were remarkable in the apparent strength but actual extreme brittleness of their defenses. They were strong only as long as a highly unified, rigidly crystallized life role turned out to be something to which they were culturally well adapted and which they found rewarding.

But their brittle shell covered a mental poverty or insecurity which had no other defenses once the shell was cracked. It seemed to make little difference whether the shell was broken from without or within. The result was rapid transition to a bodily ailment.

Just as the hard work is less responsible than the emotional conditions which led to it, so the heart-disease patient's characteristic carelessness of health, irregular eating habits, frequently excessive use of tobacco and coffee, disregard of sleep and so on are danger signals. They are not necessarily dangers.

In some cases, the abandonment of these bad habits is likely to set up a new emotional disturbance even worse than the one replaced. Such people usually have a self-destructive tendency—not necessarily as strong as a definite suicidal impulse—which is usually repressed but is often expressed in their moods of depression.

The Mind and the Heart

Before it is safe for them to give up the bad habits they already have, they must be helped to understand why they have them. Otherwise, they will perhaps fly to even worse habits and an even more difficult disease.

Usually they respond to treatment rather more readily than the fracture patient. That is because they have had long practice of working out things for themselves, instead of leaving them to others as the accident-prone like to do, and so they begin to work out their own cases. Generally they have done a great deal of thinking, even as children. Throughout life their physical reaction to an emotional problem was far more likely to be in words than in impulsive action. They will brood over their illness in solitude instead of talking it over with those three greatest sources of advice and repositories of confidences in our society—the neighbor, the druggist and the bartender.

The sufferer from heart disease should not take comfort from the fact that he has always been a cheerful patient, treating his illness as a joke. That feeling generally hides a very poor adjustment indeed. In the series of patients studied at the hospital, those who were the good sports about their illness were the most likely to die.

This type of patient generally has strong guilt feelings about sex. Promiscuity or sexual indulgence, to which many of them are drawn, conflicts with their ideals and principles. One of the results is that they frequently ask the physician if they should not give up sex altogether. This is usually an unconscious expression of the patient's need to discipline or punish himself. Actually, it is far better to relieve the patient's sense of guilt by showing it for what it is than by agreeing with his proposal to restrict his normal marital life.

There are thousands if not millions in this country whose cardiac and emotional histories are like that of a butcher who was admitted to the hospital one day complaining of a peculiar feeling around the heart. In many ways he was a model citizen and had enjoyed good health for all his forty-eight years, although he had suffered somewhat from indigestion for five and had been taking mineral oil for ten. He said his ancestors all lived to be past eighty, and the only serious illness in the family was high blood pressure in the case of his mother, but she had got over it.

An only child, he had been two months old when his father died in a railroad accident. Twelve years later his mother married again, and the boy got along so badly with his stepfather that after seven months he ran away from home and made his living for a year selling newspapers. Then he got a job in a meat market, and by the time he was eighteen was able to support his grandmother, who came to live with him.

When his stepfather died, his mother married again, this time a man twenty years her junior. The son objected violently but fruitlessly. He decided to forget about it, and get married himself. He was only twenty-one, and the girl he selected was a year older, but she thought they were both too young to marry. She consented after some urging and he bought a butcher shop with his savings.

From that time on he worked hard, rising at six and working until eight in the evening. He never took a vacation. One of his reasons was that he was determined to be a better parent to his four children than his mother or his two stepfathers had been to him. He had, however, taken his sex life lightly, professing not to be upset when after the birth of their fourth child his wife lost interest in sex, presumably because she had been treated with radium. The butcher insisted it did not matter to him because the children were really all his life. He was extremely ambitious for them, and desperately anxious to be a good father, saying:

"I never gave them a piece of bread that it wasn't divided equally. I would like to send them to college but I won't send one until I can send them all."

There was no evidence that he had ever asked them whether they wanted to go to college any more than he had considered, in dividing the piece of bread, whether they were all hungry. He was going to be his idea of a good father. So in his exaggerated straining for equality, he showed a characteristic avoidance of any attempt at intelligent discrimination. One of his children might have been happier as a secretary than as a college girl, another in a trade rather than a profession and a third might really have been college material. But the mentality of so many coronary patients is not geared to thinking of these things. Nor would it occur to them, if there is no obvious choice to be made on the basis of talent or inclination, to send the oldest child to college when he is ready and worry about the others when their time comes. It does not occur to a man like our butcher because his real problem is not the children at all, but how to deal with his own emotional reactions.

This particular patient thought his life was further complicated by the fact that the pressure of business had led him to take a partner. Their shop did well, but he was irritable merely because he was not entirely his own master. He was sure it was bad for him to lose his equanimity, but he could not help it. He stuck to his business partnership largely for the sake of his wife and children, but said:

"After all, a lot of business is personality and if you get irritable you can't do much anyhow. Having a partner makes it much more difficult not to get irritable."

Yet he repressed his anger, and was easily upset by fighting or talk of it. He said that he had been made much worse by a fight between two other patients in his ward. It was obvious that the same repressions had blocked expression of his lifelong anger, which had been directed in turn at his early difficulties, his mother's remarriages, his inability to send his children to college, his partner and his customers. Just after his second son was graduated from high school and expressed a desire to go on to college, the butcher was seized with his first severe attack of pain. It came just after a heavy lunch, and the doctor diagnosed his gall bladder as at fault. A second doctor said it was hardening of the arteries. A third suggested aluminum poisoning and prescribed a powder which gave relief. Four months later, the butcher suffered new pains so severely that he again consulted a doctor, but this time powder gave no relief and after ten days his wife persuaded him to go to the hospital.

He did not seem very much disturbed by his illness, and was the "good sport" type of patient. After three weeks he was discharged, and he seemed very much better.

"I've made up my mind to go home and be all right because my family needs me," he said.

Obviously, there had been no success in showing him what his real troubles were. He did not understand the emotional conflict, the resentments and the suppressed aggressive tendencies which had gone into the making of his personality. Failing to understand them, he could not offer them any release and they remained untreated and dangerous. Within a year he was readmitted to the hospital and died in an oxygen tent ten days later.

§ 4

Metamorphosis of a Nuisance

ANOTHER type of cardiac patient is the one whose trouble used to be deemed not so sensible as that of the butcher but was labeled the result of sheer folly. Later it was found to be neurotic, and now is sometimes treated as a disease and not a nuisance. More dramatic than most, but following essentially the same pattern as thousands of others was the case of Mrs. O., an exceptionally attractive young woman whose story is as typical as that of the butcher.

Mrs. O. had been born to middle-class, moderately well-to-do parents. She was the third girl in a family of four daughters and a son. From the day of her birth, she had been exposed to incessant conflicts between her parents, both of whom were highly nervous people. All her sisters suffered from hay fever and asthma (in both emotional factors are known to play a major role) and the brother had tuberculosis. In the family quarrels, Mrs. O. had been torn between her parents rather more than most children. While she was inclined to prefer her father, he constantly disillusioned her and she turned to her mother, whom she regarded as more virtuous.

She did well in school, and took a great interest in dramatics, hoping in girlhood as she did when she was grown up that she could make a career for herself in the theatre. In part at least, this rather stronger than normal feminine desire to be a great actress was an outgrowth of shyness and self-depreciation, for which she sought overcompensation in dramatic behavior and dress.

Her family could not afford to send her to college, so she took a teacher's training course but was married before she finished it. Her husband had a large income of his own and belonged to an extremely wealthy family, but he turned out to be not the most desirable mate for a girl whose own emotional life was not very stable.

Three days after their marriage, she woke up to find that her husband was masturbating and apparently talking lovingly to another woman. He confessed that he had done it all his life and begged her to help him get over it. Mrs. O. herself had suffered one of her own emotional shocks partly in connection with this problem, and it had been complicated by her strong father identification. At the age of twelve she had been playing baseball— her father was interested in sports—contrary to specific maternal decree but with high paternal approval. In the course of the game she broke her ankle, which she was inclined to regard partly as punishment for disobeying her mother and partly as a penalty for her own masturbation, which had begun just a little while before.

The impression made upon her by this incident had been heightened by memory of what she regarded as a similar "punishment" which God had inflicted upon her father when she was six years old. Although both her parents had strict religious principles, her father had begun to be unfaithful to his wife, and brought his infidelities to a rather unsavory pitch on Christmas Eve by bringing one of the objects of his defection home to help him trim the Christmas tree. Mrs. O.'s mother sat upstairs and wept while this ceremony was going on, and by the time it was finished, the husband and his girl were relatively tight. While taking her home, he slipped on the ice and broke his leg. Mrs. O.'s earliest strong recollection of him was seeing him carried into the house helpless and being told that it was thus that God had punished him for his sin.

The daughter had been so impressed that after she broke her

ankle she gave up her own "sin," and when her husband sought her help, she was not inclined to regard the problem lightly. After six weeks of having Mr. O. confess in the morning that he had broken his promises of the day before, she consulted a doctor who told her to forget all about it, adding that most men masturbated and all women did. This last offended Mrs. O. all the more because it was not true of her, and she was bitterly disappointed to think that there was no hope of medical help for her or her husband.

In this mood, she discovered that she was pregnant, and one morning while rearranging the furniture she strained her back. After some weeks of pain, her physician suggested treatment which included a therapeutic abortion and would involve nearly a year in bed in a hospital.

"Can it be that I welcomed the idea?" Mrs. O. wondered a long time afterward. "I don't believe that I really needed the operation, but I couldn't get divorced, and this seemed a heaven-sent opportunity to get away from my husband's masturbation."

Probably it was, but Mrs. O. made use of her respite to fall into the rather common error of deciding that if she had a child, her marital problems would grow easier. Of course the resulting baby only caused more complications. The first one was a war of grandmothers. Mr. O.'s mother, who had never approved of her daughter-in-law, became a constant visitor in the later stages of Mrs. O.'s pregnancy and gave orders and advice to all the household. Mrs. O.'s own mother adopted the same tactics, and neither of the two older women could abide the presence of the other.

Into this angry atmosphere, Mr. O. intruded his own brand of emotional disturbance. He decided that two or three months' abstinence from sexual intercourse was going to have a bad effect upon his health and his business efficiency. After the child was born, his problems continued, accentuated by a new habit of heaping reproaches upon his wife. In spite of his wealth, he disturbed himself over the additional expense of a child, insisted that his wife keep house on $15 a week, including parties and liquor, and finally moved into a smaller apartment. The little boy was two years old by this time, and in the new home frequently had to sleep in the same room with his parents. Mrs. O. had learned enough about child care to be seriously worried about the effect on the child of exposure to the nocturnal conflicts between her and her husband.

About this time Mrs. O. managed to fall in love with a mutual friend, a married man who was a business associate of her husband. Neither her upbringing nor her personality as developed by the whole course of her emotional life nor her sexual experiences up to this time had qualified her to treat lightly a liaison of this kind. After the first phase of her affair had passed, she retired to the country for two months to repent and persuade herself not to see her lover again.

At this point in Mrs. O.'s career, the moralist may see in her nothing more than a neurotic, flighty woman whose sense of duty is blunted, who therefore deserves all she will get. The physician will be impressed by the toughness of a human being who can go through an emotional life such as hers and retain even some shreds of sanity.

Obviously she was ripe for a thorough psychosomatic diagnosis. In fact, treatment at a much earlier stage would have been indicated. But, like most people, she had not so much as thought of the possibility of a little preventive psychotherapy. The great majority of patients wait until there is a serious bodily ailment which will yield to no other treatment before they turn to psychiatry. Mrs. O., therefore, wrestled with her problems alone in the country, and was so far from solving them that in spite of her strong feelings of guilt about adultery, she made an appointment with her lover for the day she was to return to town.

The evening before, she attended a gay farewell party. As had happened often before, her shyness broke out into exhibitionism, in the course of a rather well-lubricated occasion. She later told the hospital physicians that she had been doing gymnastics and supposed that she had pulled a muscle. She also managed to get herself knocked down, and thought she had broken a rib.

At the time, she was struck with a feeling of great relief. She thought that it would now be unnecessary for her to sleep with either her husband or her lover for quite a while. That hope was disappointed when it was established that the rib was not broken, but the same purpose was served by a continuation of her pain, and the next day she was sent to the hospital. Here a heart condition was diagnosed, and the attitude typical of the cardiac who has developed his illness under circumstances similar to those of Mrs. O. was displayed when she said:

"I was reading a book; the Lord strikes knives into the hearts of his children who err. I guess that's what happened to me."

This conception of a vengeful, not to say sadistic Deity, is not confined to cardiacs, of course, but it is notable how often they attribute their disease to such a cause. Mrs. O. spent a month in the hospital while various heart ailments were considered. She was discharged finally, not as cured, but as able to be treated at home. Her trouble at the time was set down as an acute form of rheumatic heart disease.

Back in her home, Mrs. O. stayed in bed for two months. Her illness, it will be noted, still prevented her from having to make any unwelcome decisions about her sex life or about any of the other domestic difficulties which she had found too much for her. But a few days before Christmas she got up for a party. Her lover and his wife were among the guests, and the old conflict returned in full force. On Christmas day she was again in the hospital.

Her stay this time was two months. At first she was far too ill for a complete examination to be made. She was put in an oxygen tent, and required oxygen for several days. The signs of heart disease were much more apparent and complicated than on her previous stay, but the hospital note on her case said:

"Her diagnosis was extremely obscure."

Several more possibilities were discussed by the physicians, but at last she was discharged, apparently very much improved, although this time the discharge diagnosis contained question marks, reading: "Active rheumatic pericarditis? Arthritis of rheumatic fever?"

Early in May, Mrs. O. was allowed out of bed again, but with strict limitations of activity. Since the difficulties of her home life had not decreased, she arranged to visit an aunt in the country, but had hardly arrived when another attack sent her to the hospital for the third time. When she was ready to leave a month later she herself asked for psychiatric treatment, although both the attending physician and her husband recommended against it. She was taken to her summer home in an ambulance, and remained in bed. Her only visitors were her mother and mother-in-law, the two people of whom she was most afraid.

Under these circumstances, more frequent visits than once a week were impossible for the psychiatrist. Nevertheless, Mrs. O.'s personality soon became clear. It was apparent that she tried hard to be a good mother to her child, but was constantly thwarted by her husband. The child's shortcomings, however, seemed to her to expose her own inadequacy rather than that of Mr. O. She was bothered by feelings of guilt, depression and unworthiness. She was extremely tense although inclined to be inconsistent and flighty in manner. She smoked too much and drank too much, both liquor and coffee. At the root of her trouble was the gradual sense of her failure in her marriage as well as in the sphere of all her personal relationships, intensified into really "sick-making" proportions by the shocks of her emotional experience.

These facts had emerged at the end of five sessions. Two months later Mrs. O. was allowed to get up for dinner, and once more the guests were her lover, invited as her husband's business associate, and his wife. Next morning, Mrs. O. woke up gasping for breath and with all her old symptoms crowding upon her.

The attending physician and her husband made arrangements to rush her to the hospital once more, but she insisted upon sending for her psychiatrist. Both husband and trained nurse were obviously agitated by the time this specialist arrived and they apologized for having permitted a useless trip. Mrs. O., they explained, was barely conscious for a few minutes at a time and then powerless to speak. Nevertheless, when the psychiatrist walked into the room, Mrs. O. was both conscious and able to talk. She was propped up in bed, her whole body rigid and a look of terror in her eyes.

"Well, you were almost too late," she gasped in a hoarse whisper which was broken by her struggle for breath. "I am going to die, but I wanted so much to wait till you came. I wanted to confess. I'm no good. I guess I'm done for. I can't help being attracted to A———. I hate my husband. I'm being punished."

"I think you're very angry," was the reply. "Look at your fists," both of which were tightly clenched.

"That's the pain . . . knife in my heart." There was a pause. "You think I want to sock someone. Nice girls don't do that."

For the first time, her features relaxed in a somewhat wry smile, and as if in spite of herself she took a deeper breath. Her pulse had gone down from 150 to 90.

"What about a long slow breath?" suggested the psychiatrist.

"I couldn't," she protested, "the pain would be terrible."

"You just did, and it didn't hurt, did it?"

Mrs. O. looked amazed at that, and began to speak in her normal voice, asking:

"Do you really think they can do anything for me? They haven't yet."

"Perhaps not, but you can."

"What?" Mrs. O. spoke in obvious astonishment.

"You might begin by unclenching your fists, at least till the right person comes along to sock, and then breathe naturally," the psychiatrist proposed.

"My toes are all clenched too," Mrs. O. remarked after a pause. "I guess I was mad. Why won't the doctors let me see my friends? People I like. Instead of keeping me in prison, tied to my bed to be tortured by my husband and mother-in-law and mother?"

"We'll see about changing that tomorrow. Now what about taking away those pillows and having a good sleep?"

"I didn't think I could breathe lying down," Mrs. O. replied doubtfully.

"Let's try it."

At this point the young woman was able to relax a little more, and murmured:

The Mind and the Heart

"I feel better. You don't think I'm no good, the way the others do?"

"Quite the contrary. We'll talk about that in the morning."

"Then I'm not going to die tonight?"

"Why should you?" the psychiatrist retorted. "Your pulse is normal. You can breathe, and there isn't any more pain, is there?"

The patient sighed deeply and went to sleep almost immediately. The whole interview had lasted about half an hour, and husband and nurse were waiting outside still. They greeted the psychiatrist with dark looks and Mr. O. exclaimed:

"Well it's all over this time, isn't it? I was going to have the ambulance if she was alive in the morning."

"You stayed quite a long time," the nurse broke in. "Can I give her her next injection [morphine] now?"

"She's sleeping peacefully, so I wouldn't disturb her," the psychiatrist answered, to the obvious surprise of the others. "I think she'll be all right in the morning."

Mrs. O. was actually so much improved next day that the physician in charge decided it was unnecessary to take her to the hospital. Instead, arrangements were soon made to bring her back to her apartment in town, where she could receive more adequate psychiatric treatment. In about a month, she was able to be up sufficiently to manage her household and take care of her child. Four months later she was able to hold a full-time job as well. Twelve years have passed since, and she has had no more heart attacks and no more accidents, nor have her activities been limited in any way. About two years ago she was remarried and is very happy in her relationship with her new husband and her child. She has continued her job with increasing satisfaction and increasing health.

The basic treatment consisted in taking Mrs. O.'s troubles seriously—all of them—and establishing a good relationship with her so that she realized that her physician regarded her as a person and not as a problem. She obviously was headed for invalidism, a permanent organic damage to the heart or death. These were averted, and Mrs. O. herself explained how, saying:

"Until you made me face what was really bothering me, and showed me I could do something about it, life was impossible except when I was sick. It may sound funny to you, but it used to be a relief to have a real pain to fight, instead of my husband, and all the people I hated and felt despised me. What I used to call the knife in my heart hurt so much that it blotted out everything else, everything that bothered me. It was like being drunk but even more potent."

§ 5

Heartache and Heartbreak

THE PHOBIAS which patients like Mrs. O. develop are by no means typical of all heart-disease sufferers. There is no single personality pattern for these illnesses. For example, the butcher tried to fulfill his desires for the liking of his family and to satisfy his self-esteem by active competition in the world of men and by hard, not to say excessive work. Mrs. O. sought to reassure herself and gain the approval of her friends by playing to the gallery. Where the butcher went home determined to get himself well so that he could take care of his family, Mrs. O. allowed herself to welcome illness as a defense. Having subdued her own angers and resentments in the interest of being liked by others, she had those emotions turn in upon herself. She convinced herself that she was "no good," and that she was a failure in her human relationships because of shortcomings in herself, and she tended toward self-injuries as a result.

The tendency of certain types of personality to acquire certain types of heart disease is marked, but it should be applied to any given individual only with a great many reservations. A very large number of factors go into the making of any personality, and it is only when an overwhelming proportion of them conform to an illness pattern that there can be any certainty in diagnosing a particular type. Most of these factors, furthermore, do not lie on the surface. The physician had to bring them to the surface.

Bearing all this in mind, it is still true that coronary occlusion

The Mind and the Heart

(an obstruction in the coronary arteries which supply blood to the heart muscle) seems to occur with special frequency among persons who are or would like to be top dogs in their own worlds. The spasmodic heart troubles happen in similar proportions to the prima donnas and the big frogs in little puddles. Rheumatic fever and rheumatic heart disease are often the ailments of teacher's pets and martyrs. Men and women suffering from cardiac arrhythmias or the irregularity of heart action which leads to attacks like those of Mrs. O. have a good deal of the prima donna in them but give a stronger impression of being children in the dark, and afraid of it.

In treating these people, a special approach and a good deal of special knowledge is required. Once the case is diagnosed, it would seem simple for the patient to go it alone or seek the advice and comfort of a friend. But few of us would take this course with a broken leg, although most laymen (and doctors, too) know a good deal more about broken bones than they do about cracked emotions. The mind requires just as expert attention as the heart.

The goal of treatment is not so much to make the patient act differently than in the past, but to make him feel differently. There would have been little gained by requiring the butcher to quit work unless he could have been convinced emotionally that this was desirable. Even when the situation cannot be changed materially, many people can regain their health if they understand what they are up against.

Rose P. was a case in point. About the same age as Mrs. O., she had a less spectacularly upsetting childhood. Rose was the second of five children; her father kept a small grocery store and both he and her mother were sociable, so that the house was always full of friends. Rose enjoyed company, too, and went to work in her father's store after a year of high school. This decision she was inclined to regret. She was not, however, an aggressive or very decisive person, so she remained. While she liked dancing, she did not mix much with other young people except for a girl her own age and a man ten years older, to both of whom she was devoted.

In the space of sixteen months in her eighteenth and nineteenth years, she was exposed to a series of shocks connected with heart disease. First, news came that her mother's brother had died, which greatly upset the mother. A month later, Rose's older brother died suddenly of peritonitis after an appendectomy. Then her father was stricken with a long series of anginal attacks. Rose helped him through many of them, but while she was still eighteen, he died in her arms. Rose herself suffered from palpitations for several hours, and in this emotional crisis her two best friends stayed with her constantly for a few days. In a week, Rose announced her engagement to the young man, and they were married when she was twenty.

For five years she was extremely happy; her husband, who was a taxicab driver, seemed bent on making their romance exactly like a fairy tale—a type of fiction to which Rose was addicted in a large way. But then he began to stay out at night; his fond attitude changed, and she soon began to suspect his fidelity. She began to have attacks like that which she had suffered when her father died, with the additional feeling that she was suffocating. These attacks came, however, only when she was waiting for her husband to come home or when she saw a pregnant woman. She would run home to Mother on these occasions. She began to lose weight, and by the time she was admitted to the hospital at the age of twenty-eight, she had a definite cardiac lesion. By the time she got to the psychiatric clinic, this was a serious organic condition, and she was treated over a period of nearly three years, at intervals ranging from once a week to follow-up sessions every three to six months.

Rose had been prepared psychologically for some type of illness. The fact that it turned out to be heart disease may have been due to an inherent weakness or to the emotional factors or to a combination of both.

In discussing her fears with the psychiatrist, Rose experienced an overwhelming sense of terror. She had attacks of palpitation and her lips turned blue. Her fear of pregnancy was of long standing, dating back to early childhood. She had a vague idea that women were likely to bleed to death in childbirth, but she had never dared discuss the point with her mother for fear of losing her parent's indulgent affection.

"Mother had just had my baby brother," she explained, "and I thought 'how awful if she would die.' He was the only member of the family she liked better than me, but after a while she didn't do that any more."

Like so many sick people whose illness has its roots in the emotions, Rose got a really substantial benefit from her ailment. Her husband, who had been "both a father and a mother to me" since girlhood, would not really leave her, she felt, while she was sick.

The psychiatrist discussed with her the fundamental psychic reasons for this. Her resentment against her mother and her fear of losing her mother's affection were brought into the open. The realities of her fear of pregnancy were faced, but she now decided that her economic situation was responsible for her unwillingness to bear a child.

Rose left the hospital a relatively well woman, and stayed that way for two years. Then she returned to the clinic to ask whether it would be safe for her to have a child.

"It's funny," she confessed, "I want one now when we have less money than we had before, when I thought we couldn't have one because of lack of money."

Before this question could be dealt with in detail, Rose became pregnant by accident. She began to dream of her father and to contrast him in her mind with her husband, who still neglected her. She spent most of her time at home alone, reading love stories. At the end of the second month of her pregnancy her best friend's father died, and at the cemetery Rose grew very nervous. Next day, she felt ill and the sense of walls closing in, which had been a feature of her early heart attacks, returned. All of a sudden she hated the idea of being pregnant and at the end of the next month, after an automobile ride, an abortion took place. Rose was relieved, she admitted, but she returned to the psychiatric clinic and the new situation was discussed against the background of the old.

Examinations at the cardiac and gynecological clinics showed that it was safe for her to have a child, and after a few months she became pregnant again, this time because she wanted to be. Nevertheless, she began to dream of her father again, and the fear of seeing pregnant women returned. From these, she was relieved in about six weeks, and she proceeded with the normal course of pregnancy, bearing a son without complications. Her husband's attitude toward her had not improved, but she had made herself less dependent upon him, and she got over the habit of running to her mother in every difficulty. In other words, her attitude toward an unpleasant home situation had changed; the situation remained the same.

Rose had been headed for invalidism and tragedy, but in the eyes of the physicians who first attended her at the hospital, her case was a very usual cardiac ailment without psychic complications. She was seen in the psychiatric clinic only because she came to the hospital during the time that a series of psychosomatic studies involved an interview with every patient admitted.

The emotional factor in such illnesses was emphasized by a review of the cases of a series of patients suffering from cardiovascular disease who had been in hospitals for the specific illness from one to fifteen times. Among them they totaled nearly 300 periods of hospital care and treatment. Brief psychotherapy devoted to the emotional factor in their illnesses was given to each. Only three of them were hospitalized for the same illness afterward during the next three to twelve years—the average time of this follow-up was five years. This does not mean that all cardiac patients will be cured as if by magic if they get psychotherapy. Some of them will fail and some will not be treated because the organic damage has proceeded so far that they could not stand the treatment.

The nature of the emotional disturbance from which these patients suffer makes it difficult for them to bear objectively any feeling of being judged, even by themselves. They should never be put on the spot in their own minds, but they have a tendency to do just that to themselves. Failure in that segment of life to

The Mind and the Heart

which they have attached their ambitions can lead them to invalidism or death.

There was a motorman in New York, Oscar, whose whole life was bound up with his job, obviously because of a strong attachment to his father and a desire to live up to his parent's standards. He was the fourth generation in his family to be a motorman or locomotive engineer, and was very proud of the record. Nevertheless, he was never at ease with authority, although he could never mention his father without emotion.

As a little boy he had been stubborn, and at the same time easily terrified by stories. Until he was eight years old he was afraid of the dark. At ten, his reaction against authority led him to run away from home, and the licking his father gave him on his return was the only one he remembered. He never tried to run away again, but at school he was constantly challenging the authority of his teachers. He pestered his father to let him quit school and go to work for the railroad, but the older man refused for a long time and steadily urged the boy to give up the idea of following in his footsteps. Finally, when Oscar was thirteen and had amassed quite an impressive record of truancy, his father gave in and permitted him to go to work. At first odd jobs were all he could get; then he served during World War I, in both the Army and the Navy. After the war, he got a railroad job, worked his way up to becoming an engineer, like his father, and then transferred to the city transit system as motorman on the subway. This job absorbed his attention and his interests, although he was a healthy, athletic fellow, married and friendly.

Oscar took his job so seriously that he was constantly under emotional strain. He felt his responsibility for his passengers keenly, was intensely proud of an excellent work record and very anxious over the little mishaps which were bound to occur. Then he had several near accidents, and they affected him so deeply that he could not stand on a subway platform and hear a train come in without having a feeling which he said was just like fear.

When Oscar was thirty-six and had been a motorman for seven years his beloved father died of a heart attack. Oscar himself developed an ailment of the circulatory system right afterwards, and this coupled with a waning sexual potency which, he felt, cost him prestige in the eyes of his wife, caused him a good deal of concern. Shortly afterwards, a man committed suicide by plunging in front of Oscar's train, and after that he drove with one hand constantly clutching the emergency brake.

His disease grew worse, and he was advised to get some less exacting work. He tried a job as a clerk for a few months but was so unhappy that he begged for and got a transfer back to his motorman's cab. However, his problems were far from settled, and he would wake up in a panic with palpitations of the heart after dreaming of accidents. This went on until, two weeks before his collapse, another motorman ran down a sailor and was so shaken that he was taken off the job to recuperate. Three days later he died of what Oscar was sure was a heart attack. Oscar himself brooded a good deal over his friend's death for several days. Then, at the height of the subway rush, he drove his train past a switch. He realized at once that it was his fault, stopped the train and rushed to the nearest communication point, which fortunately was only a few feet away. He telephoned the control station in time to avert an accident, but on the way back to his cab he experienced pain in the region of the heart and could hardly catch his breath. Although the danger was past, he suffered so severely that in a few minutes, he said, he felt "as though a truck drove up on me and stayed there." He was taken to the hospital where his ailment was diagnosed as coronary occlusion.

As he talked, it was obvious that he was failing in many spheres of his life, but that the one which bothered him most was his sudden inefficiency on the job. He was sure that after the near accident, it would never be safe for him to take the controls of a subway train again. He had judged himself.

He was wrong about it. Although he was seriously ill and getting worse, he took a quick turn for the better as he began to understand that it was no innate failure in himself that had caused his trouble, but the anxiety imposed upon him by his own identification of himself with his father, particularly in the matter of their common skill. He improved, but before his understanding of himself was complete, he was obliged by unavoidable circumstances to live over again in his own mind the whole sequence of his emotional conflicts. A man has to be strong indeed to take this twice in succession. Oscar was not yet sufficiently recovered to stand it, and the second experience killed him.

There still remains enough mystery about the heart and its diseases to keep it in the realm of literature. On the other hand, the relationship between the particular kind of cardiac trouble which an individual develops and his whole background of psychic experience has been well established. The physician may not be able always to trace that relationship along all the blocked and tortuous channels through which it has passed, but it is clear that he will have a better chance if he starts early.

Preventive psychiatric treatment when the heart first becomes suspect can avert a good deal of the tragedy of invalidism and death which are today's toll. The heart does not exist all by itself, isolated from the rest of the body, like the bit of chicken heart which Alexis Carrel kept "alive" for years. In human beings the heart is inseparable from the whole individual. If the whole individual is kept well, the broken heart can be left to the poets.

[CHAPTER X]

"*The Hygiene of a Quiet Mind*"

§ 1

"RELAX, pal," was the favorite phrase of a jovial but rather flippant porter in an office building I used to visit frequently.

"Relax, pal," he would say when one of the men in the office snapped at him for carelessness, grew impatient with his lethargy or swore angrily over some trifle.

If he had been a physician and had couched his advice in a little more erudite form, that porter could have commanded substantial fees. If he had been able to give the office men effective lessons in relaxation as well as advise them to do it, he would have been worth those fees. For the inability to relax is one of the most widely spread diseases of our civilization, and one of the most infrequently recognized. Most victims do not even suspect that they have it until it has been complicated by some other ailment. Teaching them how to relax is one of the most valuable of the psychosomatic techniques.

Hypertension is more common and has been called more deadly than cancer. It is above all others the great health problem of middle age, and it kills one out of every four men and women over fifty. This is because it is a contributing factor in a great many other diseases.

"The Hygiene of a Quiet Mind"

Tension is not always obvious either to the sufferer or to the physician. A great many seemingly calm, untroubled people are concealing from themselves and from others an inability to relax. They think they can take it, but that is true only up to a certain point. Beyond that point they experience no sudden collapse but rather a gradual wearing out like a rubber hose which has been left out too long and stepped on too often. The typical victim of hypertension would be someone like this:

1. He would have an even chance of heart disease in the family, but would be almost certain to have been exposed to it or to the sudden death of a relative or friend at a susceptible period in his life. Of our cases, 49 per cent had a history of heart disease in the immediate family, but 98 per cent had suffered the shock of witnessing the illness or death of someone close to them.

2. He would probably be nervous (three out of four) although he may avoid outward manifestations of it, showing them only when he is on the road to being cured.

3. He would have a more than average record of previous illnesses—operations, pneumonia, stomach upsets and allergies. The women in our study generally had poor pelvic histories.

4. His parents would have been inclined toward strictness, with the mother as queen bee of the home. In his own family he would attempt to be the boss, but would combine his desire for dominance with demands for a good deal of care and attention. Our patients had about an average marriage rate, but more than the average number of children and fewer divorces.

5. His intellectual capacity would tend to be above the average, but he would be inclined to choose an occupation somewhat below his real abilities because of his fear of failure. At the same time he would strive to work to the top in whatever he did attempt, but usually would fall short of his ambitions. He would tend to lose any early interest he may have had in religion; a relatively small number were reared in strict piety.

6. He would be hypersensitive as well as hypertensive, inclined

toward shyness and anxious to fit into whatever cultural pattern he found around him. He would seek release from this shyness in drinking or excessive use of tobacco or coffee, plunging into rather blatant affairs or breaking into song when in his cups in a manner which would not be at all like him when sober. He would be inclined to seek out friends as reassurance.

7. He would be poorly adjusted sexually, with a need to demonstrate superiority over his spouse and often promiscuous, less from any real sexual urge than from a vague compulsion linked to a feeling of insecurity. The men in our group were frequently impotent and had an unusually high venereal-disease rate. The women were usually frigid and had had a surprisingly large number of abortions on the average.

8. He would be over-weight and broad in frame. Only about one in seven of our hypertension patients was thin, but when the disease did strike a tall and lanky individual, he seemed to be among the worst sufferers. One-fifth of all our cases actually had been treated for obesity, and two-thirds of them had been worried about their weight. Their interest in food was well above average.

9. He would have a strong desire to please, combined with a habit of suppressed rage often so deeply submerged that he would not be conscious of it until he was sufficiently relaxed to appreciate his reactions to his environment.

10. He would alternate between a tendency to seek satisfaction within himself and a steady drive toward the achievement of some long-range ambition. One typical patient would be a solitary reader, a devotee of non-competitive sports such as hunting or riding or fishing, a fellow who liked to take long walks by himself. Another would be an incessant worker who gave himself entirely to the task of getting ahead in business and providing for his family. The first type would find in his illness an excuse for his own inadequacy and insist that it entitled him to special consideration. The second would stoically ignore his illness and plunge back into work as soon as possible.

§ 2

The Story of a Good Boy

THESE ten points make up a sort of composite portrait of a great many sufferers from tension. It is as true of medicine as of photography that a composite is never an exact likeness of anyone. Almost certainly the individual who thinks he sees any resemblance to himself in some of the description would be no more likely to have a hypertensive condition than one who sees no resemblance at all. The presence of several or even most of these characteristics does not call for alarm. The point is that most hypertension patients have most of these traits and a recognition of it is important to them in combating the disease.

Harry H—— was a good illustration of such people. The oldest of three children and the only boy, he had never liked his father but concentrated his filial affections upon his gentle and sympathetic mother. He was given to temper tantrums as a child, as well as to moods of depression which he remembered later in life.

"When things were too much for me I would go off by myself for hours at a time, trying to figure things out," he said. "Sometimes I would talk to mother, who was very gentle, but she couldn't help me much."

At the root of the child's feeling that life could become too much for him was his emotional reaction to his father. A stern man at best, the elder H—— developed physical disorders which made him increasingly cranky and depressed when his son was ten or eleven years old. He even reached the point of wanting to commit suicide. He died of a combination of heart disease, kidney trouble and dropsy when his oldest child was twelve.

"It was a great relief," Harry admitted quite frankly, "except that I had to give up school and go to work."

He found a place as messenger boy in a bank, went to a night school and started a steady but not spectacular rise in his job. As he grew up, he became a reasonably sociable fellow, joined the Masons and the Elks, enjoyed gambling but not sports, drank a bit. He apparently preferred casual sex relations to those of the married state, for in the hospital although he said that his life with his wife was "all right," there seemed a mental reservation in this addition:

"I guess sex isn't very much fun in the home because there's too much responsibility."

Harry married when he was twenty-seven and had become a moderately well-paid member of the bank's staff. His wife was an epileptic, suffering from the *petit mal*, as he knew at the time, but he was a great deal more concerned by the fact that his mother was very ill just then and he was afraid his marriage might make her worse.

Under these circumstances, it is hardly surprising to learn that his wife left him after nine months, whereupon he sold his furniture and went home to mother. A short time later, however, his wife asked him to take her back, and he agreed upon conditions which do not seem calculated to promote happiness in married life. He insisted that they both remain with his mother, and his wife accepted. But the strain of this triangle must have been great. At any rate, her epileptic attacks turned into the *grand mal*, and they remembered that a physician had told them that childbirth would be a cure. They decided to make the experiment. A son was born to them, and sure enough the *grand mal* attacks ceased, but Mrs. H—— continued to have those of the *petit mal*.

The baby may have had some beneficial effect upon the young woman's health. He did not in the least contribute to restoring harmony in the home. Wife and mother-in-law bickered constantly, and Harry found himself striving desperately to keep peace between them, even to the point of cleaning the house, cooking the meals, changing the baby's diapers and preparing his formula.

Harry had recovered from his temper tantrums although still given to solitary brooding, but he was frequently angry with his employer and even more so with his wife, who for various reasons reminded him of his father. For the most part he managed to suppress his feelings of rage, especially at the office, but he sometimes broke out at home. On one such occasion, while he was sitting quietly "wondering what to do about my troubles," his wife pulled the chair from under him. In a rage, he struck her in the face and broke her nose. His special brand of remorse was well illustrated by his comment on the incident:

"It cost me eighty dollars to get her face repaired, and I just sort of felt that was too much to pay and everything was against me."

When Harry was thirty-four his mother died of diabetes and a stroke. His characteristic dependence on her and his feeling of inadequacy were indicated in his belief that she had somehow been killed by his marriage seven years before. He did not even find his life made easier, for he continued to do the housework, his wife being so helpless in this respect that when he was sick she sent their son to her grandmother because she did not know how to take care of children. Harry said he enjoyed cooking, but he obviously had developed a pretty severe emotional conflict by unconsciously comparing his subservient, feminine role at home with his increasing importance at the bank, where he was "handling a million dollars."

Two years after his mother died, Harry's bank was absorbed by another and all the old employes were fired. Harry was in no condition to withstand the emotional shock of losing in this way a job for which he had worked for twenty-three years. He had been smoking too much, especially at night when he lay awake worrying. Furthermore, the worry did not make him thin. The hospital weighed him in at 216 pounds, and a note on his medical chart reported: "Patient always eats regularly and well." His health record had been none too good. Long a sufferer from hay fever and stomach disorders, he had pulled through one bout of pneumonia. He had never been able to convince himself that he was a better man than his father, although this had been a major goal for him. Now, with the loss of his cherished job and security, he was sure "fate was too strong for me," and he decided:

"I had too much of my father in me."

A tendency toward alcoholism had manifested itself earlier in his life, and Harry reacted to this latest blow to his emotional stability with a prolonged drinking bout which lasted with insignificant breaks for a year and a half. Finally he took a poorly paid clerical job and just managed to support his family, thanks to a lucky win of $500 in the Irish Sweepstakes. But he felt so inferior to his old friends that he gave up seeing them.

Reduced to being a household drudge and poor provider, Harry nevertheless begot himself another child. Soon after it was born, he was brought to the hospital where his ailment was diagnosed as hypertensive cardio-vascular disease, cardiac hypertrophy and insufficiency. Tension had reached the breaking point at last. Three times in nine months he was admitted to the hospital, but it was too late to help him. He asked for psychotherapy, but the complexity of his situation at home—his wife was panicky about his absence because she did not know how to take care of herself, much less her children—combined with the seriousness of his physical condition handicapped his response to treatment. The hospital managed to get him on his feet three times, but six weeks after his third discharge, Harry died. He was forty-one years old.

Like so many hypertensives, Harry, because of his passivity and indecision, was not colorful; so that his death may not seem a tragedy. On the other hand, had he been enabled to use his capacities he might have been a dynamic person and his death might have been averted or at least regretted. He remains "an almost but not quite" person. To paraphrase one of our poets— "The saddest words of tongue or pen, are the words, he might have been."

§ 3

The Girl Who Liked to Laugh

THE INABILITY to relax plays its part in a great many diseases which are not hypertension. The emotional development which prevents a person from practicing what the U.S. Naval Bulletin once described as "the hygiene of a quiet mind" may result in any one of a large number of unhygienic bodily consequences. Nervous indigestion, inability to swallow and constipation are some of them. Others are back aches, tics and a tendency to have unnecessary accidents. Hypertension is also likely to appear with certain kinds of heart trouble where the patient has little success in organizing his energies in the direction of his major life goal and where the personality organization is weak.

Alice was a good example. The twenty-seven years of her life had been a long running conflict with various authorities and an attempt to realize a strong ambition. Despite her emotional disturbances and partly because she did not recognize them altogether as such, she was often a cheerful patient. Her descriptions of her own experiences and reactions to them were almost invariably preceded by the phrase, "it's all very funny." She did not mean humorous.

Alice was the eleventh of twelve children with no remarkable childhood history of illness or accidents. She was, however, reared with impartial sternness, which she herself described:

"Mother was a strict Catholic and never let me go to dances. When I would go she would wait up for me, make me undress and then beat me. Once she hit me so hard with a strap on my left arm that it was disabled for several days. It broke out into boils all over."

"Mother was funny," the patient laughed as if she thought this really was funny. "She couldn't stop beating me even after I was married. I would never cry out loud but I cried afterwards. My husband gradually put a stop to it.

"I never cared much for Mother and Father; they were very strict. My brothers and sisters never meant much to me either. I felt better when I left them. Two years after I left home Father died of a stroke. He never kissed me in all my life. It was right after that I got married."

At the end of her first half year in high school, Alice had been obliged to go to work. For three years, until she was seventeen, she worked in a silk mill and went to night school at the same time. Then she got a job as a cashier in a restaurant. She also did spare time work as a model, but found leisure for fun, too. She enjoyed parties, was attractive and good-humored.

"I like people and always get along well with them," she said. "I laugh everything off that bothers me, and people like my sense of humor. I can make jokes about myself, too."

She was twenty when she married. While she had an all-too-common ignorance of the physical aspects of marriage, she was not frightened by them. Her reaction was one of guilt that she should find them pleasant, and she said:

"In the beginning I enjoyed sex, I am ashamed to say."

Alice had lost a good deal of the freedom and satisfied ambition which she had enjoyed while she was working. The fact that she had seven pregnancies in five years did not improve her adjustment to family life, although she was no longer beaten. Five of the pregnancies were terminated in abortions—the other two resulted in a boy and a girl—but Alice would not use contraceptives. She said she had lost her belief in religion, but when asked why she preferred abortions to contraceptives, she replied:

"I know both are forbidden, but you don't have to sin so often if you have abortions as if you use contraceptives every time."

After the fifth, she added, she lost her enjoyment of sex and almost immediately had her first heart-disease symptoms. Hyper-tension followed soon afterwards. She was then twenty-five. She alternated between the relief which the illness afforded her in her family situation and depression because she could not realize her ambitions, could not take care of her children and suffered intermittent pain. Sometimes she flung herself into housework, keeping the place over-fastidiously neat, brushing and scrubbing the children constantly, pressing her husband's suits needlessly. Then she would beat the children, weep and enjoy her suffering. She was quite unable to organize her life consistently along either of these lines.

"I never wanted children," she complained. "They drive me crazy. I scold and beat them and yet they won't eat. But I love them. I could eat them up when they are asleep. I never say a cross word to my husband though because I'm afraid he might get angry. Mother was the same with Father. I guess women have to swallow their anger with men because men are stronger.

"The one thing that relieves me is to have the children sick. When my boy was in the hospital with a fracture I was perfectly well. As soon as he got back home, the pain and breathlessness began again. The only thing that would relieve it was to beat him."

In the course of treatment in the hospital and at the clinic afterwards, she got further relief from her symptoms, but as the pain in her heart subsided she acquired bruises on her left arm for which she could not account except that they must come from her heart trouble.

"It's funny it's always my left shoulder and arm that has the pain," she said. "I wonder if it was brought on by my mother's beating me? But that's a silly idea because that's the kind of pain you get with heart trouble. Father's left arm was paralyzed when he had the stroke and died."

However, after one of the clinic doctors explained to her that if the bruises were the result of her heart condition they would appear on other parts of the body than just one arm; she did get them in other places. But the release from pain did not check her feeling that she had made a big mistake in getting married. She thought she might have "amounted to something" if she had kept her job and continued to advance. She felt unable to break through the confining limits of her life and could not get reconciled to living within them. She reacted by submitting to her husband while swallowing her resentment of his domination, by beating her children and by wallowing in her own symptoms.

"That seems to be all there is left for me," she explained. "With my broken health I can never amount to anything."

Alice had never recovered from some of her childhood neurotic traits. She had been subject to temper tantrums and had horrible nightmares in infancy. She still did, although she allowed her temper to be loosed only against her children, never against her husband, or her mother, who was still alive "and healthier at sixty-eight than I am at my young age."

Although the case of Alice was not as clear-cut as some of the others, the pattern of both the hypertension and the coronary victim's personality is plain enough in all her life story. Once that pattern has been recognized, the lesson in relaxation may begin. The sufferer will soon find out if he can take it.

§ 4

Lesson in Relaxation

THE BUSINESS of learning to relax from tensions which have become settled and unconscious habits can be difficult. The lesson should accompany treatment designed to remedy the emotional situation which led to the tension in the first place.

The ideal can be seen in the behavior of almost any domestic pet. Junior's dog, for example, will give a fine demonstration of relaxation every time he comes bounding into the living room, turns around three times and settles down with a sigh and a flop for a quiet snooze before the fire. Every muscle goes limp; the animal appears to be completely at ease. Even dogs, however, continue an inner tension which makes them move their legs as if running or growl in their sleep. And Gantt leaves us no doubt that Nick, the dog with the accident habit, was a hypertense creature whose inability to relax was responsible for his lapses from the best canine house manners as well as his tendency to hurt himself.

If even dogs, apparently so well able to relax and snooze whenever the opportunity arises, can carry over tension into such disorders as accident habit, lack of urinary control and so on, how much more likely to do it are human beings with their more complicated emotional make-up, their larger responsibilities and their greater demands for adjustment. The tense muscles become a sort of armor to protect inner strains and repressions which have never disturbed the conscious mind.

In the course of learning to relax, the new pupil will perhaps find that he can readily do it with certain parts of the body. Arms and legs may be limp at the command of the brain, but the abdominal muscles, the shoulders, the back of the neck or something else may remain rigid and set. That means the mind is using this as an escape mechanism from the inner tension. The next step is to shift this tension to attention; in other words, to bring reason to bear on the problem of why the refractory muscles won't behave.

This lesson in relaxation is all very well if the victim of tension can learn just how to achieve "the hygiene of a quiet mind." This requires an understanding on his part of the real causes of his emotional disturbances. The blunt question, "What's worrying you?" is a poor beginning. The usual answer is either "Nothing" or a recital of fears about health which are really secondary. The basic start is for the tense one to talk about himself as a person, not as a medical case. This, under the guidance of an experienced physician, will bring out the psychosomatic facts a great deal better than blood-pressure tests, X-rays and so on.

Nor is it enough just to identify a particular anxiety. The victim also has to know where it came from and why, although his first discussion of it often will provide him with a good deal of relief. This relief should not be confused with cure. It comes from the identification of a symptom—the anxiety—but there still remains the problem of getting at the full emotional background and reaching a solution of the essential problem. It may be a deep-rooted hostility on the job which can be helped by a change of employment, or occupation. It may be the effects of sexual tension, requiring a course of sex education or the use of contraceptives. It may be any set of emotional factors in the past life. But whatever the causative factors are, the effect is to deprive the victim of the power to relax.

The most usual treatment for tension in the past was complete rest in bed with no disturbing visitors and no talk of anything more interesting or exciting than the idlest of pleasantries, "How are we this morning?", "Beautiful weather for the time of year," and so on. But for many, this is an aggravation of the disease. Every physician has seen patients in hospital wards lying back against their pillows with every muscle taut and pitifully frightened expressions on their faces. The fright is likely to increase after a dose of soothing platitudes murmured in what is considered to be an appropriate bedside manner, and sedatives may bring nightmares.

Actually a little mild exercise and not such mild conversation if properly directed are more effective. A round of golf frequently lowers rather than raises the blood pressure of these people. An emotional recital of their troubles will produce quite often a superficially alarming state of excitement, but after it is over the agitated patient will actually relax, saying:

"I feel so much better now I've got that off my mind."

The clue to what they have on their minds is often found in their perfectionist inclinations, their abnormal distaste for dirt, their compulsive behavior and speech, their dislike of fuss and fury, their tendency to seek intellectual and emotional satisfaction within themselves. The clue crops out in these actual quotations from the records of hypertension cases:

"I am a person who tries not to get angry because people don't like you when you're mad. As a child I always tried to reason rather than fight."

"I was afraid of not being loved, so I tried to do things perfectly and never be mad. Not to be loved makes you feel inferior."

"I always keep things perfect in my bureau drawer. I straighten it out when I'm nervous and mad. I'm awfully quick tempered and sensitive. I get hurt when anyones makes cracks at me, and throw shoes around. Then I straighten everything and start fresh."

"I have had to keep down a great deal of feeling. Sometimes I think I am going to tell people just what I feel, but when I'm face to face with them I haven't the heart."

When the bodily illness overtakes them, the hypertensive react in two ways. One group, including those who acquire a cardiovascular disease, show the coronary characteristic of trying to ignore their ailment and go on in spite of it. The others flop limply into the arms of authority and ask to be taken care of. Typical was a patient who explained that much as it hurt him to be dependent, his friends had taken care of him since he got sick. He could count on them no longer, so he expected the hospital to support him and his family. He was quite indignant when he was told that he would have to do something about it too; he was not that sick. In either case, as they undergo psychotherapy, these patients are likely to show an outwardly increased nervousness as they learn the lesson of relaxation. They get quarrelsome and jerky or they show a tendency to have minor accidents. Actually this is a sign that their symptoms are being relieved, and they work through it to a poise which leaves them as calm as they were when they were repressing their emotions and as relaxed as if they had never suffered from those emotions. They find it easier to eat less and, where necessary, work less.

The case of Mrs. "H.P.3," described in Chapter IV, shows how the lesson in relaxation works. Her mastery of it was the key that opened the way for her to do her thinking for herself and adjust herself to a highly unsatisfactory life situation. A summary of the ten sessions in which this was accomplished will illustrate how the hypertension victim can be taught.

In the first session, Mrs. 3 was so angry at being sent to the psychiatric clinic at all—she had the usual idea that it was insulting and imputing some disgrace to her to question her emotional stability—that she spent the first part of the interview stalking up and down the room alternately weeping and shouting. After she had expressed herself, the physician agreed with her that it was silly of other doctors if they had really told her that her pain was imaginary; that pain on an emotional basis is just as real as pain on a physical basis. Mrs. 3 then was persuaded to lie down; her extreme muscular tension was pointed out to her and the impression imparted that no matter what else might be wrong, it would help her to learn to relax.

At the second and third sessions, Mrs. 3's history was taken, but she was asked to relax as much as possible during the interviews. The fact that her attacks of pain, breathlessness and palpitation seemed to occur in relation to certain specific emotional experiences was pointed out. At the fourth session, Mrs. 3 confessed her murderous fantasies and her fear of picking up a knife one day lest she kill. At this point it was necessary to hold her back a little to prevent her from keeping on with these impulses to the point where she might carry them into action.

In the fifth interview, Mrs. 3 reported having been able to sit quietly and relax at home, and even to talk about business to her husband without losing her temper. By the sixth session she had stopped having nightmares, but it was necessary to talk about her vague fears. At the seventh session she reported that she realized it was up to her to make the best of her life, that she had known it all along but had been too sick to think about it. The remaining three sessions were devoted to working over past points to make this last one quite clear.

Mrs. 3's complete cure may be contrasted with the partial cure of Steve, a Greek restaurant keeper of forty, who linked his hypertension to business worries. Steve had come to this country when he was eighteen and went to work as a dishwasher, fifteen hours a night for $29 a month and his keep. He kept at it for a year, and then began a steady advance which ended when he owned two restaurants of his own, doing a good business. Then they began going downhill (the average life of a restaurant is only eight years) and Steve thought his illness dated from the failure of his second restaurant.

Like most sufferers from both hypertension and heart trouble, he glossed over his troubles at home, but they followed a pretty usual pattern. As a boy, the youngest of seven children, he had been devoted to a somewhat dominating mother and strictly brought up by a father who tolerated no back talk from his offspring. There was no history of heart disease in his family. Both his parents were alive and well at seventy-nine and eighty-two, respectively, but Steve had suffered a series of shocks when one of his brothers was killed in the war and three sisters died, two of pneumonia, and the third, his favorite, in childbirth.

His plan for being the boss in his own household was carried out when he was twenty-seven by marrying a Greek girl of seventeen who spoke no English. It was from her that the hospital authorities learned of his family life, for Steve was garrulous enough about his business and his pleasures, but reticent about his wife and child. He objected to the young woman's attempt to learn English, explaining that she would never need it, since she would never do anything but housework. She resented it, and since she was apparently a stronger character by nature, his attempts to make her completely dependent upon him were failing. Their sex relations were quite unsatisfactory, which was not surprising after Steve explained his attitude:

"It's better to have all that outside the home where you can pay your money and be through with it."

Steve boasted that he had always kept himself under control and never was one to speak out, although he admitted that he felt better if he did. His self-control did not extend to his figure, as he had been eating and drinking too much since his business troubles began. In five years his weight had risen from 180 to 225 pounds. Although he was sure overwork had brought on his illness, he announced rather defiantly that if he could not find light work when he got out of the hospital he would go back to his regular routine of toiling ten or twelve hours a day. Steve had no psychiatric treatment except the single interview for diagnosis, at which the facts of his life were brought out. He was slimmed down a bit in the hospital and discharged, but told to report for periodic check-ups. There was also a psychiatric follow-up note which quoted him as saying that he believed he was better off as night counterman in another fellow's restaurant than he had been as a proprietor. But he was gaining weight again, had been sick a couple of times.

"Before I used to get very angry, but now I just hold myself," he said. "Any time I get angry I get sick. You see, my whole system gets out of order. My heart pumps too fast, and my head gets dizzy. I feel like 200 pounds when I walk. At the time I got sick I had a lot of aggravation over worry. Now I don't worry so much."

Obviously the fundamental conflict had not been resolved. The inner tension had not been eased. For him and Mrs. 3 life had posed the same questions: "Can you take it?" Mrs. 3, after eighteen years of invalidism and negation had discovered how she could answer that in the affirmative. Steve had not even discovered that there was a question at all. With a better health record than Mrs. 3, he had not learned to take it because no one had pointed out to him why he should and how. He had not learned to relax.

[CHAPTER XI]

Mental Indigestion

§ 1

MEN ENGAGED in a rather wide variety of business and professions are convinced that in their line of work ulcer is an occupa-
tional disease. Publishers, advertising men, taxi and bus drivers,
lawyers, merchandizing and industrial executives all claim it—
some of them with a certain odd pride. This triumph of arrogance
over pain stems from the legend that ulcer of the stomach or
duodenum is above all others the affliction of tycoons and so may
be considered as a badge of success, or at least of superior quality.

Ulcer, they say, comes to the Go-getter. But in actual fact that
is not true. All this particular kind of Go-getter really gets is his
ulcer.

Nevertheless, the legend does reveal some popular understanding of the real nature of the disease—that it is a combination of
physical and psychic factors which are all necessary to this particular kind of a sore interior.

There are four steps which go into the making of an ulcer—very
few victims ever have more than one at a time although the pain
is usually enough to make them refer to it in the plural—and the
interplay of body and mind is decisive. The development is
this:

First of all an unduly large number of impulses, caused by emotional disturbances, are transmitted to the nerve fibers which run through the mid-brain to the intestinal tract. This part of the brain is believed to have, among its functions, that of emotional expression in the involuntary nervous system; that is, the nervous system over which man has no conscious control. It regulates the automatic functionings of the body, and these cannot be consciously willed to behave thus and so. But they can be affected involuntarily through the involuntary nervous system.

Second, these impulses get passed along to the stomach and intestine where they affect the production of hydrochloric acid. This is their normal function; it does harm only when the acid is produced in larger quantities than are necessary for digestion. The immediate result is likely to be hunger pangs which in health are an indication that the body needs food. In this stage of ulcer development they prompt the consumption of more than is actually needed, so that the more the person eats the worse he gets.

Third, tension develops in the smooth muscles, whose work is especially beyond the power of the voluntary system to control. The even contraction and relaxation of these muscles is disturbed. This may interfere with the normal rhythm of those muscles which govern the traffic between mouth and stomach. If their signals get mixed, the stomach will naturally be irritated by vomiting. Food which is kept in the stomach instead of being passed along in the normal course of digestion also irritates the lining.

Fourth, the victim then may eat something scratchy or irritating to the mucous membranes lining the stomach or intestine. The hydrochloric acid and the muscle tension combine to aggravate the slightest blemish caused on the wall of the digestive tract. The sore becomes noticeable, painful and infected, and can be seen by X-ray as an irregularity on the stomach wall. That is an ulcer.

Treatment in the past has generally worked backward from the symptom. The sore was the obvious seat of the trouble, so doctors tried to remove it by prescribing a soothing alkaline diet which would heal the ulcer, or they went to more drastic extremes and cut the ulcer out. Recently there have been experiments in severing the vagus nerve, which carried the offending impulses. This last seems very much like cutting the telegraph wires from Washington to avoid hearing bad news. It does not halt the march of events, and the bad news will reach us one way or another. Probably it will come as all the more of a shock for the delay imposed by the roundabout route.

While the actual sore has to be healed, the permanent solution is to stop at their source the sequence of events which lead up to an ulcer. This has been recognized by medical practitioners for a long time; in fact, almost as long as medicine can be considered a science. The relation between the mind and the gastro-intestinal disorders has been accepted ever since Hippocrates, in the year 640 B.C., was reported to have cured King Perdicas of Macedonia by the analysis of a dream.

§ 2

A Pattern for Ulcer

THE EXISTENCE of an ulcer is usually not a matter of any doubt to the physician. Yet there are times when the location of the sore and the reactions of the organs may conceal the irritated tissue from the fluoroscope. The facts may be revealed by a study of the victim's emotional problems, for the typical ulcer personality is not difficult to recognize if the physician has had adequate psychosomatic training.

I recall a young woman named Dorothy who was referred to a clinic as a purely psychiatric case. For more than a year and a half she had been complaining of pains which were definitely suggestive of gastric ulcer, but all the tests were negative. The doctors who had examined her became convinced that the symptoms were hysterical in origin, for they could recognize that she seemed to be laboring under a good deal of emotional strain.

They were right about the strain, but at the same time it was apparent that Dorothy followed the psychic pattern of the ulcer victim. It was not difficult to get at the bottom of her emotional problem. Unmarried and living alone with her mother, who had decidedly Puritanical reactions to her daughter's social activities, Dorothy was carrying on a love affair with the husband of one of her close friends.

Dorothy had a personality which inclined her to depend upon her mother for affection and support. At the same time she resented her emotional dependence on her mother and her mother's economic dependence on her. She could not shrug off her mother's views on virtue because she was accustomed to relying upon the older woman's judgment and needed to feel that she was approved. On the other hand, she could not accept the limitation on her own activities which this attitude implied.

She responded readily to treatment which revealed this situation to her, and the pain subsided. However, she could not be regarded as cured. She had a living to earn, and her job kept her from continued attendance at the clinic. When she was discharged, she was warned to have a medical check-up at least once a year, and that if in between these check-ups the symptoms returned, she was to come back to the psychiatric clinic at once.

In due course the pains did return; Dorothy's emotional system had not been as thoroughly stabilized as would have been possible if she had been able to continue treatment. But when she arrived at the clinic, the psychiatrist happened to be on vacation, and she was referred to a neurologist.

For three years he treated her with sedatives, but at last the emotional and physical strain grew greater than drugs could cope with. Her lover decided to divorce his wife and marry Dorothy, a complex situation in which the young woman felt that she owed it to her friend to break off her affair with the man altogether. Immediately afterward she suffered hemorrhages, and for the first time became aware of the fact that she really had an ulcer.

"Last week," she wrote to the psychiatrist, "I was so sick I called in a doctor from the neighborhood and he said I was having hemorrhages from an ulcer in my stomach. If this is what you were treating me for six years ago, why didn't you tell me?"

She was promptly asked to come back to the clinic, and this time the existence of the ulcer could be confirmed without any trouble.

Mental Indigestion

In fact it had progressed so far that she required blood transfusions. But for the accident of getting to a neurologist instead of a psychiatrist on her first return to the clinic, she might have been helped to avoid this suffering. The possibility was more than hindsight, for at the time her job had prevented her from continuing psychiatric treatments, this note was added to her chart:

"This patient should be followed in Medicine (that is, by the general clinic). Although the immediate emotional problem has been relieved and with it her symptoms, she has the specific reaction pattern to any type of stress and strain which is characteristic of the ulcer patient."

The recognition of that particular pattern would do a good deal to prevent ulcer. However, the possessor of it does not usually consult a physician, particularly one trained in psychosomatic techniques, until the disease has developed to the point where a sore is actually present.

Therefore, the first step in treatment of the ulcer is to get rid of the sore. This can be done by diet, although often the obvious regime of milk and mush is psychologically harmful, or it may be necessary to operate if the ulcer has proceeded too far. Once the sore has been healed or removed, intensive treatment of the basic trouble can begin. In the meantime, psychotherapy can help prepare the patient either for an operation or for acceptance of his diet and pave the way for serious consideration of the underlying mental indigestion.

The rather clear pattern of emotional life is a good deal of help in treatment. Ulcer patients generally are a bit above average intelligence, often very much above, and like to talk about themselves. They know very well that there is some sort of nervous or emotional basis for their pain, although they are inclined to blame other factors than the real ones.

"This happened to me because the government has made it so tough for us business men," they will say. Or, "My wife drives me nuts." Or, "I've had so much hard luck, Doctor, that it worries me sick."

Actually, these worries are more superficial than the majority of men like to think. Their trouble is deeper, but once they understand that fact, they co-operate quickly with the physician. That, too, is characteristic.

We find that most ulcer sufferers have always been feeding problems. If we can talk to their mothers, we learn that they usually had nursing difficulties in the very first few months of their lives. They were subject to colic later on. They may have inherited an organic weakness which predisposes them to ulcer when the necessary train of psychological explosive has been laid. One investigator has prepared statistics to show that among his ulcer patients, only 10.8 per cent were children of parents who had both been free of ulcers all their lives. In another 25.7 per cent, one parent had suffered from ulcer. That left the substantial majority as children of parents both of whom had been afflicted with the disease.

This indicates that the popular acceptance of ulcer as primarily a disease of men has little foundation in fact. For twenty-odd years, there was this much justification for the story: Most of the people who had ulcers were men. But that was only between 1914 and 1936. Since then, the proportion of women has been increasing, until now the sexes are about evenly susceptible. That this change in the sex distribution of ulcer is no phenomenon peculiar to the atomic age can be seen from the fact that until about 1900, the chief victims of ulcer were women.

The truth is that the cultural conditions of the time, reacting upon the peculiar emotional system of the ulcer type, has a determining influence. The impulses passing through the mid-brain are altered by the conditions of life under which people find themselves.

This cultural element in disease is not confined to the digestive tract. There are men and women still living who can remember when a special kind of anemia called clorosis was quite prevalent. It struck only at adolescent girls, and was widely discussed in the medical literature of the day. Today it has departed from life and even been dropped from the medical textbooks. The reason is that girls no longer live as they did in the late Victorian era. Both their

Mental Indigestion

physical and emotional lives have been liberated from constricting influences. The emotional upsets which used to be channeled into clorosis by the tight clothing and lack of exercise now find outlets in some other ailment, or happily do not exist at all because of the additional emotional freedom which has come with the change in costume and habits.

The ulcer patient in his childhood usually is devoted to his mother, and yet he cannot be satisfied with the dependence which that devotion implies. As he grows older, he is continually torn between his impulse to lean upon his mother, wife, friend or employer and his compulsion to assert his own independence. It is his desire to escape from his own fear of being a clinging vine which causes him to reach out for responsibility and gives him the appearance of the go-getter—and often causes him to climb quite high in the ladder of worldly success.

There is not in this personality the drive to excel which characterizes others, the coronary type for example. The ulcer patient's ambition and activity are merely a cloak for his dependent pull. He wants only to be active and escape from his own suspicion of inferiority; he does not necessarily seek to rival others, to climb over them, to impress his superior abilities upon them.

§ 3

The Real Go-Getter

THE BEGINNINGS of his personality troubles start early—earlier than in the case of most other sick people. The desire to remain a protected and loved babe begins an early conflict with the more conscious desire to assert individuality.

The reason that this conflict results in ulcer rather than in some other form of physical disturbance is to be found in the relationship of body and mind in this emotional situation. The child's first feelings of being cared for are associated with the act of taking in his nourishment. He sucks in milk, and his nervous system transmits impulses of well being. The nerves most immediately affected are those which lead to the stomach. Before the child has proceeded beyond his earliest helpless stage, a conditioned reflex has been set up. The stimulus of food has sent soothing messages through the involuntary nervous system. In the potential ulcer victim, there is a reversal of this soothing process—the early feeding problem, the nursing difficulties, the colic.

As the nursing becomes associated in the emotional system with the maternal protection, the drive to get away from the dependence, at once desirable and hateful, results in nerve impulses which are just the opposite of the normal infant's reaction to food. Because of this fact, the prescription of a milk diet may not turn out to be the best in all cases. The stuff is soothing to the mucous lining of the stomach, but it throws the patient back into an infantile status which may be thoroughly exasperating to his adult insistence upon independence. The resulting stimulus to the production of hydrochloric acid in the stomach may offset much of the benefit of the milk. For these patients, a dietary regime more closely approximating the grown-up table will often be beneficial.

Before the ulcer has developed, however, the predestined victim has rejected for himself the dependent position which one part of him desires. This is very different from those other patients who develop diseases from emotional upsets caused by withdrawal of the affection they need. The ulcer patient is not the inert victim of unrequited affection. His mother, wife or friend may be quite ready to supply the protection and love. But the ulcer personality has to assert his own self-sufficiency; he cannot yield to what he would perhaps regard as his weaker impulses if he were aware of them.

The adult ego, rejecting a desire to be loved and to depend upon others, pushes this feeling deeper and deeper into his mind. Concealed at last from himself and casual observers, his desire cannot be gratified by the ordinary circumstances of his daily life, for he is too busy impressing his independence upon his associates and his family. Finally the yearning for love seeks an outlet through a more primitive channel, the yearning for food.

This is something different than the condition which we describe as hunger. Hunger is merely an absence of food. The yearning for the act of eating, which the ulcer patient has developed as a substitute for his desire to be protected, does stimulate the nerves in the same way. Instead of the production of hydrochloric acid to digest a food, however, the stimulus results in the production of acid which helps create an ulcer. In short, the nervous system has been reduced to cheating the stomach. It gives the stomach all the stimulus it normally gets when about to receive nourishment, but no nourishment materializes.

It usually takes some time before this sort of deception bears its final fruit. Mr. Dooley, who anticipated so much of the wisdom of future generations, noted that in its normal condition the stomach was a mighty tough mechanism and would go to work cheerfully on a lump of coal. But when not even the coal is provided to satisfy its industrious habits, the stomach will finally get sore—but literally.

It should not be neglected that the early upsets connected with eating are the same factors which ultimately bring on ulcers. In order to overcome his hidden wish to be mothered, the ulcer patient will exaggerate his ambitious and self-assertive traits to the point of appearing positively aggressive. He refuses help; he reaches out for new responsibilities; he assumes unnecessary burdens. Insofar as these qualities make for success in business or professional life, the typical ulcer personality is an asset in propelling its owner to the top of the ladder. But the individual himself is just as likely to get the same satisfaction out of excessive work and emotional drive in the operation of a truck as in the conduct of a vast interlocking empire of industry.

The fact that women are being permitted to join in the scramble for independent achievement in our economic life is a factor in their increasing presence on the rolls of ulcer patients. Where the cultural habits of the community prevent a woman who has the ulcer pattern from engaging in any activities which allow her to struggle for self-sufficiency she will tend to develop some other ailment.

The attitudes so typical of the ulcer patient, whether man or woman, can be made to serve in treating the basic cause of their troubles. In general, they react to their illness with a complete reversal of what they and their friends regard as their usual form. From assertively independent people, they rapidly become exaggeratedly helpless, like babies. They give in to the long-repressed impulses with unhappy abandon. As a result, they are frequently healed (so far as the sore in the stomach is concerned) by a simple rest cure. They give themselves up to it, relaxed and contented, fussed over by family and attendants. The emotional conflict is halted, so that often they are feeling in fine fettle within a surprisingly short time. But if that is all that has been done for them, the conflict has been stopped by a truce rather than a peace. As soon as they return to their normal lives, the emotional process that leads to the illness starts again: the sore reappears. But if they are helped to understand themselves, they can make the cure permanent.

One of my patients, a major in the Army at the time, was benefited a great deal by the very quality of his independence and aggressiveness, once he understood what he was fighting against in his emotional background. He read some of the medical literature on the cause and cure of diseases in sheep which have proved so useful in our understanding of men. He learned that sheep can become neurotic by being subjected to strain. He read about experiments in which petty annoyances built up in them ailments similar to his own.

"I'm damned if I'm going to be just a sheep," he declared forcefully, and set out to show by getting well that he was a man.

Such men can gain control of their emotions—or at least enough control to prevent the development of new ulcers—when they have brought the essential conflict to the surface of their minds and begin to grapple with it intelligently. It is not too hard for them to strike a balance between their desire for love and their drive toward independence; few of us find ourselves in a position where these are incompatible altogether. The ulcer patient's trouble is that he seldom realizes the true state of his emotions.

Many resemble the middle-aged man whose chief difficulty was the unconscious attempts he made to establish his wife in the same relationship which he remembered enjoying with his mother, who had been dead for some years. Actually he had never permitted himself to be babied, even in childhood. He regarded himself as a rather strong character and was proud of it. But his marriage was being made unhappy and his stomach ulcered by the fact that his conscious self-assertiveness and domineering attitude in some matters conflicted with the other side of his emotional nature. Once he realized the facts, it was relatively easy for him to reconcile the two. His mind ceased to stimulate his stomach all the time. He became a real Go-getter; he got rid of his ulcer.

§ 4

The Man Who Changed Himself

THERE is more to the ulcer personality than his conflict over dependence. Once the digestive tract has started to acquire a sore spot, other emotions can contribute to the progress of the disease. Anger, fear, hostility and resentment are the most common, but any serious emotional shock stimulates the ulcer-forming or ulcer-irritating process.

Popular speech has linked these emotions to the stomach in dozens of picturesque phrases. We say we hate so-and-so's guts, or we admire the guts displayed in an act of bravery, or we go to the guts of a question. We can't stomach injustice or hypocrisy or somebody's manners. We refuse to swallow an insult. Our style is cramped. We propose to digest a problem. We abase ourselves when in the wrong with an expression of our willingness to eat crow or humble pie. We choke on all sorts of feelings, and it is a fact that a good many of them can give us the sensation of having a lump in the throat, just as more intense emotions can cause a more severe physical upset of the stomach.

Every ulcer patient illustrates the truth of some of these sayings. Walter S— proved the aptness of most of them. As the oldest of three children he had always, he said, regarded himself as sort of responsible for his younger brother and sister. They were not very practical people, he explained, and were likely to get into all sorts of trouble if left to themselves. Their parents? Well, of course the father had always provided well enough, but both mother and father were impractical, too. They needed guidance.

At first, Walter gave the impression of being the sole prop of the whole family. Actually he had never contributed to the support of any of its members because they did not need it. He was always seeking to "make things easier" for his parents by urging them to tell him what they needed, but they seemed quite content to live modestly on Mr. S—'s little retirement income. Walter had not so much as seen his sister for years, but he knew she had four children and a husband who did not make much money, so he thought he ought to do something for them. The only trouble was that they wouldn't take anything. His brother was in even easier circumstances than Walter himself.

The family had been a close-knit one, as Walter described it. But he had felt a little apart from it. His mother had a great many interests outside the home—clubs, the suffrage movement, study courses—and he was sure she liked his younger brother better anyway. Walter thought that was fitting; the youngest as the most helpless should be the favorite. His father naturally, he said, preferred the daughter. The boy had been competently cared for as far as his physical needs went, but he had had little further attention in the home. He remembered being told that he had colic all the time. One of his earliest recollections was of crawling up on a sofa to put his arms around his mother affectionately, only to be brushed aside without anger because she was reading. The indifference, he said, made more impression on him than a blow would have done.

There was no ulcer history that he knew of in the family, but his mother had complained frequently of minor digestive disorders. His father and his sister had suffered from asthma and hay fever, and at seventy his father was told that he had a mild heart condition and ought to take it easy. Walter could not remember that his mother, now sixty-five, had ever been seriously ill except for a vague and protracted siege some years before which he assumed had been related to her menopause. He himself, in addition to the

Mental Indigestion

usual childhood diseases, had been through an appendectomy and a long bout of pneumonia during successive summers in his teens. He remembered them vividly, he said, because they had spoiled his holidays.

Walter had left college in the last half of his senior year in order to get married. A friend of the family had offered him a place in a small but thriving business, and it seemed a wonderful opportunity to become independent of his parents. The job paid enough to support a wife if they were careful, and the girl was willing. Walter was just twenty-one, and plunged into the work of being head of a household with a great deal of energy. Within a few years he had been made a partner in the business, had two children and was quite generally regarded as a highly successful young fellow.

By the time he was thirty, he began to have mild stomach trouble. At first he thought he got it from eating irregularly in the course of business trips, but when he stayed home for months at a time and stuck to rather simple food, the attacks grew even more frequent. They were not, however, unbearable, and so he did not bother to consult medical advice. He saved that for a few years later, and then he went to see a doctor because he had had a series of bad colds and sore throats. He did not mention his stomach upsets, considering them unworthy of serious attention. He was advised to have his tonsils removed and did so. Thereafter he was free of what he considered major troubles for several years.

Finally, however, the pains in his stomach grew too much for him. He went back to the physician, and ulcer was readily diagnosed. Diet and avoidance of worry were prescribed. The first was easy—Walter confined his meals to milk and eggs and mush—but the second was beyond his powers. He really had nothing much to worry about superficially, and often his personal life was so uneventful that he was reduced to worrying about the iniquities of the government, the decay of politics in our time and the state of the world in general. His ulcer gave him a good deal of pain, but there were intervals when he was almost unaware of it. Curiously enough, he was nearly always free from serious discomfort when he was on his business trips; his worst attacks were saved for the privacy of the home.

On several occasions, his ulcer was so bad that he went away for rest cures. These always did him a lot of good. He threw aside business responsibility, family responsibility and care, forgot about the people he didn't like and allowed himself to be taken care of in every way.

The vacation from his dislikes was particularly important. While not a man given to outbursts of temper, Walter had developed a collection of pet hates, anxieties and fears. He had become a confirmed pessimist, and the world being what it is he was frequently confirmed in his gloomy predictions.

At the same time, Walter was no bitter misanthrope shunning his fellows. He liked cards and parties and gatherings at which his business associates met for wassail and jubilee, even though he no longer took part in the wassail. He was popular enough, telling a story well and willing to listen, too.

He was forty-five when he was advised that surgery was the only hope for him, but he was advised at the same time that there are psychic factors about an ulcer which he ought to investigate. He decided to investigate both, but his ulcer was so far advanced that there was nothing for it but to operate. Psychotherapy, except for helping put him in a better frame of mind to undergo the operation, came later.

Walter began, after some rapport with the physician had been established by talking freely of his feeling of responsibility for his father, mother, sister and brother. His mother did foolish things—taking trips and buying clothes or furniture which she couldn't afford—and his father did nothing to stop her. That angered and worried him. His sister failed to ask his advice, although she knew he was ready to give it to her, and he gloomily predicted that his bachelor brother was too irresponsible to come to any good end. He himself, he confided, was the only practical one of the lot.

It was pretty plain that his relationship with his mother had been one of resentment because she was not sufficiently dependent upon him and dissatisfaction because he had never been able to get himself babied. It was equally plain that neither of these sentiments was understood by him in the least. And still more plain was the fact that his curious reticence about his wife and children was based on an even more disturbing emotional conflict.

As the case eventually developed, it appeared that when he married her his wife had all the mannerisms of the helpless and fluttering female who was seeking to attach herself to his strength for protection. But as their married life settled into domestic routine, she showed a certain aggressiveness which was mainly directed toward furthering his career. She was a nagger, in short. Walter had to work pretty hard to keep himself believing that he held the upper hand in the more obvious areas of family decision. He could not relax for a moment and sink into the role of the pampered husband if he was to retain his self-respect. But he had a very obvious yearning to play that role. The degree to which he repressed it was measured by the intensity of his ulcer pains.

"Sometimes," he said, "I get so mad at that woman I have to get out for a while. But she adores me really, and there isn't anything I can do to change her."

It would have done Walter no good to have changed her. It was himself he had to change. Peace, and freedom from any recurrence of his ulcer, came to him when he finally understood that it was in his own emotional conflict that his troubles originated.

§ 5

Back to Babyhood

ULCER is not the only recourse for the dammed-up clash within the personality which can accept neither the dependent nor the independent role in life. Other disturbances in the digestive tract may take ulcer's place, and usually it develops that there are slight but significant differences in the personality of the person who gets colitis, say, and the one who has an ulcer.

As a rule, the colitis victim is less mature emotionally than the sufferer from ulcer. He is likely to be more lonely, and it has been found that for those colitis patients who are obliged to undergo operations, the presence of close friends or relations in the hospital the night before helps to prepare them for the ordeal of next day. It is important for the physician in charge to observe carefully and, if an operation is actually necessary, to time the operation with an upswing from the patient's generally self-destructive drive. If their attention is focused on dying, they will die no matter how the operation is performed.

The behavior of parents and close friends of colitis patients provides some clues to the forces that help develop the illness pattern. Just as the colitis patient has his attitude focused on dying, partly out of hopelessness, partly to make those who should have loved him sorry, and partly to punish himself for his unworthiness, so his loved ones react to illness with feelings of hopelessness and guilt, even to the extent of becoming ill themselves or dying as a reaction to the death of the colitis sufferer. Dr. Lindeman felt the reaction of the relatives to be so important that when such colitis patients were on the danger list, he asked the closest friends or relatives to spend the night in the hospital; not simply because he hoped that they might help the patient, but because he wished the opportunity also to do a little preventive medicine. He wished to save the relatives from their own reaction to the death of their loved one.

That a somewhat more infantile type should choose colitis is quite natural in view of the very simple fact that one of the earliest forms of resentment which an infant can express has to do with his bowels. The process of elimination is the most important in the life of a baby, next to breathing and eating. During the last thirty years an imposing amount of information has become available on the psychic aspects of this bodily function.

As eating becomes a symbol of desire to be loved, to lean on someone for security, to receive emotional or material good or to take it by force if necessary, so elimination becomes a symbol of possessiveness, of pride in accomplishment, of the tendency to give and of such hostile impulses as desires to attack or soil or disparage.

The importance of this function is a by-product of civilization.

Mental Indigestion

Its emotional importance is emphasized for the child during what is usually his first educational experience—toilet training. His introduction to conformity with the (to him) incomprehensible customs of society is generally associated with praise, tokens of parental esteem either material or affectionate such as candy or kisses and in some cases penalties for failure. Under these circumstances the child naturally associates this function with possession of something valuable, and the relationship of this in later life to preoccupation with money is one of the best established of psychoanalytic concepts. The exaggerated disgust which can easily follow the infantile pleasure is simply the reverse of this medal.

As the child grows older, these emotional attitudes disappear from his conscious thinking. But they remain rooted in his personality, and are at work within his body. Later still, any disturbance of the function of the bowels is greeted with an exaggerated fear or concern, which further intensifies the emotional disturbance. The wish to receive affection and material tokens of it is countered by the unconscious desire to make up for that dependent desire by assuming new duties and obligations. The individual feels called upon to make extra efforts in his work, to support or help others, to give until he develops frequently a reputation for great conscientiousness. At the same time there is the opposite pull toward relaxing these unnatural efforts, to cease the exertion, to relapse into dependence.

When this conflict becomes too great to find expression in actual day-to-day activities, the colitis or other disorder of the bowels may be substituted. Therefore in many cases of colitis, the relief which can be obtained from sedatives, rest cures and diet will often be made permanent only by the addition of psychotherapy, so that the cause of the ailment can be removed along with the symptoms. As early as 1930, a study of a number of colitis cases in a New York hospital led to this passage in the resulting report:

"Of seven men . . . all were tied to their mothers except one who had found a mother substitute in an older sister. Several of these men had never been away from their mothers for more than thirty days in their whole lives. None of these men was married, and for the most part the onset of their colitis was associated with the conflict between the mother-tie and the desire for marriage—psychologically a repetition of the birth experience. . . .

"Of the five women . . . three were married as follows: One to a man her own age who had been virtually living in the home of his wife's parents; the second was married to a man twice her age—an inadequate father substitute—from whom she tried to free herself, but got colitis in the attempt; the third, E. P., was secretly married. Of the remaining two women, one, C. M., was engaged, but her colitis and her unconscious mental attitude were interfering with marriage. The other was unapproachable on the subject of marriage."

Hemorrhoids are an even more avoidable expression of this sort of basic conflict than colitis, and represent an even more infantile personality. This ailment is usually associated with anger, too, the physiological response to an emotional stimulus being diverted from what we have come to regard as the normal sphere. The expression "grind his teeth in rage" describes the usual reaction. But in this personality, the grinding is transferred to the sphincter muscles and becomes a rectal spasm. If this continues, the veins are constricted and hemorrhoids are formed. Further continuation may result in a chronic rectal condition. Contributing emotional factors are fear of pain, which tends to constrict the sphincter muscles further, as well as hidden guilt and spite reactions.

The necessity for grappling with the psychic elements in all these diseases of the digestive tract seems clear enough. Perhaps one of the most convincing demonstrations of the high degree of suggestibility of the human being in relation to this part of his anatomy was made more than twenty years ago in a hospital by a physician who may sound like a practical joker in medical school but whose experiment has some value. He described it as follows:

"A physician ordered sugar solution as a medicament for patients on a ward. Shortly afterwards he rushed in, appearing perturbed and declaring that by a mistake a harmful drug had been given. He said it would be best if everyone could vomit; otherwise a painful pumping out of stomachs would be necessary. Almost every patient vomited immediately."

In this prompt obedience of physical function to the emotional stimulus of fear lies the direct connection between psychic experience and digestive disorders. Mental indigestion becomes a reality, a psychosomatic reality.

[CHAPTER XII]

Allergy con Amore

§ 1

THE BRIDGE over the chasm between our understanding of bodily and of emotional factors in illness is nearer completion in allergies than in any other field. The chasm itself is neither narrower nor shallower; the difference is in the progress made on the bridge. So if it sometimes seems that the relation between an attack of hay fever and the sufferer's emotional state is closer than in the case of some other disease, that is only because we know more about it.

We are so familiar with it that we can call it by nicknames and label the underlying factor "smother love." Whether the victim has had it heaped upon him or whether he goes burrowing for it himself seems to make little difference.

Knowledge about this group of ailments and about the emotional factor is comparatively recent. The word "allergy" itself was not coined until 1906. It means literally "altered force" and may be defined as a person's altered capacity to react to a specific stimulus. That alteration may show in a reaction to pollen, dust, food or something of the sort on the part of the skin, the nasal tissues, the bronchial tissues, the stomach and so on. It may show itself as hay fever or asthma or a rash.

The condition is usually not hard to recognize. The substances to which an individual is sensitive usually can be identified through skin tests. More obscure are the reasons why one person sneezes in the presence of ragweed and another because of cat fur, while a third breaks into a rash after contact with a certain dye and a fourth has no allergies at all.

Susceptibility may or may not be an inheritable characteristic. It has also been suggested that substances which are responsible for the allergic reaction may be present in the placental fluid, and thus transmitted to the foetus before birth. The same substances may be absorbed by an infant with his mother's milk, or even with cow's milk. Whether the reaction will be hay fever, a rash, asthma, nausea or nothing at all, however, will depend upon emotional as well as hereditary and physical environmental factors.

This last fact is not a new discovery. Hippocrates himself knew that an asthmatic attack could be brought on by some violent emotion. What is relatively new is our current knowledge of how these emotions work and what can be done about them. As early as 1922 a Dr. Costa, writing in a German medical journal, described how he had cured a woman who had been suffering uninterruptedly for four months despite the use of the whole bag of tricks then believed to be effective. He abandoned the drugs she had been using and resorted to hypnosis. In the first session he planted the suggestion that she would sleep well, and she did. Another session relieved her anxieties, including a fear that she would die of tuberculosis. She was apparently cured in eighteen days, but two months later had a new attack. This time she did not respond to hypnosis, and Dr. Costa proceeded to try analysis. In response to one of her questions, he mentioned that the same sort of thing happened in the intestines, and in a few days the patient developed an intestinal disturbance. Ten days later both that and the asthma had disappeared.

There may be some question as to the permanence of this cure. However, the methods of men like Costa have been improved upon in the twenty-five years since he wrote, although for a time, until only a few years ago, the discovery that an asthmatic's specific allergies could be identified led to a subordination of the emotional factor. The allergists concentrated on their tests, theorizing that if the patient could be kept away from every substance to which he was allergic, he need never suffer more.

For the person who is allergic only to a few substances which can be avoided easily, the course is clear. A city dweller whose only allergy is poison ivy, can learn to recognize the plant and stay away from it. A farmer or a woodsman might have more difficulty, at least in staying away from it.

When it comes to the asthmatic who reacts positively to a long list of common substances, the problem becomes more complicated especially if he rides in the subway. Here, for example, is a representative list of items to which one man was sensitive: The pollen of elm, oak, sycamore, ash, hickory, birch, grass, Russian thistle, pigweed and ragweed; the hair of goats and hogs; wool, tobacco, flaxseed, pyrethrum and household dust, and finally, but only slightly, fifteen different foods.

Even assuming that he had unlimited means and leisure, this man could have spent a lifetime running in vain from contact with any of these. Most people are bound by family, jobs, friends and income to the environment and the climate in which they and their allergies find themselves.

But the asthmatic, for example, who can actually get away from those substances to which he is allergic is not necessarily safe. Time after time, an emotional reaction will bring on an attack which cannot be connected with any of the things to which the individual's skin reacted. On the other hand, relief from emotional conflicts frequently gives a sufferer complete or partial relief, even though he remains exposed to the pollens and dust to which he is sensitive.

Of course the skin tests are useful. There seem to be two categories of asthma. One, sometimes called "extrinsic asthma," is caused by external factors such as dust, pollen, food, animal hair. The other, "intrinsic asthma," is due to disturbances of the endocrine system, the emotional system or faulty metabolism—internal causes. The two can be and often are found in combination. The first type if existing alone can be benefited by removal from contact with the external substances which cause it. But the others cannot get away from their own bodies and their own minds.

In the treatment of this second group, the allergist and the psychiatrist are an inseparable team. Perhaps this psychosomatic relationship is never so obvious as in the work that has been done in recent years on hay fever and asthma. Dr. Leon Saul states the case when he offers the thesis that "the emotional state leads to physiological changes which either 1) imitate the allergic symptoms or 2) render the tissues more sensitive to allergens [which are the substances to which the victim is allergic] or 3) do both." Thus the choking brought on by a pollen may be intensified or relieved by the emotional state, and the choking originating in the state of the emotions may become worse because of the pollen.

There are certain specific emotions which seem to be linked especially to asthma and hay fever. A conflict about longing for mother love and mother care is one of them. There may be a feeling of frustration as a result of too little love or a fear of being smothered by too much. A second emotional conflict characteristic of the allergic is that which results from suppressed libidinal desire, often closely connected with the longing for mother. The steady repetition of this emotional history of "smother love" in the asthmatic is as marked as the contrasting history of hostility and unresolved emotional conflict in the sufferer from hypertension.

Of course, nearly everyone has a certain and usually very keen longing for mother love. The longing and the pollen (or dust or food) must be considered in their relation to each other and to the individual. Just as almost everyone will have his membranes irritated by dust but does not get asthma, so the longing for a mother is almost universal but not necessarily toxic.

There is a special pattern of mother-child relationship which seems quite constant in asthma cases, and also seems to be related to the nature of the disease. There is a reason why, given a predisposition to it, the disease should be the result of this particular emotional setup.

[*185*]

Asthma derives from a Greek word which means "panting." The victim has difficulty in breathing, wheezes, chokes, nearly suffocates. It appears that the bronchial mucous membrane becomes irritated and inflamed. The inflammation obstructs the passage of air through the bronchial tubes and causes phlegm, which makes for further obstruction. It appears also that the controlling bronchial behavior muscles become subject to spasms, and these block the passage of air, too. In any case, the important fact for the victim is that he finds it hard to breathe, the difficulty ranging from a gentle wheeze which is hardly noticeable to rather acute paroxysms. But always asthma is a respiratory problem.

Now the first experience of a newborn child is also a respiratory problem. The infant, as the first independent act after birth, has to start to breathe, and that begins with a cry. Crying can be delayed only at the risk of the baby's life, which is the reason for the traditional slap which starts the cry, the breathing and the child's independent life. It is probable that the child had a feeling of suffocation until that first cry started the air pumping in and out of his lungs.

Crying soon fulfills another purpose for the infant. It will bring someone—usually the mother—to administer aid or comfort. Crying has been fixed, therefore, as the solution to problems which are too difficult for the infant to deal with himself. Frequently in adult years the asthmatic will find that an attack subsides when he bursts into tears—real weeping, not the watering of the eyes which is a symptom of his disease—for he has managed to achieve a form of emotional release which most grownups take a good deal of trouble to suppress. It is noticeable, too, that asthmatic children cry less than the average of their years. Asthma may be a substitute for weeping.

As the child grows older, his longing for a mother's love is accompanied by fear of losing it. This, too, is pretty nearly universal, but some children will have a certain kind of emotional system combined with a certain kind of respiratory system which converts that emotion into asthma. This is how:

For any one of a number of reasons, the child is not sure of his place in the mother's life. Sometimes he is jealous of brothers and sisters. Sometimes the mother feels (consciously or not) that the child interferes with her career or happiness. She may be neglectful or seek to compensate for the feeling by an overly protective attitude. Sometimes she will seek to break the child's habit of helplessness by making the infant prematurely independent. Sometimes the birth of another baby before the first is old enough to stand alone will divert really needed maternal attention.

§2

Children in Search of Love

STUDIES of actual asthmatics show a more intense than average dependence upon the mother. This is followed later in life by dependence upon someone whom they set up in the mother's place—wife or husband, relative, friend, physician. Among those sufferers from asthma whose ailment is either derived from internal stresses or a combination of these with external allergies, such cases as the following are not exaggerated.

Mr. A. had slept in the same bed with his mother until he was eleven years old, and he had remained dependent upon her emotionally all his life. Even when he got married, he repeated toward his wife exactly the attitude he had assumed toward his mother, down to sleeping in the same position as he had when a child and looking to her for maternal rather than connubial affection. Mr. A. had ceased to share his mother's bed only because he had touched her breasts one night, and she decided he was getting to be too big a boy. She had sent him away to camp, his first separation from her, and he promptly got his first attack of hay fever. At twenty-six he married against her wishes, and got his first attack of asthma.

Mr. B. had had asthma since he was four. His father was an actor and both parents were away from home for long periods, but as a boy Mr. B. had been delicate, and his mother took him into her bed to be close to him in his various illnesses whenever she was available. Actually this continued off and on until he was

[187]

twenty-one, and he was constantly with her except when she accompanied his father on tour or at intervals when he was sent away to seek relief from asthma. It was noticeable that he was much less troubled by the disease during these periods of separation, regardless of the climate.

Mrs. C. had felt herself the unloved child in a family of four which was dominated by the mother. The girl developed asthma at six, when her sister was born and began to share the mother's affection with their older brother. From the time she was thirteen until she was fifteen, she was away from home and free from asthma. She relapsed at once on her return, remained asthmatic until she left home again at twenty-nine, and had no asthma again until she repeated in another city the psychological pattern of her home life.

Mr. D., born in Poland, had been babied by his mother because he was the sickliest of her children. He had developed a rash at the birth of his first brother, of whom he was very jealous. Frequent asthma attacks began when he was eighteen, and was out in the world on his own, and hay fever followed when he came to the United States.

Mr. E., a successful businessman, had developed asthma and hay fever early in life, along with a rash for which no allergy had been found, and which finally disappeared. He, too, had been immensely drawn to his mother, an aggressive but attractive woman. She had, he thought, alternately stimulated him to become an important person in the world and "slapped down" any budding attempts to do it.

Miss F., suffering from asthma since she was a little more than two, had been very jealous of her brother, who was only fifteen months younger. Her attacks began when she was sent away from home because of her mother's illness, which she later believed to have been a pretext to get rid of the children for a time. Miss F.'s childhood was a long history of domestic discord and separation, which was not eased by the divorce of her parents when she was seven.

Miss G., the product of a difficult delivery, had weighed less than four pounds and apparently suffered from asthma at the very outset. Despite her small size and delicacy, she had little mother care as an infant because of Mrs. G.'s long illness. As a little girl she was rather ostentatiously placed on her own by her mother.

These seven are typical of the asthmatics whose ailment has a large emotional basis or factor. Perhaps their strong dependence upon the mother will seem somewhat exaggerated. That exaggeration, however, comes largely from the admission of feelings and experiences which are usually not discussed and may be so severely repressed that it takes a long time to get at them even when the discussion is in the privacy of the physician's office.

§ 3

Children of Fear

MOTHER is not the only problem of asthmatics, of course. In fact, one of their most common difficulties is a sexual problem, often very closely related to the maternal. In general the allergic have had a strong sexual curiosity and temptation—not necessarily a strong sexual desire—and they tend to be afraid of it. Their usual fear is that any expression of their curiosity or any attempt to gratify the temptation will cause them to lose the maternal care or affection. As a rule, the mother has contributed to this by completely avoiding talk of sex with the child or else making it appear shameful or evil or at best somewhat dirty. In our seven representative asthmatics, the records along these lines were rather convincing.

Mr. A.'s mother had been very strict about keeping talk of sex out of the home, and she had managed to instil into her son so strong a belief in the shamefulness of it all that it survived his marriage, which was made extremely unsatisfactory in large part by his sexual attitude and deficiencies. Perhaps the plainest indication of his combination of mother love, sexual temptation and resulting fear was that when he was twenty years old he got almost to the point of intercourse with a girl, but he was so entangled in his own emotions that at the last moment he jumped out of bed and ran home to confess his "sin" to his mother. He was naturally bothered by feeling himself to be less than normally potent, and his sexual life with his wife was mutually unsatisfactory. Sexual emotions tore Mr. A. so strongly and so noticeably that he could even get attacks of asthma at apparently irrelevant moments, which when traced back turned out to be brought on by watching his employer's wife cross her legs, or some equally mild stimulant to his curiosity or temptation.

Mr. B.'s mother also had a tendency to repress firmly any curiosity he might display about sex. Her son developed a strong conflict between his dependence upon women and his sexual desires, with asthma resulting.

Mrs. C. never received any sexual information from her mother, not even about menstruation, but as an adolescent she was simply forbidden the company of boys. Naturally she evaded this order, and while still in her teens became pregnant as the result of a clandestine affair. Her mother forced her to marry the man— apparently a gay, charming but weak youth, who came to live with her family after their marriage and fell easily and happily under the domination of his mother-in-law. It was after his death that Mrs. C. left home and became free from asthma.

Mr. D. remembered his terror as a child that he would be punished for any sexual escapades. His father was the chief object of his fear, although he was afraid of his teachers and priests also. His curiosity and the course of his education in sex might have been that of any other lad, asthmatic or otherwise, but had left a more than usual impression, and all his life he had been drawn toward women who would mother him.

Mr. E.'s difficulties in his own mind were more neurotic than asthmatic. He entered the group of cases here discussed not because he wanted treatment for his asthma, to which he had apparently resigned himself, but because he had developed a strong distaste for any physical contact with women and had secret homosexual obsessions.

Miss F.'s stories of her childhood were completely revealing whether they were true or not. She managed to remember—and it was as real to her as if it had happened—a rather horrifying history of beginning masturbation at four, inordinate sexual curiosity and sexual play with her brother and a sixteen-year-old housemaid a few years later, actual attempts at intercourse with her younger brother when she was ten and submission to being "raped," as she put it, by a young man that same summer. These memories revealed the youthful curiosity and temptation, along with the unhappy emotional reaction to them. It was also significant that Miss F.'s mother had not helped much by confining her discussion of sex to complaints about her own disgust with the sexual act and her nobility of spirit in yielding herself to her husband, who was pictured as a cruel and inconsiderate not to say coarse fellow because he desired his wife.

Miss G. had been informed about sex by her parents quite as inadequately as Miss F. She, however, developed in adolescence a rigid code under which sex was as sternly outlawed as her parents could have wished. The repression turned out to be as emotionally disturbing to her as Miss F.'s more violent or more imaginary experiences.

Just why these seven people should develop asthma rather than some other ailment is probably dependent upon more than purely emotional factors. For instance, all of them except Miss F. were known to have had asthmatics among their immediate relatives, and the hereditary or pseudo-hereditary element in setting up a susceptibility to allergies is one of the best-known circumstances of this branch of medicine.

It is also obvious that the disease tends to intensify the very emotions which in turn are likely to aggravate the disease. The asthmatic child has a very understandable and practical fear of being alone with his attacks. The helpless, choking sensation leads him to depend more than his healthier brothers upon the ministrations of a mother or a substitute for a mother. Thus a vicious circle is drawn within the individual's life, with the need for a mother's care and the longing for it strengthening each other until both are harmful and require medical treatment.

Asthma may also serve as a means of getting attention which

would otherwise be diverted to others, and will finally become an unconscious reaction if the individual is deprived of what he thinks is his due. Of course, this is not confined to asthmatics; many sick people get this sour-grapes satisfaction, but in the asthmatics it is strong: "If I can't get what I want in one way, I'll try another," they say, and asthma is often the other way. Mr. B., for instance, found that his attacks gave him the protection of mother. Mrs. C. had mighty little care from her mother, who hated illness, but was nursed tenderly through her attacks by her father. Mr. D., who remembered that as a boy he had been taken into his mother's bed only when he was sick, remarked; "I guess I learned that I could get with mother by being ill."

Another factor in emotional development which may tend toward asthma rather than something else is the frequent repression of the impulse to cry, despite a rather sensitive nature. Frequently asthmatics turn out to have been children who had acquired the habit of suppressing their tears because of fear. Crying is closely connected with the respiratory system. As the natural outlet for the emotion is blocked, it turns into the nearest or most closely related channel, the breathing apparatus. The resulting asthma may be long delayed, but the theory of a connection is strongly supported by the relief which many asthmatics experience if they can burst into tears instead of into wheezes.

§ 4

They Breathe Again

EVERY sufferer from asthma soon finds from bitter experience that certain emotional storms will bring on or intensify an attack. By the same token, a calming of the storm or an avoidance of it will relieve or prevent asthma. This principle, applied by a variety of psychiatrists and psychoanalysts, has resulted in freeing a great many slaves of the wheezing, choking, sniffling and itching of various allergies.

One of the most illuminating studies in this field was made between 1937 and 1941 at the Chicago Institute for Psychoanalysis where twenty-seven patients were studied from periods ranging from two weeks to forty-three months. Among them were the seven who have been described in the preceding pages.

Of course all of these patients were aware of some emotional conflicts in themselves—or their parents were, for eleven were children. They would not have been at the Institute otherwise. Therefore, they are significant as showing what can be done through a psychosomatic approach where the patient understands that an emotional problem is involved. Although fifteen did not complete the full course of analysis mapped out for them, the results in the twenty-seven cases were:

Symptom-free 11
Much improved 8
Improved 1
Unchanged 7

The course of treatment by which these results were achieved was prolonged analysis of the victim's emotional life and problems, plus the attentions of a competent allergist. Avoidance of some of the substances to which the individual was most allergic was plainly helpful, but since most of them could not be completely eliminated, the acquisition of emotional stability seemed to be the chief ingredient in the improvement of those who were helped. It was significant that the seven who remained unchanged had severe and far-advanced neuroses. The less firmly crystalized the behavior pattern, the easier was the cure.

The earliest relief experienced by many of them from their treatment came when they were able to confess rather freely episodes, thoughts or desires which they had never dared mention before or which they thought they had forgotten. Confession, whose soothing effect has long been known in the religious world, seemed to have much the same effect upon an asthmatic as a fit of weeping. Then, for those who came to regard the analyst as a substitute for the mother they longed to have care for them, there would be a period when they interrupted the treatment in a burst of independence, just as earlier in life they tried to get free from parental domination. Usually, the patients of this kind were spared asthmatic symptoms as long as they were able to maintain their self-sufficient attitude. But if that weakened, either through internal strains or the pressure of some new development in their lives, they came back to the analyst suffering from asthma, or perhaps some other allergy, all over again.

The ones who were most helped were those who finally were able to understand how their longing for a mother or her equivalent—wife, friend, analyst—was in opposition to their sexual impulses and set up emotional disturbances, why they simultaneously strove for and feared genuine independence. The record of our seven sample cases is explanatory.

Mr. A. began to improve when he was shown how his dependence first upon his mother and then upon his wife led him to doubt his own manhood, and how this in turn led him on to desires for sexual promiscuity which he never satisfied. At the start of his treatment, the analyst provided him with a substitute mother and satisfied his yearning for attention by devoting an hour a day exclusively to the most trivial details of his past. When the flattering routine was interrupted by the analyst's vacation, Mr. A. was so upset by the withdrawal of this daily attention that he had a bad attack of asthma. Gradually, as he came to a complete awareness of the reasons for his dependence, his attacks grew weaker and finally disappeared. One of the incidents which brought this home to him was an unusual but severe asthmatic attack in January—up to this time his disease had been seasonal, never having appeared in the winter. He began to suffer just after a near seduction which he did not mention to his wife, and he remained sick until he realized that his fear of his wife's reaction if she learned the real facts of the incident was the basis of his trouble. After that he had no more asthma, even in the spring and fall. His relations with his wife became much better; they were finally able to achieve a reasonably normal marital life, and for four years he has been rid of asthma and suffered only mildly from hay fever.

Mr. B. was a more advanced neurotic case, diagnosed in the Institute as a paranoid personality, strongly inhibited. Although he had always felt uneasy in the presence of girls, he had heard that marriage would cure asthma—a superstition which suggests some understanding of the facts long antedating scientific explanations. So at twenty-three he advertised for a wife, and picked his mate from the replies sent in, displaying little judgment in his choice, a rather coarse woman who scorned him sexually, emotionally and intellectually. He was thirty-nine when his treatments began, and still financially dependent upon her. In view of their marital relations, it was hardly surprising that Mr. B. had incessant desires for other women, but he never felt sure enough of himself to do more than think about them. It took months before his suspicions and fears were sufficiently allayed to enable him to ease himself by talking to the analyst about his manifold doubts and terrors. Despite his really advanced neurotic state, the recognition of his symptoms finally enabled him to deal with them fairly effectively. He managed to stand on his own feet economically. He also divorced his wife and married a woman with whom he could live more happily. His attacks of asthma, formerly perennial, were now confined to the hay-fever season. His bodily well being was improved in direct proportion to his emotional betterment.

In the case of Mrs. C., the clue to a solution was given by the two periods in her life during which she had been free of asthma, when she left home. The disease's return a third time occurred when her situation paralleled that in her parental domicile. Her attacks then began when her superior in the New York store where she was employed (a man) began to give preference to another woman. The feeling of being neglected by someone on whom she relied for protection was the same as that which had characterized her home environment. Up to this time, she had supposed that the air conditioning in the store kept her well. But now, despite the air conditioning, she suffered.

She moved to Ohio, getting a better job, and brought her daughter, Edna, who had been left in the South with Mrs. C.'s parents, to live with her. Edna nursed her through a number of asthma attacks and several nasal operations, until Mrs. C. easily drifted into a feeling of emotional dependence upon her daughter. Edna was jealous of any man who came near Mrs. C., and the older woman was not in the habit of celibacy. Between desire and fear of losing her child's love, her asthma grew worse.

Finally, she moved to Chicago for treatment, leaving Edna behind. After a time, she improved greatly, then relapsed when her life became rather emotionally complicated once more. This time she managed to fall in love with a doctor who had a jealous wife and at the same time took as her lover a married man who was also asthmatic. The doctor soon dropped out of the picture, but the affair with the other man dragged on. He could not leave his family, and Mrs. C. suffered from a feeling that she was bringing nothing but sorrow both to herself and to the man's inoffensive wife and children. Finally she insisted in true movie fashion that he choose between her and his lawful spouse. In the same fashion, he chose his wife, and to her surprise Mrs. C. became relatively free of asthma.

At about this time, Edna came home from school and resumed her motherly role. Mrs. C. had only the mildest attacks. But when last heard of, despite a long analysis in which she had come to understand something of her emotional make-up, she was shaping up for a relapse. She was again dissatisfied with the absence of a man's love, but was again afraid of losing Edna if she brought anyone else into their life.

The allergists had given Mr. D. up as hopeless. The analysts doubted that they could help him either. There was no chance of getting him away from his environment which contributed materially to his suffering. The only job he had, or could get, was with the railroad where he had to work constantly in and around cattle cars—and he was allergic to cattle hair. His wife, a fat and sloppy woman, disgusted him, and he was constantly angry with her because of her appearance and his opinion that she was not a good mother to their children. He derived considerable material benefit from his disease, first as the source of a pension which he received as a partially disabled veteran of World War I, and secondly because his fellow workers out of pity did a good deal of his work for him—and Mr. D. was constitutionally lazy. Finally, he had suffered so long and so acutely from asthma that there was some organic damage apparent in the lungs.

Despite all these handicaps, and without improving his physical environment, he won some relief through understanding his own condition and emotions. It took a long time—303 hours of psycho-analysis—but Mr. D. no longer gets acute asthmatic attacks while at work in spite of cattle hair. He suffers them at home only when he gets angry with his wife.

"I hate and am dissatisfied with what I have," he said after this result had been achieved, "but it's better than nothing."

Mr. E.'s problem was his impotence and his homosexual fan-tasies. The course of his treatment was an analysis, long and rather arduous, in which he found that he suffered asthmatic attacks be-fore and just up to the point of confessing his sexual complexities. Then, when he brought himself to actually talking about them, he would experience relief. Finally he was able to establish his own sense of security in the world of men and women, especially women, and his impotence disappeared. He suffers from asthma now only intermittently and the attacks are relatively mild.

Miss F. was diagnosed as a victim of prolonged adolescence as well as asthma. She recited in the course of her analysis a long his-tory of sexual and homosexual promiscuity. She was unable to make up her mind whether she would prefer to be babied and pampered or settle down to an adult life with children of her own. Attacks of asthma punctuated the struggle until at last she came to the conclusion that she was grown up. She married, got a job, reconciled herself to relatives with whom she had quarreled—and had no more asthma.

Miss G., who had not had her first attack of asthma until she was twenty-one, began her treatment three years later. Her specific allergies were identified, and so were her chief emotional conflicts. She herself felt that these latter were the more responsible for her condition. Two and a half years after her analysis was interrupted, she reported that she had tried small quantities of the foods to which she was allergic and had experienced no ill effects. Further-

more, she said, she never had an asthma attack any more if she
was able to cry.

These cases were part of the first real study of the effectiveness
of psychoanalysis in treating asthma. Since then a good many short
cuts have been found, so that the time required for psychotherapy
of allergy sufferers has been greatly reduced. However, asthmatics
still require more than most because the pattern of their emotional
conflict sets in so early and is so compulsive.

§ 5

Fondle But Don't Touch

ONE OF the delayed-action mines of childhood explodes, appro-
priately enough, on the surface. The explosion takes the form of
the common skin diseases, and the fuse is usually shorter than that
of most other such mines. Eczema and its medical relations generally make their appearance while the victim is still young.
Smother love has enveloped them so completely that, in a sense,
their body is covered by it, and the skin is the part most immediately affected.

"Mummy," one small sufferer exclaimed, "I'm going to itch and
scratch if you don't love me."

Tracing back the psychosomatic nature of skin allergies, it must
be remembered that a baby feels through its skin what the mother
feels and does it even before any other faculties have developed.
Furthermore the skin, of all parts of the body, is obviously the one
of which everyone is most conscious all the time. It is the medium
through which we feel all sorts of sensations, pleasant and painful,
and through which we express some of the most common psychosomatic relationships. Nearly everyone has responded to emotion
by perspiration, and the soldiery of the recent war recognized a
psychosomatic truth by coining the phrase "sweating it out" when
they meant enduring a distasteful regime. Most people have felt
themselves blushing, or at least have seen others blush, from
purely emotional causes, usually a feeling of inferiority, guilt or
shame. More than forty years ago a couple of experimenters

showed the intimate relationship between mind and skin by rais-
ing blisters on their subjects by hypnotic suggestion. They were
real blisters, too, which took some time to heal and left scars.

So when a child is relieved of pain from bruises and scratches
because "mamma will blow it away" or "papa will kiss it and make
it well," there is sound psychosomatic basis for the "cure." The
homely wart is cured nowadays by relatively simple suggestion.
In reverse, annoyance or frustration can bring out a painful or
itching sensation. There was a woman who suffered from weals on
her body every evening for ten years. It developed that her brother
called on her daily, so that she was never able to be alone with her
husband. When the connection was explained to her, she never
had them again. There was a girl who had hives whenever she had
any intense longings which could not be realized at once. An allergist could find no reason for it; then it was discovered that if
she wept from frustration she did not have hives.

The outstanding feature of the typical sufferer from skin disease
is a deep-seated emotional conflict between desire for affection
and a fear of being hurt if they seek it. "Touch me and comfort
me," they seem to say in one breath, but "don't touch me" in the
next. Many of them are lonely people, even though they are sur-
rounded by relatives and acquaintances. They seem unable to
achieve strong and lasting friendships, drifting from one to another
but never permitting themselves to drift into a real friendly inti-
macy.

Usually their parents have been kindly, with the mother more
likely than the father to be the hub of the domestic universe.
Allergy is present in a great many of the family histories, but the
skin ailment seems to be caused as much by copying the symptoms of elders as from actual heredity.

Despite the general leniency of the home environment, the skin
sufferers have been hurt in childhood at the same time that they
developed their strong craving for affection. Later many of them
react by an exaggerated self-consciousness, shyness, a striving for
correctness in behavior and appearance, a shrinking from notice

and a desire to please and be accepted. They are sometimes described as painfully conventional. They go in for competitive sports rather than intellectual interests, apparently as much from a desire to win approval as to win a game. Their sexual adjustment is superficially good, but the women incline to resent anything more than petting while the men tend to be promiscuous, explaining that they never seem to find the right woman.

Their illness is usually associated with a personal loss. Someone or something to which they have become attached is taken away from them. It may be a mother who died young, and the child mourns her not as one who is dead but as one who deliberately deserted him. Once the behavior pattern has been established, an attack may be induced by nothing more serious than the loss of a purse. Often they derive an exaggerated compensation from their illness, which makes it difficult for them to fight the disease. Their exhibitionism is soothed by the obvious signs of their ailment. Their desire for care is partly satisfied by the application of ointment and the hope of sympathy.

They incline to be afraid of responsibility, and even blame almost anything or anyone but themselves for their illness. "I was left with too much responsibility," they will say, or "I felt afraid all the time" or "I don't want to be dependent on her but yet I can't break away." They choke back anger and are proud of it, like a bellboy who used to break out in a rash when he failed to get as big a tip as he expected, but prided himself on maintaining his politeness. (Of course this does not mean that rudeness is a sign that someone is avoiding skin trouble.)

Margaret, for example, was a girl whose emotional stability seemed well established until the cause of a severe attack of eczema was looked into. She had suffered from mild attacks of it on her body from time to time since she was six years old, but when she was twenty-two it spread suddenly to her arms, neck and face, and remained for weeks. It began to clear up when she saw the connection between her skin eruptions and various emotional maladjustments of which she was not previously aware.

Allergy con Amore

Margaret was an only child, on terms of deep reciprocal affection with her parents. She was especially fond of her father and for six years helped to nurse him while he was an invalid. At the same time, she said, she had lots of friends, enjoyed going to parties, liked dancing and as a child had been much interested in sports. She was compulsively neat (a characteristic of women with these skin diseases) and said of herself:

"People call me a fuss-pot. I like things to be in order. If somebody throws a dress on the bed I pick it up immediately. I'm that way at work, too." She was a secretary. "Everything has to be orderly."

When Margaret was nineteen, an air-force soldier to whom she had become engaged was killed in China. Then she became engaged to another man nine years older than herself. Three months before her violent attack of eczema appeared, her father died. Margaret herself connected the death of fiancé and father with the eruptions on her skin, for she had been holding back her feelings.

"I feel nervous inside," she explained once, "but never show it." And again: "I can't say anything that will hurt people. I don't see any percentage in that. I never remember getting mad. When I was a kid I took a cuffing from others but never fought back. I want people to like me."

She was eager to get married, she said, but would not until she could find an apartment near her mother. This, under current housing conditions, seems a little perfectionist, but then patients of her type often are. "I won't live with my mother, though," she said, sensibly. "Two families living together never works out."

A more dramatic example perhaps was Frances, who dated her eczema to an emotional explosion which was more obvious than most of the mines of childhood. Her parents had been separated when she was twelve, and four years later her mother, with whom she lived, had an illegitimate child. Frances and her brother and sister were separated, the two younger going to an institution and

Frances back to her father. Between shame of her mother—she had never mentioned her illegitimate brother to her husband although they had been married five years—and dislike of living with her father, she had her first attack of eczema. She did not, however, bear a grudge against her parents, and remained attached to her legitimate brother and sister. She was constantly trying to help them, although they did not reciprocate.

"People shouldn't have children if they are not wanted," was her nearest criticism of her parents. "You can't love people if they don't love you. My mother didn't want us and my father didn't either."

Frances had been fond of basketball and swimming, liked dancing and parties, got along well with others, saying: "I never get mad at people." She had been a waitress, salesgirl in a department store and a telephone operator until after her marriage and some months before her baby was born. One of her chief worries about her illness was that it made her ashamed to take her baby out for fear people would think she was a bad mother who let her child risk catching a contagious disease. She went down side streets so no one would see her, but she never asked a doctor whether her skin trouble was contagious.

In Frances as in Margaret, there is the same dominant desire for affection and fear of being hurt. Strongly suppressed, the emotion had sought its outlet through the most obvious channel, the skin. Their problem was to hold on to someone they loved, but they never felt quite secure. In times of definite insecurity, when the loved one was taken from them, the illness would break through their rather weak defenses.

These cases have been relatively simple ones, but a great many people have several allergies at once. Skin diseases, asthma, hay fever and a certain type of digestive upset occur in frequent combinations. A physician experienced in the psychosomatic aspect of these conditions can often predict with accuracy whether a patient suffering from one of them today will come back with another at the next visit.

§ 6

Oh, My Poor Head!

PSYCHOSOMATICALLY migraine is related to the allergies. The personality pattern, the psychic factors are the same, although in these patients the smother love operates without the assistance of ragweed. Migraine can be one of the most painful of ailments, and at one time the psychic factor was recognized indirectly by the theory that it was chiefly a disease of hysterical women, and would be cured if they would only use their heads instead of filling their heads with nonsense. Since it is not really confined either to women or to hysterical types, the theory has fallen by the wayside.

However, the importance of migraine to the general public as well as to the physician can be estimated by the fact that next to low back pains, headaches are the chief complaint of the visitors to doctors' offices. The unsatisfactory nature, from the standpoint of permanent health, of treatment which simply relieves the pain but does not consider the real source is plain if it is remembered that headaches come from all sorts of causes. They are symptoms, however, and a preoccupation with a single aspect of the illness may give some temporary relief at the expense of a more serious illness later.

Migraine is only one type of headache, although a common one. It and others are attributed to various physical disturbances. Dr. Max Goldzieher attributes them to pressure inside the cranium caused by an increased flow of water to the tiny blood vessels of this area because of an abnormal retention of salt in the tissues. He was very successful in treating these cases with medication which removed the excess salt, and decreased the irritability of the walls of the blood vessels, and by recommending a salt-free diet.

He found, however, that some of the factors responsible for the condition of the blood vessels in the first place were "psychogenic influences, nervous strain, emotional difficulties, overwork."

When the migraine patients are separated from those who suffer from other kinds of headaches and examined as complete human beings rather than as an ingeniously contrived assortment of chemicals, the pattern of their personalities accords with that of the sufferers from the various allergies. Treated psychosomatically in the same way, they respond as readily. The removal of their symptoms, the headaches, can be followed by the removal of the cause.

Instead of the "fondle me but don't touch" attitude, the victim of migraine has at once a strong desire to inspire love and is so afraid of being hurt in the search for it that his headaches get worse on holidays. He does not like to take this time off from his less emotionally upsetting occupations to be with his family, and the headaches give him the secondary compensation of being able to avoid that contact.

Now this is far from being the purpose of the patient himself. He would much prefer not to have the headaches, and the benefit he derives from them is a better-than-nothing, secondary compensation. Nevertheless, it becomes strong, frequently interfering with treatment because it is hard to rouse in these patients their desire to fight the disease. In common with the victims of asthma, hay fever, and skin disease, the sufferer from migraine is so swathed in the soft folds of smother love that it is difficult for an outsider to get at him or for him to escape from the folds. One patient in this group summed up the whole sad, sweet story of the emotionally smothered when she said of her mother:

"She has made me too dependent on her. She does all the work in the house and minds the baby. She doesn't even let me cook for my husband, and I'd like to. She does everything for me, so how can I hurt her by saying anything? I'm not going to do that to my child if I can help it."

[CHAPTER XIII]

Failure in Chemistry

§1

SCIENCE has discovered no way to reverse the process by which milk turns sour. Until recently the same thing was true of the human personality. There were cases of individuals who did change back again, but no one was quite sure how or why. There were more individuals whose bodies just couldn't handle sugar. The more they were deprived of it, the more they craved it, and the worse their afflictions became if they got it.

They had diabetes, and were usually a considerable strain upon the patience and good nature of their families. The disease was said to have spoiled their dispositions. In many cases, however, their dispositions had been spoiled before the disease was in evidence. They turned sour as a result of emotional churnings which were not at all obvious.

Gradually the interplay of psychic and somatic forces has become better understood. The physiologists have been building upon studies of bodily reactions among diabetics. The psychologists have learned a good deal about the corresponding emotional factors. A bridge is being pushed out from both sides of the chasm of our ignorance on the subject. Construction has progressed so far that one physician wrote after discovering that a diabetic's passing of sugar rose alarmingly without any change in his hospital regime but solely because he heard that his corporation was about to retire him:

"It is interesting to be able to measure the power of emotion in terms so tangible as ounces of sugar."

It is more interesting to be able to restore sweets to the sour. Through the combination of advances made in our understanding of both the emotional and bodily aspects of the disease, that is just what psychosomatic techniques often can do. The failure of the body to handle sugar and the alibi which the mind makes for the emotional counterpart of the physical symptom are jointly the target of the psychosomatic approach.

Diabetes is a failure in chemistry. The pancreas stops producing insulin, the substance which enables the body to assimilate its sugars and make use of them. Twenty-five years ago two Canadian physicians succeeded in producing insulin and opened the way to relief for millions.

But diabetes remains a serious problem to the medical profession and the millions of people all over the world who suffer from it. In the United States this problem in chemistry is seventh on the list of causes of death and fifth among the reasons for chronic invalidism.

While there seems little doubt that emotional factors can contribute to the failure of the pancreas, no method has been discovered either in psycho or any other therapy to restore the normal functioning of the organ. But diabetes has such a strong psychic effect in most cases, and the patient's emotional state reacts so strongly upon his physical condition, that psychosomatic research and the application of psychosomatic techniques offer a good deal of hope for reducing invalidism. The chronic disability which is often attributed to diabetes can more properly be laid at the door of the emotional consequences of the disease, and therefore can be obviated by helping the patient achieve emotional stability.

The psychic development of the diabetics follows a very clear pattern if we keep in mind that these generalizations are true only when we look at the pattern displayed by the composite records

Failure in Chemistry

of thousands of patients but will not apply at all to every individual case. This pattern works out something like this:

Heredity—About one-third of diabetics have a history of the disease somewhere in their families, but there is no difference in the progress of the ailment as between them and others. As a group, diabetics have a rather high proportion of nervous disorders in their ancestry.

Previous Health—Diabetics have a better health record than most patients, with an average number of accidents which tends to increase after diabetes sets in.

Family Life—In early childhood, most diabetics develop a strong emotional conflict between resentment of parents and docile submission to them. There is a large proportion of "spoiled" children among them, and a strong jealousy of brothers and sisters. Among the men especially there is a history of domination by the mother with strong ties of affection and dependence.

The whole pattern tends to repeat itself in the relations between the diabetic and husband or wife, with the result that their marriages are not outstandingly successful, since the diabetic partner often wants to be babied more than is usually compatible with mutual happiness.

A surprisingly large number of these patients talk about divorce and separation without ever coming to the point of action. Their frequent dislike of the sexual act keeps many of the men single and the married ones have a smaller than average number of children. The women, frequently frigid, often complain of what they regard as the excessive sexual demands of their husbands. As might be expected, these diabetics make pretty poor parents, having a strong tendency either to scold their offspring unmercifully or worry about them excessively.

Attitudes Outside the Home—Superficially diabetics seem to get on well with their fellows, but they are bothered by feelings of insecurity in their relations with others so that they tend to alternate between a self-conscious initiative which sends them more than half way to meet people and an inaccessible aloofness which prompts them to withdraw suddenly from friendships. Their strong compulsion to win sympathy often has just the opposite effect.

In their work, they incline to a commendable industry but without much display of initiative. They shrink from responsibility and scatter their energies among a multitude of tasks, often ignoring the important for the trivial. This inability to follow a consistent course of action prevents them from developing their intelligence and abilities, which are frequently above the average, even to the level of the average.

Personal Behavior—Diabetics include more than their share of people with markedly infantile personalities. Generally careless of their health, they seek to blame others for any trouble they get into. They tend to shy away from participation in competitive sports, and to seek work where they think competition will not be too keen. They procrastinate and postpone decisions, but try to shift responsibility to others if there are any unfortunate consequences.

There is among diabetics a high proportion of men and women with homosexual tendencies, expressed or not, and a generally unsatisfactory adjustment to sexual relationships. As a rule they take little save a perfunctory interest in religion except when some special maladjustment, especially an awareness of homosexuality, rouses a sudden fervor. This then usually takes the form of an extreme asceticism or fanaticism.

Diabetics in childhood seem to have complained more than most, but took few positive steps to remedy the condition of which they complained because they had no confidence in themselves. While they are willing to be kind and helpful if they do not have to assume any responsibility for others, they tend to give little and demand a great deal.

Reaction to Illness—Diabetics have the strangest ideas about how they contracted their disease. By the very nature of it there is usually no sudden attack, only a gradual process of pancreatic deterioration; but the first discovery of it is frequently the result of some emotional crisis which exaggerates the symptoms sufficiently to bring them into the open. Yet I have known patients who attributed their diabetes to giving up liquor, to falling off a kiddy-car, to being struck over the heart, to a shell-shocked husband who attempted to strangle the patient long before her illness, to an unwanted pregnancy, to worry over a husband's or wife's failings, to a childhood fright from a dog.

The general run of diabetics enjoy being taken care of; they find their illness either an alibi for inadequacy or a prop for weakness. They can be remarkably clever at evading a prescribed regime and then blaming the physician or the injustice of fate for a setback. They are equally acute at persuading the unsuspecting practitioner to play mother to their childishness.

§ 2

Curdled Emotions

SOMETIMES caricature is more readily recognizable than a portrait. Sometimes an object is more easily studied if it is magnified. Similarly, the general characteristics of diabetes and its emotional factors may be clearer in a patient whose case, on the psychic side at least, was an extreme exaggeration of the run-of-the-mill diabetic.

Such a patient was Roger R———, who was of special interest. He came with a mental problem and became the first reported case of a patient who had received psychoanalytic treatment prior to the onset of diabetes. At the time I first treated him, the characteristics of the diabetic had never been systematically studied or compiled and, of course, he was not then diabetic. But years later I was startled—and impressed—to discover that the notes I had made on Roger's personality fitted with amazing precision the "typical" diabetic. No suspicion that he had diabetic tendencies had ever entered my mind or the mind of any other physician whom he had consulted. Yet eight years after his original treatment, which had enabled him to recover sufficiently from his schizophrenia to make a good vocational and social adjustment but was interrupted by the necessity of accepting an out-of-town job, he returned with diabetes. Although the onset of diabetes is slow and insidious and although diabetes, like hypertension, often remains undiscovered for several years, in this case the time of onset could be fairly well defined. A year previous to his return to me he had an operation for hernia, with careful physical and laboratory examinations indicating perfect health.

Roger was what some readers may at this point in the book have mistakenly decided is an oddity in our civilization—the much-wanted child of very happily married parents. He and his brother—older by two years—were the central interest of the R—— household, and they lived in a home equipped with everything which kindness and money could provide. Roger and his brother, as he remembered it, were treated with scrupulous fairness, indulged in all their desires and encouraged to develop their own careers in their own ways. The elder brother thrived under this system, and became a university professor.

Although remembering his father as the kindest of men who never punished his sons, Roger was as an adult resentful and suspicious, bitterly jealous of his brother whom he successfully avoided after early childhood, and convinced that Mr. R—— sent him to school only to deprive him of his mother's care.

Roger's first memory was of waking to consciousness with his mother and a woman doctor bending over him after he had been kicked in the temple by a horse. He was then five years old and had already conceived a strong fear of horses. He was surprised to learn this from his mother nearly twenty-five years later, for he had developed a highly successful amnesia about the whole phobia. He also had no recollection of the occasional punishments which his father meted out in an effort to end what Mrs. R—— called Roger's "terrible tempers." Mr. R—— would lock the boy in a closet where he would kick and scream until he collapsed from exhaustion. His mother said this always took half a day at least, but Roger had completely forgotten the incidents.

A shock which he did remember happened soon after. Waking from a frightening nightmare, he ran to his parents' room for comfort, only to hear what sounded like a struggle and his mother's voice saying:

Failure in Chemistry

"Henry you're wild. If you keep on you'll go crazy like your father!"

Terrified, Roger crept back to bed unheard, but the reference to his paternal grandfather scarred him emotionally. The old gentleman, later committed to an institution for mental patients, suffered from the delusion that he had committed the unpardonable sin and was responsible for the World War of 1914–18.

At five, Roger was sent to kindergarten with his brother, but the older boy was soon promoted to the first grade. The younger displayed at this time both his violent jealousy and a strong compulsion to excel. He grew to hate his teachers, the school and even to a degree his parents because, try as he might, he never caught up with his brother. He studied in a frenzy (also forgotten later) but he had an abnormally strong desire to make people admire him, and plunged into athletics and the quest for popularity.

At ten, he decided his life was ruined because he was obliged to wear glasses. He felt he must give up athletics for fear the glasses would be broken, and he decided that little girls wouldn't like him because "my face was not perfect any more." He retreated into loneliness, kept away from people because he was afraid they would laugh at him, fell into a state of really anguishing anxiety over such trifles as losing a paper on which he had been writing or drawing. Later, when he discovered masturbation, the sense of sin which he managed to build up around the practice intensified his neurosis.

He entered college, but rebelled against a life which failed to recognize what he thought was his great poetic genius. At the same time he felt himself an unfit companion for others, and decided to retreat into the country with his books and be his own teacher. He really did make a sort of solitary school life for himself, studying all alone on a regular schedule, reading far into the night, taking the usual school holidays. His parents allowed him to continue this life for two and a half years, until he was twenty-two.

Meanwhile, in the summer he was twenty, he had his first experience of sex, and an unhappy one. He was seduced, or at least so he liked to think, by a married woman twice his age, but Roger proved impotent. He was thoroughly disgusted with the whole affair, so much so that he gave up masturbation almost entirely. He was inclined to blame his father for his impotence because when he was little Mr. R——— had frequently washed and examined his genital organs, explaining that there were things which little boys could do to themselves which would prevent them from becoming fathers. Roger got the idea that there was something wrong with his own organs, probably that they were small.

His impotence accompanied a strong homosexual tendency at this time, and his period of seclusion in the university of his own making complicated his neurotic difficulties to seriously pathological proportions. He wrote a Dadaistic epic which was to be a life masterpiece and then, in the belief that it was mere mental masturbation to excite himself over a poem, he threw it into the fire. But he went on writing verses, strangely defiant pieces with a good deal of strong imagery and fine feeling for words.

The summer after he emerged from his seclusion he indulged in what even several years later he called the greatest love affair of his life with the wife of his best friend. He was still impotent; apparently the "greatness" lay in the abnormality of undertaking the affair with the husband's consent.

At the end of that summer, his father and the friend urged him to return to college, and he allowed himself to be persuaded although convinced that he knew more than the professors. He tried a couple of other unsuccessful love affairs, proposing double suicide to the objects of his affection with no more success, although he once attempted to throw himself in front of an automobile. On another occasion he kept his father waiting in a hotel all day while he spent the time with a girl. At first he thought he did it to show his love for the girl; then he decided he had avoided Mr. R——— for fear he would kill him.

Shortly after this, the girl rejected his proposals. She wrote him that she did not want to kill herself with him and that her husband found his letter distasteful. Roger thereupon removed from his

Failure in Chemistry

clothes all marks of identification except her letter, walked up to a policeman on the street at midnight and demanded:

"Who are you? Are you God?"

He said later that he thought he would like to spend a week-end in a mental hospital to gather literary material at first hand. He remained in the institution for nearly a year, which he remembered as the happiest in his life, but he was finally discharged as much improved. His father obtained for him a poorly paid job in a store, and he settled into the routine of doing his unexacting work, returning to a dark, unattractive room to read and write, imagining to himself that he was God and the Messiah and appointed to save the world by teaching it destruction. He was sane enough, however, to spend the week ends at his parents' comfortable home.

Roger was twenty-nine when he came to me for treatment. The whole pattern of his emotional development became clear as he returned at frequent but irregular intervals for a good many months. The larger than lifesize picture of a diabetic (although I was far from recognizing it at the time) emerged from his talk and his memories. There was the spoiled jealous child, the conflict between resentment and submission in the home, the superficial popularity and retreat into solitude, the shrinking from responsibility, the desire to blame others, the homosexual tendency and sexual maladjustment, the infantile personality, the waste of energy and talent.

In due course Roger began to understand himself. He survived even the depression, which threatened his job and swept away all of his father's money. Roger took the lead in organizing the store employes for mutual protection. He began to concern himself with the business, talking to the boss about it and actually qualifying for, asking and getting a raise. He even managed, after a few more frustrating attempts, to prove his potency to himself by having successful intercourse with prostitutes.

Before his treatment was complete, however, Roger was offered an excellent managerial job in another city and he took it, for the salary enabled him to help his parents. For three years he was perfectly well mentally, and no one would have believed him to be a former schizophrenic. Then his father died, and Roger's sense of responsibility began to undergo a strain. He gave up a girl he had planned to marry—"no time for such things"—and worried about what he ought to do. What he actually did was to develop a hernia, for which he was operated successfully. The examination made at the hospital at this time could hardly have missed physical diabetic symptoms if any had been present. His urine was free from sugar but his personality at this time was not investigated for diabetic traits.

Shortly after Roger left the hospital, his mother came to live with him. He gave up his own social life to make her happy, and emotionally went back into his childhood when she had taken care of him. At the same time, he worked harder than ever before and began to take his business responsibilities more seriously or at least with more anxiety. He gave up seeing girls altogether. Some of his old neurosis returned. He became, he said later, "obsessed with masturbation and cigarettes." In this state of mind, nine months after his mother had come to live with him, he avoided the schizophrenic pitfalls but visited a prostitute and picked up a gonorrheal infection. This turned into gonorrheal arthritis, and when he went to the hospital for treatment, it was discovered that he had diabetes too.

§ 3

The Last Pleasure

ROGER R—— gives the diabetic pattern in something more than lifesize, and his treatment—the same sort of help in understanding his emotional difficulties which had brought him out of his mental ailment—was successful in preventing invalidism and recovering a normal way of life. Yet it is only in degree that he differs from more commonplace examples. At first sight the emotional history of Jenny, who came to the hospital with diabetes when she was twenty-four, does not appear strikingly unusual. This was her story:

"I've always been mother's favorite [she was one of six]. If I swallow my feelings and listen to her, she'll give me anything I want. That's the way I learned to get my own way. Father is no good, but he has to listen to her too."

Jenny left school at the end of the sixth grade to help support the family, working as a waitress in restaurants and for private families.

"I could never get along with people," she said. "Both at home and outside they are nice in front of you and mean behind your back. If you buy anything, they are suspicious about where you get the money. . .

"When I would get disgusted with the work I would go to my room and cry. I would never fight back. Then I would think about getting another job; then I'd be afraid I couldn't get one, and try to stick it out. After I changed my mind a good many times I usually did get another job. I didn't realize how lucky I was, working."

This last remark was prompted by dissatisfaction with her marriage. She had liked to skate, but gave it up after her marriage. She was bitter against her husband, whose carelessness, she said, had resulted in her having a child.

"I knew my husband for a year before I married him," she explained, "but I never knew any other men. I didn't like the idea of sex but I wanted to get out of the home and I thought he would take care of me. I never had any satisfaction in sex and was disillusioned when I had to have the baby. . . I think I'm the type that was meant never to marry. I keep thinking about leaving my husband but he sort of has me caught. I would be afraid of being left alone with the child. . .

"There's nothing I'd like better than to work now and let someone take care of the child, but my husband won't let me. I'd much rather put in a day's work than take care of a child. She gets me aggravated all the time. She's afraid of me. I get so nervous I don't care what I do to her.

"Mother brought me up to go to church, but since I've been married I stay as far away from it as possible. The priest would scold me about not wanting to have more babies. . .

"I'm afraid of responsibility. . . I resented having to have responsibility about supporting the family. . . I didn't realize the responsibility of having to have a child. . . I like girls better than men. It's easier to make them do what you want."

Jenny's angry reaction to diabetes was as typical as her mental attitude before it.

"It seems like the last insult," she cried. "My husband gave it to me by making me have the baby. Now I don't care what happens to me. I don't care whether I get well or die. I can't follow my diet because I don't want to give up the only pleasure that's left in life, eating what you please."

In her thoroughly commonplace way, Jenny had all the emotional difficulties which had befallen Roger R———, and she, too, had diabetes.

§ 4

Return to Sweetness

No amount of emotional stability is going to give the diabetic back his former degree of ability to produce insulin from his own pancreas. But emotional stability will cut down the physical reactions to the disease—the fatigue, the debility, the loose co-ordination, the irritability. Furthermore, it often allows him to adjust to the necessary diet and even increase the diet while eliminating the necessity for insulin.

The first great difficulty in helping diabetics to achieve this stability is their reluctance to discuss their real emotions. They have a few other handicaps in making a satisfactory adjustment to their illness, among them their facility at inventing reasons for unhappiness which appeal to their ideas of their own importance but are not usually related to any facts. Then they have a tendency to deny the existence of any conflicts at all. They develop a good deal of ingenuity in placing blame on others, and their enjoyment of the attention which illness brings often stifles any desire to get well.

Allowed to follow the easiest path of their inclinations, they will gradually subside into chronic invalidism. But the diabetic, like other people, has the qualities of his defects. The physician

Failure in Chemistry

using a psychosomatic approach can often find in the very characteristics of the disease itself a handle for successful treatment.

One of these handles is the intelligence which the diabetic usually possesses even if it is sometimes hidden under a mask of idleness and stupidity. They are more than usually susceptible to an appeal to reason, especially if the appeal is coupled with an attitude of sympathetic respect for their point of view and their sufferings.

Another handle is the familiarity which these patients acquire with tests for sugar. Through these, they can be shown how their emotional conflicts intensify the severity of their illness. They often feel that they are getting a new lease on life when their anxieties are relieved by an understanding of them. This not only more than compensates for some of the secondary pleasure they derive from illness, but enables them to deal with their home or social environment in realistic terms. It can prolong their lives while enabling them to avoid invalidism. It can make them happier people and give them enough support so that they can stand on their own feet—literally and in solving their problems.

That is what happened to Rose, the diabetic near-invalid whose reticence about her emotional life has been mentioned in Chapter V. When it was finally broken down, the course of her disease, dating back to the earliest psychic factors possible to trace, had followed the pattern which psychosomatic studies have led us to expect.

As the oldest of eight children born in Austria, she was obliged to leave school early to help keep the house although she dearly desired to become a teacher. She insisted that her mother "loved me least of all" of the children, but she was her father's favorite and deeply devoted to him. She both loved and envied her oldest brother, who was the only sickly member of the family, suffering from nervousness. Her love was inspired by his resemblance to their father, her jealousy by his attainment of the goal she had desired for herself, teaching. In all this lies the first emotional conflict characteristic of the diabetic—submission to and resentment of parental authority, and jealousy of others in the family.

[217]

Rose came to this country, hoping to study some more, and became engaged to a cousin here who had helped pay her fare. The engagement was broken, however, ostensibly on the ground that she did not speak English. The cousin then proceeded to become engaged to Rose's younger sister, and the jilted girl attempted suicide by shutting herself in the bathroom and turning on the gas. She was rescued, and instead of repeating her suicide attempt, she promptly married a fruit-stand clerk "to prove to myself and the world that I could get a husband if I wanted to." She also hoped that he would take care of her, but he could not support the family—they soon had a son and two daughters—without her help, and Rose became a seamstress. The husband had long periods of unemployment, and his wife said:

"I often think if he were a real man he would try harder to get a job when he sees how numb my arm gets from sewing. My day is never done, and he, even when he has work, comes home and settles down just to have me make him comfortable. He forgets about everything else."

In this, too, the desire to be babied crops out, and Rose complained like so many diabetic women of her dislike of the sexual act. She felt, too, that she failed with her children. Her daughter had married a man of whom Rose disapproved on the ground that he was too much like her own husband. Her son, whom she urged to study hard and be brilliant so that she could realize in him her desire to be in an intellectual occupation, responded by flunking his examinations.

Rose liked to talk to educated people, and would seek them out. Her industry was considerable, but she resented the responsibility she had been obliged to assume.

Her illness began to manifest itself after a series of emotional shocks. These were the death of her father in World War I, her broken engagement and her marriage to a man she did not respect. The birth of her son, upon whom she pinned high hopes, relieved her of her symptoms for a time, but when the boy and her daughter and her husband all seemed to be failing her at once, she acquired diabetes. She was saved from invalidism, for which she seemed obviously headed when she came to the psychiatric clinic, because she acquired an understanding of how her situation in life affected her emotions. Although she was unable to change her situation, she was able to change her attitude toward it.

Thanks to the combination of treatment for the bodily symptom and understanding of the emotional factors behind it, a great many sufferers like Rose and Jenny and Roger have been saved for usefulness and diverted from becoming a burden upon their families or society. If we have not been able to turn the cheese back into milk, we have at least been able to make it content to be cheese, to show it that there is a secure and comfortable place for it.

§ 5

Too Big for Comfort

MUCH HAS been said about the unhappiness and illness that may come to those who eat more than the chemical plant of the body can handle. If what you stuff into your mouth has the purpose of feeding a starved ego, what usually happens is that the body gains in size and the ego loses its stature.

Dr. Charles Glenn King, who is scientific director of the Nutrition Foundation, writes that persons up to 15 percent overweight have a death rate 22 percent over average. Those overweight 16 to 25 percent have a death rate 44 percent over average and those more than 25 percent overweight have a death rate 75 percent above the average. Insurance men say wistfully that if only Americans were less frequently overweight they would have the best longevity record in the world.

One out of five in the United States between the ages of twenty and fifty-four is overweight. The extra pounds are a serious hazard not so much in diabetes as in heart disease and other ailments of the circulatory system.

The afflicted are likely to say, "I just can't help getting fat," or, "I was made that way," or, "It's my glands." But they say this only because they are looking for a reason for something that has confused them for almost as long as they have lived.

It is probably true that only one percent of obesity can be attributed to glandular disorders. But what does that mean? It has been said that the endocrine glands translate the tempo of the nervous system into the tempo of metabolism and vice-versa. But sometimes the glands are the pacemakers for emotion and it works both ways. Body chemistry can become defective with or without blowing a glandular fuse.

The glands, subjected to excessive stimuli in early developmental phases of the organism, may become worn out or over-stimulated. Most children manage to maintain an equilibrium even when they have been subjected to noxious external or internal agents, but the capacity of the organism to recover its balance after a physical or emotional upset may have been decreased because too many such adjustments were required too early. The adult who was one of these children may find himself with a five-ampere fuse when he needs a fifteen-ampere fuse. Sometimes when this happens it may take the doctor a long time to find just where and when and who crossed the wires that made a short circuit.

Take the case of Elliott, who grew from a little boy of ten to a big fat man of fifty and whose only obvious unhappiness in all those forty years was his own dislike of his bulbous shape.

Elliott was the youngest of a vigorous, healthy family who professed and seemed to feel a great attachment to one another. They all loved Elliott, and laughingly said that they always had spoiled him. What they meant by that was that they gave him everything they thought he would like, but hardly ever bothered to find out if he really liked it. They told him what games to play, and with which children, what to wear and what to eat, when to go to school and when to come home. By the time he was ten, Elliott was using most of his quite adequate intelligence in devising ways to be by himself. His best consolation was a bag of candy or a slab of cake. He felt himself regarded as very much the least member of the family, and his only compensation was to get something the others didn't have. More food than they ate was the one success he achieved.

Failure in Chemistry

His bulk and awkwardness increased his loneliness as he grew into his teens. The family redoubled their efforts and supervision because they thought poor Elliott probably was too stupid to take care of himself. A very sweet kid, though, they said.

In college Elliott kept aloof from extra-curricular activities, but did not study very much either. He was graduated in the lower half of his class, an amiable fellow almost unknown to most of his generation. To the great relief of his family he married almost immediately after graduation a girl they admired.

Eloise was a brisk, cheerful, efficient young woman with a decided manner and complete assurance that she knew just what she wanted. She also knew how to get it. She took over the management of Elliott's life, and both of them loved it. At his mother's suggestion Elliott had planned to go to law school. Eloise ridiculed the idea. He'd be a struggling lawyer for years, she said, and she wanted him to be a success. She had studied to be an interior decorator herself, and Elliott had really good taste.

So they were married and went into business together. They were very successful. Eloise ran everything from behind the scenes, and Elliott turned out to have a wonderful way with rich clients, conveying to them his own enthusiasm for Eloise's designs. Their friends marveled that they could remain so devoted when they were seeing each other all the time.

Elliott no longer avoided companionship, but he continued to eat as much as ever. He kept a box of candy in his desk; dinner for him wasn't over unless he had two desserts; he knew all the best places for ice cream for miles around. He had a wonderful life. He loved the seashore, and they spent two weeks there every year. Of course when they got a country home, it was in the mountains. He turned out on week-ends in violently colored shirts, but Eloise saw to it that he wore only sober gray ties to work. She decided what shows they would see, what friends they would visit, what civic activities they would join. The one faint ripple of discord in their lives was that she tried to curb Elliott's eating.

"Now Elliott!" she would exclaim disapprovingly when he reached for a sweet.

With a guilty smile, he would withdraw his hand, only to snatch the bit of candy when her back was turned. It was a game. Even after he had passed forty-five and 260 pounds, he enjoyed it, although a succession of minor illnesses plagued him and one doctor after another ordered him to lose weight.

Instead he lost Eloise. After twenty-eight years of married life, she died suddenly, and for the first time in his life Elliott had no one to tell him what his next move should be. His surviving brother and sisters wondered if he could be left alone safely because, they said, he'd never known enough to come in out of the rain. They wondered who would run the business now that he didn't have Eloise to lean on.

Their worry was wasted. Elliott mourned deeply and sincerely. He missed Eloise every minute. But he proved to be anything but helpless in ordering his life alone. He worked a little harder —or at least longer hours—and if he lacked Eloise's forcefulness he made up for it in competence. He went to theatre a bit more often than in the past—Eloise hadn't cared for plays much—and sought out some old acquaintances he admired but whom Eloise had not liked. He sold the country house and rented a cabana at the beach. And, most surprising to his friends, he lost weight as if it were melting in the sun. Sixty pounds in four months, he would exclaim, for he was proud of his new figure.

"And I don't really diet at all," he added with some amazement. "I just don't eat as much as I did, and I've pretty well cut out sweets. I guess I've had so much in my lifetime that I've lost my taste for them."

Of course what Elliott had lost was not the taste but the reason for gobbling up all the candy in sight. He no longer needed to behave like a little boy. No one was making him feel like the least member of the community, and his whole outlook on life had changed.

What had happened to Elliott to make him fat was a fairly

common prelude to obesity. And, although few need so drastic an event as death to help them lose weight, the psychological development of his "cure" is also of a usual pattern. Of course the urge to overeat does not always result from being smothered with well-intentioned kindness. The sense of smothering and the urge to eat may come from indifference or neglect or confusing strictness, or any other attitude which leads to the substitution of food for love or security or assertiveness.

We have learned a good deal about obesity and how to deal with it from observing overweight children and adolescents. For it is often their emotional patterns, carried on into later life, that keep the extra pounds on overweight adults. The surplus may date back to early youth or may be a subsequent phenomenon, but the reason for it generally is to be found in a parent-child relationship.

For example, a boy of twelve was brought to a psychiatrist because, although his parents had been told he should have a high protein diet, he remained grossly overweight. The problem which they posed for the doctor was: how to make the boy stop eating starches and sweets. The obvious answer was to eliminate these from the family table.

"He's going to eat what's set before him," the mother retorted firmly. "We're not going to change our meals, his father and I, just because he's overweight."

"Couldn't you have these things for yourselves when the boy isn't eating with you?"

"He's got to learn will power and not eat things that aren't good for him," she insisted stubbornly.

"But do you have to put so many temptations in his way?" her husband protested.

"Yes, it's for his own good."

In this case, of course, the doctor's first and hardest job was with the mother. She had arbitrarily insisted that her son clean up his plate, but also that he not touch the fattening foods. Small wonder that he was confused, filled with unrecognized resentment toward his mother and more food than he could handle except by adding it in layers of fat.

One of the complications of obesity, which puts the emotional disturbance into a vicious circle, is the fat person's sensitivity to his physical appearance. Adolescents often are more distressed by this than adults. They can be as upset by a faulty distribution of weight as by overweight in general, sometimes more so.

"I don't like the way I look in a leotard," a girl of thirteen complained to the family doctor. "My thighs are so big! And I've given up potatoes and bread, too. Isn't there a better diet?"

"One small helping of everything you like," he replied, "but only one and small. You can have potatoes or anything else, but just a little bit of everything, remember."

"Oh, but, Doctor, that takes so much will power! I'd rather you told me to eat nothing but grapefruit for the rest of my life."

"You'd get fat on that, too," the doctor told her.

With good humor they discussed the question of why the girl thought she couldn't stop eating, and why she thought her food seemed to go into building her thighs rather than being more generally distributed over the body. The problem began to seem childish to her; of course she could take small helpings.

"I guess I do have will power after all," she told the doctor complacently a few months later.

She had learned the lesson, which many fat people never will, that it is an idea rather than a diet she needed. Given an idea which can be the answer to the emotional need for excessive amounts of food, the diet will take care of itself.

Such ideas, however, do not come easily. That it is possible, however, to replace the compulsion to eat with another concept is proved by the countless men and women—yes, men too—who go in for slimming because of vanity. Many of them, the women especially, are not really overweight at all, but simply trying for an exaggeratedly slender silhouette. They have plenty of will power for that. They starve themselves gladly, but shorten the lives of their husbands and sons by overfeeding them. One of the greatest hazards confronting an overweight male is the coy

Failure in Chemistry

feminine cry: "Oh, I do love to see a man eat a good meal! You must have another helping of this deep-dish blueberry pie or else I'll think you don't like my cooking."

There are no statistics to prove it, but it would appear to be true that the longer life of women in this country can be attributed sometimes partly to fashion. Fashion for many years has decreed a standard of weight which permits of no excessive indulgence at table for most of its devotees.

Nevertheless the fads in diet by which many women maintain fashionable figures are a danger when they become rules and regulations instead of an idea about how one would like to be, not just look.

People who think of their bodies functionally get a sense of about how many pounds should be hung on the particular skeleton that is theirs, and about where the pounds should be hung to balance best in order to keep the body strong as well as slim.

It's silly to fight your body because it's "gotten big" like the parents you wanted to fight. Remember it's your body and in order to be happy, make it happy—sort of the way you would take care of a child. Height and weight tables are no guide, but just as you can learn to understand what makes the people around you work well and happily, so you can get a sense of what makes your body work well, and hence healthy and happy. Try grapefruit, roast beef, salads, for a while, and you will find yourself hungry for something else. Have a little of something else and notice the next morning or a few days later when you're walking down the street whether it's with a springy step on the balls of your feet, or whether you're walking on your heels and slumping. This is one way your body has of telling you if you guessed right about what your body needed.

People get this body sense very quickly once they are assured that this body is exclusively theirs, not something for other people to toss around, admire or insult indiscriminately. Children whose bodies have been too much dandled, tickled, punished, dressed and undressed by grown-ups, may come to think of their bodies as playthings for *those others* and abuse them accordingly. These people are suckers for experts in metabolism who recommend starvation with vitamins or so-and-so many calories of this and that—breakfast, lunch and supper. They have an odd feeling that something is not quite right, and it's this feeling and not lack of will power that makes them unable to co-operate. They will eat themselves to death or starve themselves to death but until they get the idea their body is theirs and some understanding of how it works, they are extremely unlikely to regain their health. Children allowed and helped to learn this early rarely become obese.

[CHAPTER XIV]

"Half in Love with...Death"

§ 1

LIFE MUST come to an end for everyone, but it need not come more than once. The sound mind in the sound body can greet that end calmly when it arrives without seeking to involve itself in a lot of needless advance planning. But the sort of people who become patients are frequently preoccupied with thoughts of the tomb far beyond the normal reminders of man's mortality. They die a little bit every day.

It has been said that cowards die a thousand deaths, the brave man only one. That is even more true of many sick people as compared with the healthy. These victims of disease, not necessarily through fear, prospect in the valley of death for a long time before they need to take up permanent residence, and they hasten that moment accordingly. After enough of this anticipation, which may seem to them either pleasurable or painful, they often are reluctant to return to health. Elizabeth Barrett Browning was harking back to that stage of her own illness when, describing her psychosomatic progress in some of the finest sonnets in the language, she wrote:

"I yield the grave for thy sake and exchange
My near sweet view of heaven for earth with thee."

It is a state of mind not unknown to adolescents. They may be regarded by their elders as merely impressionable youths who will grow out of it, but there is a danger that if they are left to do so unaided, it will come back upon them with intensified force later in life. One hundred years after Mrs. Browning's eloquent cry, a girl left this even more poignant and revealing bit of verse in her physician's office:

"Oh, please God, don't stand there hand in hand,
  Don't smile and stand and say good-bye
  Don't smile and turn and walk off down the street . . ."

Brooding over the prospect of death, longing for it or being frightened by it are all variants of an emotional disturbance which plays a part in many bodily disorders. Just how big a part it is difficult to say, but the existence of it in such diseases as tuberculosis may well help to explain the apparent caprice with which the illness strikes—passing by the seemingly fragile to select the outwardly robust. There is reason to believe that a mind which has concerned itself with death helps to prepare the body for disease, and the illness in turn will intensify the mind's activity along these lines. Thus another vicious psychosomatic circle is set in motion. To break the circle convincingly, both the emotional and bodily symptoms must be removed.

The emotional state which is partly responsible for this sort of development does not just happen in a vacuum. It is created by the individual reaction to environment, and human relationships are the most important environmental factor. These are constantly changing as our society itself changes. The last few decades have seen the process accelerated beyond all previous historical precedents. Any man's mind today needs to be more alert, more agile, more flexible than was the case with men of only a few generations ago, or even one generation ago.

One of the greatest problems of modern man is how to learn to live with civilization. This means not only the technological progress represented in atomic energy, super-sonic airplane speeds, the wonders of electronics and so on, but changing customs and standards of human behavior as well. A man who has grown up in an environment where all mention of drink, sex equality, bodily functions and psychological reactions was taboo may find himself transplanted to a group where all these things seem quite natural and even interesting. Unless he can adjust himself to the new standards, he will get himself into emotional as well as social difficulties. It is not a question of approval or disapproval. A good many people do not approve of the atomic bomb or soap operas on the radio or other people's passion for getting from one place to another in a hurry. But they are willing to accept the conditions imposed by the existence of new mechanical gadgets. Similarly the man who disapproves must still, for his own sake, learn to accept the sight of other people sipping a cocktail or kissing a girl.

Those who learn rapidly to adjust themselves to civilization do not get sick as easily as those who fail. The failure is not always obvious. Some of the most brilliant men and women, who have contributed not a little to the progress of civilization, have secretly clung to the standards of their fathers. In an exciting, fast-moving urban world they cherish the ideals taught to them in a village thousands of miles away and a generation or more ago. When they get sick, their maladjustment is, at the very least, enough of a factor so that often they cannot get well until it has been straightened out.

In order to maintain a proper balance in the shifting sands of civilization, every human being who is a part of it needs to keep his head. Once the mind has abdicated its responsibility, the personality becomes a headless horseman galloping crazily to destruction. It is one of the functions of a sound mind to help adjust the whole being to its environment.

Loss of that faculty is not always apparent immediately. Time after time during the war, the persistence of old habits of behavior was shown in startling fashion. Perhaps the most striking examples were those pilots who had been wounded so severely in combat that they were completely unconscious at the controls, and yet managed to bring their planes back to a perfect landing on the decks of carriers. Now such landings are delicate operations under the best of circumstances, demanding the ultimate in physical co-ordination. Some of these men were so badly hurt that they died without recovering consciousness, but managed to carry out the full sequence of split-second movements which brought the planes down safely. Often members of their crews did not even know that the pilots had been hit until after the landing.

Some of these men recovered to tell the tale. Frequently they would remember nothing after the bullet or shell fragment struck them. They did not have the faintest idea how they found their way back to the carrier, how they received the signals to come in, how they manipulated the controls to bring the plane down.

Such strict adherence to a previously set behavior pattern is entirely admirable in a wounded pilot. It becomes less praise-worthy in a person who is in no such desperate situation but has been driven gradually to it by inability to adjust to his environment. Actually, of course, it is not a matter of praise or blame. It is some-thing that happens, usually not so spectacularly as to the pilot. Nor is its existence generally suspected until it has resulted in or at least contributed to some bodily ailment. Even then it may not be recognized immediately unless the psychic factors in the illness are studied.

These headless horsemen are the patients who so often are pre-occupied with death. They react to talk of it, even when the talk is about others. In hospitals sometimes they take a sudden turn for the worse quite inexplicably until it develops that they over-heard physicians discussing another case, disagreeing about it and finally saying: "Well, we'll know in the P.M.," meaning the post-mortem. They are the patients who, while not suffering from what are usually considered psychosomatic diseases, are affected be-cause they either thought a lot about death before they got sick or became panicky about dying after they were sick. In either case, an important element in treatment is to help them keep their heads.

§ 2

Get It Off Your Chest

Sir WILLIAM OSLER, probably the greatest medical teacher who ever lived, once warned his profession that the fate of the tubercular depended more on what they had in their heads than on what was in their chests. Osler has been dead for nearly thirty years, but the idea he preached is still a little unbelievable to many people who think that a germ or a peculiar condition of body cells is the sum and substance of disease.

Victorian novelists were more realistic than these skeptics. Their prim and prissy heroines succumbed in droves to an epidemic of ladylike behavior. Disappointed in love or deprived by the malignity of fate of some adored object, they went into gentle declines and perished with immense propriety. They never seemed to suffer symptoms any more distressing to themselves or their attendants than a becoming pallor, a flutter of the heart or lovely dark shadows under the eyes. They died of simple excess of emotion and sensibility.

A great many victims of tuberculosis today are doing the same. They only add a few unpleasant details, sweating and coughing blood, which no Victorian liked to mention. They are those baffling cases for whose ailments no thoroughly sound explanation can be given in terms of their lungs alone. They are the principal reason why nearly 55,000 people still die of tuberculosis every year in this country, making it the sixth largest of disease killers.

In 1900, when it was the most deadly of all, most of the victims came from the classic T.B. environment. They lived in overcrowded, dirty, airless rooms, were exposed to cold and wet, were chronically underfed. Today a far larger proportion of tuberculosis patients come from the well-nourished and fairly well-housed groups in the community.

Of course T.B. germs are everywhere, and always were. But we have to revise our thinking as to just why one person never gives the germs a chance and another seems to provide a virtual broth culture in which they thrive. The emotional factor has proved to have a great deal to do with it—more in some cases than any known physiological weakness or susceptibility of the tissues.

There is a personality which predisposes us to certain ailments, as well as a physical susceptibility. When the germs find lodging in a victim whose body and mind are both prepared to receive them, the virulence of the disease is often startling. The sufferer fails to respond in the slightest degree to treatment which works speedy cures in other and apparently more serious cases.

A good many physicians have learned this lesson the hard way, both for themselves and for their patients. The idea was not new to them—for a long time the state of mind of the tubercular has been known to play a big part in the outcome of the disease. The new element is a growing understanding of how the state of mind affects the body, and how the state of mind came to be what it is.

In the case of Susan C——, the interplay of mind and body was well exemplified. Her mother had contracted tuberculosis at the age of eighteen, many years before Susan was born, and had died of pneumonia when her daughter was twenty-three. The older woman had been aggressive and masculine, characteristics which her child inherited. Susan's father had been of less consequence in the home, but he added to the girl's emotional problems by becoming a mental patient who at last was sent to a hospital.

At about sixteen, Susan rebelled against the rigid standards her mother set, the rebellion being as much a reaction against the maternal coldness and aloofness as against the standards. Three years later the girl, unable to make up her mind to marry, had a child by a man who turned out to be an alcoholic. Nevertheless she had another child. Then she married the man, but the marriage did not last long. When she was twenty-eight she married an artist who was no match for her in temperament. A year later she developed tuberculosis, and was sent to a sanatorium, where, after seven months, during which she had grown worse, the staff called in a psychiatrist.

This doctor soon found that the patient's restlessness, unhappiness and dissatisfaction with her lot stemmed far back beyond the time of active disease. She had a low opinion of men, and certainly her experience with her father, husbands and sons had not been such as to give her any other. One of the children, especially, had been a problem to her since infancy and she constantly lost her temper with him. This was not so much because he gave her good reason as because she had come to see herself in him and to be as dissatisfied with the boy as she was with herself. All her life she had reacted to her hostility to men by trying to baby them and thus establish her own superiority as well as satisfy her aggressive tendencies.

At the same time she had displayed a quality which Keats described as "half in love with easeful death." The psychiatrist found in her strong suicidal drives. The Rorschach test, that extremely useful guide to the personality which shows itself to the expert through the patient's interpretation of ink blots, indicated a fear of death associated with the idea of suicide. Susan herself in describing a dream of drowning once said that it was the kind of death she had always desired. This last is the sort of remark which may have some significance. Death by drowning and death through collapse of the lungs, which is usually the fatal termination of tuberculosis, are not very different.

While her seven months at the sanatorium had left her in worse physical condition than ever, a summer in the same environment but with the assistance of psychotherapy led to marked improvement both in her health and her mental attitude. Most of the time was spent in analyzing her feeling of weakness behind her drive to maintain a surface impression of great strength. By the next summer, still at the sanatorium, the lesions in her lungs had healed and she was able to take a fair amount of exercise. Meanwhile she transferred a good deal of her emotional burden to her doctor, as many patients do in the course of treatment, and she was changing her attitude toward men largely on his account.

During that summer, one of her old friends was being courted by the psychiatrist. After a time, Susan was quite unable to make further progress under his care. In fact, shortly after she heard of the physician's marriage, she caught the flu and suffered what was at first believed to be a mild relapse of the tuberculosis.

Some months later, physically about the same but emotionally increasingly disturbed, she consulted another psychiatrist, this time a woman. She was living at home again, still unable to control her temper with her son and quarreling with her mother-in-law. Typical of the disputes was one over the older woman's treatment of the dog, which ended up with Susan crying:

"Isn't it enough that you spoil my children? Do you have to spoil my dog, too?"

More significantly, Susan was again thinking about dying. Yet she was not really very sick, the physician who had treated her tuberculosis being of the opinion that she had gained some ground in recent months in spite of her activity. She had been gaining weight, but had not been gaining in emotional stability. Under emotional stress she would have accidents, or expose herself to influenza or poison ivy. She still needed a physical symptom.

Talking through this problem gave Susan some new insight into herself. Although in the past she had referred to her mother only in terms of hatred and anger, she now spoke of what a hard time the poor woman had had in life. Suddenly she interrupted herself to remark that this was the first time she had had any sympathy with her mother. After a few weeks, she was sleeping more soundly and managed to keep her temper when she was with her younger son. The psychiatrist advised her that it might be well to stop calling him a baby and treating him like one since he was by now twelve years old. Susan was soon able to report that the boy had stopped annoying her, and even been quite nice and asked why she visited the doctor so often.

"I wanted to find out why I was so cross with you, because I didn't want to be," Susan said she replied.

Finally, Susan was feeling more energetic and was no longer quarreling with her mother-in-law. She actually felt friendly toward the older woman and was able to talk to her freely and easily. She said she was beginning to see that there was no use patching up the synthetic defenses she had built against the world. Examination by X-ray showed a corresponding improvement in her lungs. She felt that she should be herself and get along quite well.

Perhaps it is too soon since these results were attained to speak with authority of Susan's improvement as permanent. Yet the development of her case shows how real cures are accomplished. The treatment of body and mind was simultaneous; the improvement of each helped the other, but when there was a setback in one there was delay in the other. Psychic factors seem to have done as much as heredity and more than environment to predispose the girl to a susceptibility to tuberculosis. Until there was some attention paid to her emotional problems, not even the most expert physical care could halt the deterioration of her lungs. What Susan had in her head was more important.

§ 3

Case History of a Doctor

THE PROGRESS of knowledge about psychosomatic factors in such diseases as tuberculosis has been gained from the experience of a good many people, medical practitioners as well as patients. The development is well illustrated by the education of Dr. George Day, an English physician who acquired a considerable background in general practice, as staff man of a tuberculosis sanatorium and finally in psychiatry. All of these contributed to the understanding which he achieved, not only of the nature of the disease and its progress but also of the emotional factors which enter into it. Consequently we have, for a change, the case history of a doctor instead of the case history of a patient.

A dozen years ago, Dr. Day began to puzzle over the problem of why so many apparently hearty young men and women were arriving at his sanatorium. They were just at the age when their physical powers should have been at their peak for resisting the bacillus. They had not been exposed to the conditions which are supposed to facilitate the progress of the disease.

Dr. Day rejected the thesis that it might be pure chance that one was struck down while others escaped. He began to ask questions and he found that a surprising (to him) number of cases were patients who had been involved in unhappy love affairs. He looked further, and saw some other emotional difficulties coming at a time of life when young people are meeting their first problems of independence. The emotional stresses involved are quite severe.

Dr. Day noticed that girls who had been jilted and young men who were mixed up in unsatisfactory love affairs from which they did not know how to escape were not the only sufferers. There were youths who shrank from the prospect of becoming self-supporting. There were others—in Dr. Day's experience, mostly women—who sought to escape into a world of dreams where they were adored, pampered and showered with all the luxury of a Hollywood movie. A good many of both types found more or less conscious consolation in their sickness for the harsh realities of life. The jilted girls could make themselves and others believe that they had to give up the young men because of their illness. The unhappy youths could escape from their entanglements or the necessity for earning their living because of the sad state of their health. The women who yearned for attention and luxury found a rather poor substitute, but still a substitute, in the care which tuberculosis brought them both in the sanatorium and at home.

It became apparent to Dr. Day that unless he could change either the pattern of the patient's life or the pattern of the patient's thinking, he could do little to arrest the disease. He tells two stories which illustrate a fairly common medical dilemma.

The first concerned a girl called Peggy whose tuberculosis was discovered at an unusually early stage, who lived under what are generally considered ideal conditions for speedy recovery, whose domestic and vocational happiness seemed complete. She had earned her happiness after a good deal of severe strain and trials, too.

Orphaned in poverty at fourteen, she had supported herself as a housemaid, cook, stewardess, shop girl, chorus girl and model until she finally achieved the status of glamor girl. In this last capacity she fell in love with and married a pleasant young wastrel who drove a racing car well but contributed little to the family support. Peggy cheerfully sold her jewels and went to work in a hat shop to keep him until she discovered that he was lavishing the rent money on other women. She promptly left him, and found in his place a fairly prosperous farmer who loved her and delighted in doing things for her. She reciprocated his affection with enthusiasm, and embarked happily upon a hearty out-of-doors life. She was not able to get a divorce, but the fact that she and her Bill could not marry cast no cloud over their happiness, so far as Dr. Day could tell.

Without any qualms, indeed with keen anticipation, she decided to have a child, and the tuberculosis was discovered only when, in the sixth week of her pregnancy, she visited her doctor for a check-up. It was the merest spot in one lung, quite unsuspected and unnoticed except after thorough examination, but to play safe the examining physician advised her to have a therapeutic abortion and postpone child-bearing until she recovered. The operation was performed; Peggy was whisked to Dr. Day's sanatorium, and the complete rest and careful treatment which were to work a speedy cure were begun.

But Peggy grew worse instead of better. She did not lose her cheerfulness, but the tuberculosis spread to both lungs, then to the throat so that she could hardly talk or eat. Sitting at her bedside in the evenings, waiting for opiates to take effect, Dr. Day listened as she whispered the story of her life. And as he listened, he became aware of the fact that outward happiness is not enough. Peggy said she had never been so happy as on the farm; she had never been so fond of anyone as of Bill. But behind that happiness were the memories of her first marriage—and by no means bitter ones altogether. Dying, she remembered the delights which had accompanied the miseries—the sprees when her first husband picked a winner at the track, little celebrations, a kitten they had picked up on Christmas Eve. These things were far more real to her in the last hours of her life than the more recent idyll on the farm, which had become insubstantial as a dream. Finally she murmured quite calmly and analytically:

"It looks as if I have a need to suffer."

She died that night, leaving Dr. Day to ponder the impact of an emotional hangover upon one small spot in a healthy lung.

Some years later he wondered even more when he saw an old patient who had succeeded in living Peggy's life in reverse. This one, Gladys, was a classic tuberculosis case at nineteen. She had a family pedigree of the disease as long as the ancestry of a crowned head or a champion mare. She was coughing blood; both lungs were seriously affected, and three months in the sanatorium served merely to arrest the progress of her disease. Dr. Day lost track of her until one day she came to see him. She was married and seven months pregnant.

The danger of tuberculosis in these cases is usually not so much in the period of pregnancy as in the sudden rush which the disease seems to make upon the patient's defenses after the delivery. Gladys was no exception. Dr. Day managed to pull her through, but she was still in bed three months later when he left the district. He had warned her of the terrible dangers of another pregnancy and had supplied explicit contraceptive instructions, which Gladys received with giggles.

Seven years later Dr. Day returned to his old practice to relieve a colleague, and was somewhat surprised to hear that Gladys was still alive. He was less surprised to receive a call to attend her, but his amazement returned in full measure when he entered a tumbledown cottage to find Gladys, serene and hearty, ladling out dinner to nine children, all younger than eight years old and all hers. The ailment for which she had summoned help was slight, but Dr. Day took the opportunity to get a good set of pictures of her lungs. The huge cavities of seven years before had disappeared, leaving only a trace of firm scar tissue behind. The purely physiological facts did not explain the cure. Childbearing is not supposed to be so good for the tubercular, although recent knowledge has taught us how to avoid some of the dangers. Gladys's husband was a farm laborer and they would have been poor if they had had no children at all. As it was, the mother's diet was obviously inadequate; the cottage was the kind of habitation which is supposed to spread the germs and is considered good housing only for them. Of course Gladys was happy, delighting in her good-natured husband and noisy brood, but then Peggy had been happy too.

"Can it have been sheer contentment?" Dr. Day asked himself. "Or can it have been contentment plus the gratification of her deep creative impulse?"

Some of the answers to these questions are being unearthed as we learn more about the psychosomatic techniques. One of the features of sanatorium life which helps mend the diseased lung tissue of the tubercular is the escape which rigid routine provides, escape from conflicts in normal life, escape from responsibilities, escape from the exacting strains of a deeply felt affection. Emotional ease as well as bodily ease is achieved, and of course ease is the antithesis of disease.

For those who need the two-way escape, a healed lung is not the permanent answer. These patients need to heal the mind as well, or the bacilli will find a new home provided for them in the tissues made susceptible once more by the hospitality of emotional disturbance.

§4

The Headless Horseman

IN CANCER something of the same phenomena can be observed. Our ignorance of this disease in the psychic field keeps pace with our lack of knowledge of its organic causes, but it is apparent that in cancer, as in tuberculosis, we confront a situation in which the wrong kind of cells run wild in the body. The patient has lost the ability to have his mind maintain control of his body, and once that occurs the case is usually hopeless. In both cancer and tuberculosis, the progress is extremely rapid. In that fact lies much of the deadly force of these diseases. The value of psychosomatic techniques, therefore, lies in applying them in the early stages. At this period there is sometimes a good chance of helping the mind to keep or regain control of the body. Under that control, the treatment of the actual symptoms can proceed with far greater assurance of success.

The very different course which cancer took in two individuals whose physical condition was about the same gave some clues to the part which personality or character plays in the progress of the disease. Both were rather Junoesque women of just over forty. Both were widows and had achieved some success in business on their own after their husbands died. Both were regarded by their friends as capable and warm-hearted, able to take care of themselves and ready to give weaker persons a helping hand. Both developed cancer, necessitating the removal of a breast.

Two years later one was dying, a hopeless invalid, while the other had achieved a remarkable recovery. Not only was the latter back on the job, but she was taking on added responsibilities without showing extra strain.

Admittedly cancer still guards many of its mysteries, but the difference in the outcome of these two cases, unexplainable by anything we know of the malignancy of the cancerous growth, was partly predicted by a physician skilled in psychosomatic techniques.

Ginny, the woman who became an invalid, was the more ostentatiously brave of the two in the beginning. She declared frequently and determinedly: "I'm going to get well."

But in the intervals, she would say with an air of resignation: "Perhaps the sooner I die the better."

She was quite incapable of facing up to the fact of her disease, and she was notably fertile in devices for avoiding the truth, either hearing it or telling it. The growth in her case was rapid, more so than her doctor would have expected if he had not had a great deal of experience. He had observed, as have many others, that the progress of cancer is rapid in people like Ginny. When he advised her that a breast would have to be removed, she cried: "Oh, I wish you hadn't told me!"

The physician tried to explain to her just what the operation would be, the length of time needed for convalescence, the problems of adjustment and so on. He could tell that Ginny was closing her mind to his words. After he left her, he shook his head. The outlook for the poor woman was not good, he thought, and he was right. She never could reconcile herself to the loss of a breast, which is not easy of course, and her doctor reluctantly reached the conclusion that she did not want really to get well.

Celia, on the other hand, was not so glib about how sure she was of her recovery. Yet she did not allow herself to be plunged into despair. The growth in her case was relatively slow but it became obvious that the breast must be removed. At this point she was more honest with herself and her doctor than Ginny had been. She not only listened when he told her what the operation meant but asked intelligent questions. The blow to her pride as a woman was at least as great as Ginny suffered. One difference, however, was that Celia said so. Another was that she tried to find out how she could adjust her life to it.

She succeeded not because her operation was any less serious than Ginny's, her cancer any less malignant; she succeeded because she had the character for success.

"I never had any doubt about *her*," the physician said.

The importance of understanding the differences in personality lies in the fact that personality is not immutable. Psychosomatic thinking about illness has given clues about how to bring the attitude of a Ginny nearer to that of a Celia.

Although it is now known that the attitude of a patient toward life and toward his body may play a role in slowing up or increasing the speed of development of a cancerous growth, much more needs to be learned. But there is one suggestive point which seems to have emerged from recent research. Cancer is related to the body's balanced (or unbalanced) production of hormones. It has been suggested that men whose hormonal balance is a bit overweighted on the feminine side appear to develop cancer more readily than others. The same observation has been made about women whose balance is overweighted on the masculine side. This does not mean that the men are in outward appearance or manner effeminate, or that the women are obviously mannish. In fact they may seem to be just the reverse. The actual fatalities by sexes are not very revealing, although they seem to reinforce the idea that personality is an important factor. In 1900, one hundred women died of cancer for every sixty men. Now men have a little higher mortality from cancer.

In the excellent recovery of Celia, her doctor thought that his patient's honesty and feeling toward life were important factors in her recovery and probably accounted for her better attitude toward the operation. Many surgeons, seeking to minimize the psychological shocks of this or any other operation now give a complete outline of the procedure and even have the patient visit the operating room to see what it is like so he will not be upset by going into or waking up in entirely strange surroundings. The attempt is made to render the whole experience less frightening. The unknown seems to most of us much more of a danger than does a clearly understood hazard.

For example, one young man with a long history of illness traced all his troubles back to the day he had had his tonsils out. When he was four years old, his mother took him to the hospital, but with the mistaken idea that she would spare him the fear of anticipation, she told him nothing of what would happen to him or why. He entered the strange, imposing building—the hospital —quite unprepared.

"All of a sudden, a woman all dressed in white, with a mask on her face, came out and said, 'Now we are ready,'" he recalled twenty-five years later. "She started to take off my pants while another woman in white carried me into a white, strange-smelling room, put me on a table and put something over my mouth so I couldn't breathe or talk. The next thing I knew I was in bed vomiting blood, and I was sure I was bleeding from my genitals, too. I never saw the doctor at all, so I supposed that the women had done this to me."

The boy grew older, but in the deepest recesses of his mind he blamed the whole female sex for this outrage upon him, and he never forgave them. Nor was he able to trust women.

"They betray you," he explained with the calm certainty of one who states a law of nature.

When he said that, he was seeking treatment for an ulcer of ten years' standing, and needed a good deal of help, too, in his marital life. There were other underlying conflicts in his life of course—the mind usually succumbs only to an accumulation of often trifling experiences—but the operation appeared to have been the turning point for his future health.

Many patients have been as badly prepared for surgery, both before and after the event, without disaster, but many others turn up in the offices of doctors and the wards of hospitals with stubborn, often dangerous illnesses. The shock seems to be especially serious in childhood, partly because children have more fantasies about what might happen while asleep or under an anesthetic than the adult, who has a clearer picture of the range of possibilities.

Adults would know that the removal of pants in the operating room does not necessarily presage violence upon the genitals. But a child is always expecting that some liberty will be taken with his body against which he is incapable of defending himself and, without careful explanation, is only too likely to jump to the conclusion that the intent is to hurt instead of to help him. He may think an operation has done things to him which he cannot see or feel afterwards. And in one sense he is right. The "operation," not understood, can boomerang and disturb his physical and emotional balance in a great variety of ways.

§ 5

The Allure of Pain

OTHER BODILY suffering has its reflection in the mind. We find it in rheumatic or arthritic pains, in migraine headache, in eye and ear troubles. Exploring the emotional and physiological symptoms gives something of the sensation of scaling a mountain from two sides. The path to the top winds through quite different scenery; the view from the peak is the same.

Arthritis, for example, may be the reaction to a simple emotional problem. It may mask a deeply buried emotional disturbance. It may have created such tissue damage that it is called organic. In all three cases the joints may be equally swollen, the pain equally intense.

The first two types of arthritis patients usually are found to have experienced long-standing maladjustments of some kind—social, sexual or vocational. Cause and effect may seem as simple as the case of a housewife who was unhappy in her home and developed a pain in the shoulder which relieved her of the necessity of doing hated housework, although she would have told you in all sincerity that she was the loser in the deal.

A slightly less obvious personality was that of the man who was torn between his desire to write a book and his fear of failure, and found arthritis localized in his fingers so that he could neither typewrite nor hold a pen. The incipient genius to whom this happened had been exposed to the advice and friendly ridicule of a host of successful literary relatives and friends. He was strongly impelled to show them that he too could create a fine bit of prose. At the same time, he was horribly afraid that his pet idea would not come off when he actually got it down on paper.

In this state of acute anxiety, he was easy prey to the arthritis. The manuscript was pigeonholed perforce. As long as he keeps away from his unfinished masterpiece and tends to his own business, in which he is quite as successful as his literary family and acquaintances are in theirs, his fingers remain free from pain although they have been permanently misshapen. But on the several occasions when he has returned to his dream book, the pain returned too.

An ostensibly more complicated case was presented by a younger man who was being treated for terrifying attacks of anxiety garnished with acute fears that his knees would buckle under him at any moment. In the course of his treatment he developed a severe pain in the shoulder joint. It had all the appearance of arthritis.

The physician, also a man, discovered that the patient had developed unconscious sexual feelings for him. It is not an easy or a rapid process to convey a finding of this sort to a patient so that he will accept it, and in this case, the patient greeted the information with a rather common reaction. He declared that the real cause of the arthritis was that he had been obliged to sit in the draft of an electric fan while in the physician's office. This had happened six months earlier. He also said resentfully that he had overheard the physician discussing him with another doctor, the implied reproof being that this had something to do with his pains. As for the homosexual feelings, he repudiated the suggestion with indignation. All this is fairly characteristic of such a patient's attitude, which he expresses to himself in some such words as:

"It is not I who loves the physician, but he who wishes to harm me."

This particular patient thereupon resorted to novocaine and deep X-ray therapy in an effort to relieve the pain, but he was so unsuccessful that he could hardly move his arm, and at times the agony interfered with his breathing. Meanwhile he continued with his psychotherapy, too, and finally was convinced that his physician had been correct in the diagnosis. The pain disappeared within twenty-four hours.

In other cases, arthritis may be one of the manifestations of gout. The sort of dietary self-indulgence which is one of the contributing causes of this disease is less prevalent than it used to be, and gout is disappearing along with its particular brand of high living. But when we do find it as an interesting survival, the personality factor is of great importance in treatment. Usually it is not enough to give these patients sage counsel about refraining from rich living and outbursts of temper. They usually have lost control of their habits on both counts and are irresistibly impelled to eat, drink and get angry. Before they can follow good advice, their emotional balance has to be restored.

The restoration of that balance, in fact, will help in averting or in healing a great multitude of ills from migraine headache to incipient deafness and blindness. The disturbances of mind and body may be very different in details, but the principle is essentially the same.

Sometimes the principle is illustrated in cases where one ailment is removed almost as an incidental process in the treatment of another. The same emotional unbalance has been responsible for both.

Mrs. Z. was anxious to have a child, but she had been pretty thoroughly frightened out of the idea. She came to see me originally to find out if those fears were justified. They were not, but then they were not the usual fears which are so often implanted in girls by their mothers, who inform them that the whole business of sex is not quite nice and the less they know about it the better. Mrs. Z.'s terror was the result of more nerve-racking experiences.

As a girl she had conceived a cordial hatred of her mother because the elder woman obviously preferred a younger sister. Mrs. Z. also had become quite a tomboy despite an extremely feminine appearance. She sought to emulate the boys largely in an effort to compete with four older brothers for her father's affections. This gentleman, a Wall Street broker, had precise but not exactly modern ideas on the place of girls in the scheme of things. College was not one of them, so his daughter went to a music school instead.

Here she had her first severe sexual shock when she was raped by one of the instructors. Apparently she began to complain about her hearing shortly afterward, but was graduated with high honors.

Almost immediately thereafter, at the age of twenty-one, she married. She said later that she had been attracted to the young man because he was "so romantic," but their romance was rather seedy by the time of the wedding. A more impartial observer might have thought him rather an infantile if not a neurotic type. At any rate, his romantic nature expressed itself during courtship by taking the girl to an underground cavern, the meeting place of a secret society which no woman was supposed to enter.

In these "romantic" surroundings he would make love to her.

He developed a strong feeling of guilt, but only of guilt over the betrayal of his comrades, so he decided to confess to the officers of the society. The penalty was inflicted upon the girl, however, and she was told that she must undergo the initiation rites. The most harrowing of these was a complete confession before the assembled young men of the society of all her sexual experiences to date.

She came away from that adventure with a hearty dislike of men, but decided to go through with her marriage. She thought it would save her self-respect.

Her husband was consulting a so-called psychoanalyst at the time, and persuaded her to do the same. This man told her she was "too sick emotionally to have a child." The verdict was reinforced by an ear specialist who told her she would become completely deaf if she tried to bear a child. Within a year she got a divorce.

Six years later she tried again. Mr. Z. was an artist—Mrs. Z. with her tall, pale, good looks and fine figure had turned to modeling after her hearing was impaired. He had recently been commissioned in the Army, and between some fears of army life and her unresolved sexual conflicts she got into something of a panic. She came to me to talk about the old story of her emotional unfitness to bear children. She was extremely tense, spoke in a whisper and was unable to hear me at all. Gradually, and with no attempt on my part to analyze her symptoms, she began to speak and hear normally.

Her husband's transfer to another part of the country interrupted her treatment. I told her a pregnancy probably would not cause deafness, but I advised her to wait until she had worked out some of her emotional problems a little better. She decided to take the chance, however, and in November, 1941, was delivered of a stillborn boy. An odd feature of the case was that the child's heart beat for forty-five minutes, but he never drew a single breath. There were no obvious malformations, and the pathologist was unable to satisfy himself as to the cause of the stillbirth.

Mrs. Z. returned for psychosomatic treatment, and despite some interruptions made good progress. In February she became pregnant again. She continued to consult me through her pregnancy, and I was present when her baby was born. Her only moment of panic came when in reply to her question as to when the baby would be born, the obstetrician answered lightly and unthinkingly:

"Oh, I think before New Year's."

Persiflage is sometimes out of place in the delivery room, and Mrs. Z. was plainly heading for a blackout, having taken the poor man literally.

"In half an hour or forty minutes," I told her. "Relax; use all your strength now because it will be better for the baby if you do not have an anesthetic."

Mrs. Z. snapped to attention in almost military fashion, considering the limitations of the time and the place, and in forty minutes her baby was born. She was unconscious only for eight minutes. She came to easily, and was greeted with the information that she had a fine healthy daughter.

"All that for a measly girl!" she exclaimed bitterly, and promptly burst into tears.

By the time she left the hospital, which was not long since there were no complications, Mrs. Z. had ceased to complain about her hearing. When she was able to visit her ear specialist, he could hardly believe his own ears as she responded to tests, for her hearing was perfectly normal. It has remained so ever since. Two years later Mrs. Z. gave easy birth to a son, and her hearing remained normal.

It seems plain that the course of treatment pursued with Mrs. Z. was as important to the successful delivery of her infant, as to the restoration of hearing. The large part which emotional factors play in the course of pregnancy hardly needs much insistence. Their existence has been known both to medicine and to legend. Almost every practicing obstetrician agrees, but we are still near the beginning of our understanding of just what areas of psychic and physical functioning are involved.

§6

Eaters of Sour Grapes

NOVELISTS and poets were aware of the relationship between the emotions and the teeth long before doctors and dentists were labeled as doctors and dentists. In books, characters ground their teeth in anger or felt them chatter with fear. Of course that happened in real life, too, but its significance was not fully appreciated in the professions. Yet the prophet Ezekiel had uttered a profound psychosomatic truth when he cried:

"The fathers have eaten of sour grapes and the children's teeth are set on edge."

And Ben Jonson was almost as observant of the connection between the mind and the teeth when he wrote the line:

"Sit melancholy and pick your teeth when you cannot speak."

Only within the last ten years has attention been focused on the psychosomatic aspects of dentistry—the interplay of emotional and body factors in such disorders as tooth decay, inability to keep cavities filled, gum softening and wobbly teeth.

If Johnny grinds his teeth or chews on pencils and he is so angry he is thinking "I could really chew nails"; if Mary constantly pushes her tongue against her teeth or bites her fingernails, it is likely that anger or frustration or at least something in the child's life is making him feel uncomfortable. But those habits may also mean work for the dentist later on. They are responsible for many of the malformations with which dentists struggle—these and a few similar habits.

Dental problems are almost universal. Virtually everyone has some damage to his teeth sooner or later, if only a few cavities, and usually it is sooner than later. Half our children have at least one cavity by the time they are two; at eighteen the average American has had nine or more fillings—or needs that many— and several extractions. Authorities predict that today's children will have lost half their teeth before they are forty. All the dentists in the country working full time would not be able to take care of the backlog of unfilled cavities, estimated at half a billion, and still keep up with the new ones which form each year in the mouths of the American people.

Perhaps understanding of the emotional factor in tooth troubles might save them the impossible task. It has been established that chemical changes in the saliva during feelings of hostility and frustration are very considerable. Their effects in creating susceptibility to dental caries are highly influential, if not measurable.

It is quite plausible to assume that understanding of the emotional factor in tooth troubles might bring down the appalling figures to a more reasonable level. At any rate, a lessening of emotional disturbances would improve the chemical composition of the saliva and thus reduce susceptibility and the beginnings of actual decay. We might be able to do for the death rate in teeth what we have accomplished by preventive medicine for the death rate in children.

Popular understanding of the nature of the role played by the emotions in troubles with the teeth are to be found in such well-known phrases as "bite back the angry word." The person who snaps his teeth together to keep from saying what he thinks is only working up to some long sessions with his dentist. Just as there is an incidence of dental decay in relation to emotional factors, so there is a correlation between repressed feelings of aggression or hostility and the excessive wearing down of the teeth. In case after case the individual's tensions are expressed in grinding the teeth, often during sleep.

Sometimes grinding of the teeth is discovered in the course of treatment for something else. Anton V., who at fifty was being treated for high blood pressure, had also been going to his dentist for years to try to do something about his back teeth, which were worn down almost to the gums. Talking out his problems with the doctor who was attempting to analyze the tensions which led to the high blood pressure, Anton revealed himself as a man who was almost constantly angry at someone and frustrated about something. His boss didn't promote him as

he should; his colleagues failed to appreciate him and less qualified men were jumped over his head, he said. He was upset by
conflicts with his divorced wife over their children and with his
second wife over her behavior, which was bad only in his mind.
But he had always been slow to express his resentment either in
the office or the home.

"I keep my mouth shut; I don't speak up," he explained, obviously believing that his seeming patience and forbearance was
a virtue. Perhaps in a sense it was, but it damaged his blood
vessels and his teeth.

During a discussion of one of his dreams it was revealed that
Anton habitually ground his teeth in his sleep, although never
when he was awake. His emotions were working in his mouth
all night, apparently, busily getting rid of the accumulated rage
of the day. As Anton gained a more objective picture of himself
and the annoyances of life which he could not correct, not only
was his blood pressure reduced, but he stopped grinding his
teeth.

How much the affliction of uncontrollable decay is due to emotional disturbances no one can say with any degree of precision,
but it is fair to assume that one of the causes of the wholesale
destruction of teeth is a surplus of acid in the saliva activated
and produced to excess by emotional conflict. Such emotional
conflicts are usually the consequence of repressed hostility and
can produce an excess of acid in the mouth in much the same
way as conflicts of the same kind lead to an abnormal percentage
of acid in the stomach under emotional stress. The balance between acidity and alkalinity may be disturbed in such a way as
to produce an "inflammation of the stomach lining," which may
even lead to stomach ulcer. Some readers are probably familiar
with the Harold G. Wolff account of the man whose stomach
lining was studied directly through a hole in his stomach.* With
pleasurable emotions the lining of the stomach was normal, but
with unpleasurable emotions it became flaming red.

* *Human Gastric Function,* S. Wolf and H. G. Wolff, Oxford University
Press, New York, 1943.

Such experiments and many others have demonstrated quite clearly why children who are made to eat while they are disturbed are subject to stomach upsets. Their teeth may become injured also, or even first, in such a way as to cause them trouble throughout life. Attention was called to this fact long ago in the limerick:

There was an old man of Blackheath
Who sat on his set of false teeth.
Said he, with a start,
"Oh Lord, bless my heart!
I've bitten myself underneath."

The language is full of such expressions as "It gnawed at my vitals," and references to mordant or incisive speech. But even young children have trouble with their "bites," and until the dentist has learned something about their biting habits and their fears about being bitten, he is likely to have trouble in bringing their teeth into sufficient alignment for the job teeth are really supposed to do, which the dentist is likely to call "correcting the bite." Of course the bite may be difficult to correct even after the dentist has learned something about the child's habits, because some of these habits may need to be corrected in order to make dentistry effective. Furthermore it is well known that some older people have trouble keeping fillings in their mouths. This is not always because their teeth have not been well filled. No matter how skillful a dentist may be in restoring the ravages of decay, he wages a losing battle against the chemical composition of the saliva and the actual mechanical strain to which the teeth are subjected. Feelings and habits are factors in influencing, if not entirely controlling, both the chemistry and the mechanical stresses that are constantly present and in operation in the mouth.

A few years ago the first textbook of psychosomatic dentistry was written, and more and more dentists are thinking about teeth as related to personality and behavior rather than merely diet and constitution. But dentists are busy and a friendly conversation is more or less impossible with the patient who is questioned with his mouth held open by a number of tools and the dentist's hands. One reason people don't like dentists is that in the dentist's chair they are deprived of the ability to talk back or even to talk at all.

All this may explain why few dentists, but many doctors, are pestered by patients clamoring for unnecessary appointments. Every physician knows the hypochondriac who can't wait to get to his office for a nice long chat about imaginary, or even real, illnesses. These sufferers, as well as genuinely sick people, can and do talk their heads off to the doctor. This is an experience most dentists are spared.

The uncomfortable position imposed by the techniques of dentistry is not the only reason for this lack of what someone has called *odontophilia* (love of dentistry). Except for the skin, to most people the mouth is the most prized, and except for the genitals, is the most untouchable. It is the baby's most important point of contact with the world—for sucking and eating to keep himself alive, for exploring by putting anything possible into it, for expressing love and hate. As the child grows older, the infantile habits of gratification by mouth may continue, especially if there is emotional disturbance to keep him from growing up.

Sometimes emotional conflict about mouth and teeth results in excessive brushing which can do about as much damage as neglect. Teeth are not a separate part of the body and damaged teeth may cause illness in other parts of the body. When this fact was discovered, some people became too enthusiastic about extraction. It is now known that many damaged teeth can be saved with the aid of good physical and emotional hygiene.

It may be said in brief that the process of teething is much easier for children of parents who understand some of what has just been said. Perhaps more important is the fact that an early return to the state of the toothless babe is not inevitable when people and their dentists think of teeth as integral, not just peripheral, in relation to body and personality and co-operate in treating dental problems psychosomatically.

§ 7

Back to Methuselah

OLD PEOPLE are not only getting more numerous; they are getting healthier. A recent study showed that there are 2,000 men and women in this country over the age of 100 and suffering from no physical infirmities. Senile dementia, senility, arteriosclerosis —the once traditional afflictions of the aged—are becoming less frequent in spite of the ever-increasing number of individuals who would formerly have been expected to contract these ailments. Coronary diseases are cropping up in greater numbers among the segment of the population between twenty and forty, but are declining among the old gaffers from fifty to seventy.

It is perhaps not exactly a coincidence that the new medical problems of old age and an interest in Euthanasia should both have been recent additions to the philosophy of medicine. The activity, usefulness and happiness of people is being extended now with extreme rapidity as time is measured in the history of mankind.

The advances of public health have banished epidemics; medical progress has taught new cures for once deadly diseases; millions are spared to an age when the most successfully buried mines of childhood are likely to explode, to an age when they are susceptible to the chronic and predominantly psychosomatic diseases. This is true of both men and women.

We are nearing the time when the Biblical span of three score years and ten will be too short for the average American. At present, those who reach the age of sixty-five, which is below life expectancy for both sexes, will attain an average age of eighty-one. At the same time, the men and women over sixty-five make up just a trifle more than 7 percent of the population, but they account for 15 percent of the sufferers from chronic diseases. Thus they represent more than twice their proportional share of the nation's medical problem in spite of their increasing robustness.

It is natural that the thought of death should be with them

rather more frequently than it is with their children and grand-children. But the effect when thoughts along these lines become a preoccupation is not materially altered by age. This is a factor which must be taken into account in treatment at every age. Even two-year-olds may have it.

Those in whom illness has exaggerated the habit of brooding about the grave or those whose brooding has contributed to the illness frequently pass through a sort of intermediate stage when they are on the road to recovery. As the disease and thought of death both fade out, the patient is prone to all sorts of folly. As the serious ailment is conquered, they are likely to fall victims to something else through sheer carelessness.

There was one convalescent who improved the moments of regained activity by working in a garden, and deliberately set about pulling up poison ivy around the walls. She knew quite well that she was unusually susceptible to the stuff, and suffered veritable torments as a result.

It is characteristic of these individuals to be careless about ex-posing themselves to infectious diseases, and some of them de-velop an accident habit. In the hidden recesses of their minds is a feeling that they really are not anxious to get well. They are substituting for the disease to which they had been attached another ailment or an injury which represents the last lingering effects of the longing for death or the fear of it. The emotional nature of the secondary illness or injury seems to be established by the fact that those patients who have the danger pointed out to them do not succumb to it. When they are told in the appropriate stage of recovery that they are likely to do crazy things because they do not really want to get well yet, they pull themselves together and refrain from doing the crazy things.

Control, in these cases, has been re-established. The lost head, which has sent the rest of the body dashing recklessly down the road to illness, has been screwed back on and our "headless horse-man" ceases to be a menace to traffic and himself.

[CHAPTER XV]

"Half in Love with...Birth"

§ 1

Changes in Boys and Girls

SINCE the publication of the first edition of this book the focus of attention has been shifting from the cure of illness and post-ponement of death to the preservation of health and bringing new life into the world. Childbearing is no longer taken as a matter of course and the obstetrician is beginning to see him-self as more than a skillful mechanic. Books and articles about psychosomatic gynecology and obstetrics have been added to the literature. So much has been learned that it seemed desirable to devote an additional chapter to this subject.

The first medical text devoted to psychosomatic gynecology was published in 1951. There is still no psychosomatic textbook devoted to urology and the male's role in procreation.

There has been a change in the attitude of boys and girls toward marriage and parenthood as well as toward sex in general. At the same time many "male" and "female" disorders ap-pear to be fading out. For example, the diagnosis chlorosis, which meant the anemia of the pubescent girl, is almost unheard of. Girls today rarely get symptoms when they begin to men-struate, and even more rarely get put to bed, or are told not to exercise during their "sick time." Even the expression "sick time" is fading out, although girls semihumorously still speak of the "curse," or the visit from the aunt.

Boys no longer get pale, wan and worried about their first wet dreams or masturbation. They find it easier to take the female sexual cycle as a matter of course without embarrassment.

It used to be said that 80 percent of normal women were frigid. They were frigid in part because they were not supposed to enjoy sex, but these women, almost talked into being frigid, did not make their husbands happy and had more than the usual troubles in childbearing.

Women who are frigid today in spite of the general change in attitude toward sex have been made frigid in early childhood because of the emotional climate of the homes into which they were born. What they say about this runs somewhat as follows: They admired their fathers, despised their mothers.

§ 2

Changes in Emotional Climate

IT SHOULD not be surprising that the bodily machinery of conception and pregnancy is especially sensitive to emotional conflicts. In the families in which most of us were brought up, the genital organs were the subject of more taboos, warnings, fears and discipline than all the rest of the body put together. When the vagina in girls and the penis in boys is the object of a confusing series of explanations, silences and innuendoes which mix up toilet training with sex education, the function of these organs may become impaired.

The problem of Mrs. T. illustrates the sort of trouble that can lie in wait for the confused child when she grows up. Mrs. T., the mother of two girls and a boy, was afflicted with a wide variety of "female complaints" one after another. At last in her early thirties she consulted a psychoanalyst, mainly because, she said, she was troubled about the behavior of her husband and her son. In the course of the first interview she produced pictures of her three children. The little girls had been photographed in the nude; the boy's head alone was shown. In reply to the analyst's comment, Mrs. T. remarked:

"It's the same way in my dreams. I always see my daughters whole. With my son, I see only the head. His body disgusts me. I feel as if I would vomit when I take him to the bathroom."

"How do you feel about your husband?"

"The same way. It makes me sick to have him undress in my room, and I won't let him come into my room even in his pajamas unless the lights are off."

In the environment in which Mrs. T. had been reared this attitude toward the human body was considered quite correct, even praiseworthy. Carried into the realities of married life, it had upset the normal functioning of her own body, and was having a bad effect upon her little boy, too. Yet Mrs. T. appeared well-adjusted and efficient in her handling of social and family situations. In other areas of her personality she had no trouble. This fact certainly made it easier for her to become aware of her disgust for the male body as a holdover from her conditioning in infancy, not the real judgment of her maturity. Four months after she first showed the pictures of her children to the analyst, her husband called for an appointment.

"I just came to say thank you," Mr. T. explained. "I was always against this psychiatric nonsense, but you have not only cured my wife and son, you have made me a new man."

Women very much like Mrs. T. sometimes have a slightly different but quite unconscious attitude of disgust. They are secretly ashamed of the whole business of pregnancy and childbirth, although they may talk eloquently about the joys of motherhood. These are the women who are most likely to have prolonged spells of nausea and vomiting during their pregnancies. Women who never felt that disgust are relatively free from these discomforts.

Emotional disturbances of this kind may go even further and express themselves in what has been called by some doctors "the abortion habit." It is stated in most textbooks on obstetrics that one out of every four pregnancies ends in spontaneous abortion.

This would mean well over a million such losses a year. Whatever the figures—and abortion statistics are about as reliable as those concerning the common cold—spontaneous abortion is a problem of imposing medical proportions.

The abortion habit seems to be very closely related, emotionally speaking, to the accident habit. Those who have it resemble one another in much the same way, but they are more susceptible to the psychosomatic approach. Where the accident victim does not want to admit any emotional factor as being responsible, the habitual aborter often readily convinces herself that the loss of the baby was due to something in her own mind rather than a fall or fatigue as she first argued. Such women recognize their deep-seated fear or dislike of pregnancy and motherhood. Women who do not have this hidden or deeply buried feeling are not nearly so likely to have a spontaneous abortion, even though they are for the moment very conscious of not wanting this particular child at this particular time.

The nature of the conflict which leads to repeated abortions or miscarriages or stillbirths was brought to light in the case of Mrs. A., who at thirty had had nine pregnancies without a single live birth. The repetition of the disastrous experience had profoundly affected her and her husband. At last she decided that she never would bear a living child unless she could, as she herself expressed it, "figure out why I kill so many babies."

The process of figuring was a difficult one, especially when the real basis of her trouble began to emerge. Suddenly with tears and anger she remembered her father telling her mother that he would not live with a woman who had a baby. Paradoxically she had grown up to hate her mother for having a baby and to despise all women who were mothers. When she married, she could not rid herself of a torturing fear that her husband shared her father's attitude.

It happens more frequently than is realized that children hear comments and exclamations in low or quarreling voices from their parents to this effect. And what is perhaps more important, some husbands really do carry out the threat. What is still more important is that children who have experienced the results of such threats grow up with a fear that something like this may happen to them when they want to become mothers.

Mrs. B's. mother was actually deserted by her husband when Mrs. B. was born. In order to keep this from happening to her, Mrs. B. decided to become pregnant by her fiancé before marriage. But this did no good because he left her as soon as she told him about it. She had to have an illegal abortion about which she felt very guilty. After she was married to another man, one who "at least said" he wanted children, she was unable to carry through a pregnancy. Although obstetricians think that for a young woman to have a miscarriage or an abortion does little harm, certainly it is not as disturbing as for an older woman. This is not always true. Much depends on the reason for the abortion.

Another woman became pregnant by accident before marriage, had an abortion with her fiancé's consent. Later they were married. But it took her ten years after marriage and a long series of abortions to carry through a successful pregnancy and become a mother.

Mrs. A. had another psychological problem which seems fairly common with women who cannot carry a child through the normal term. They confuse pregnancy with elimination. In Mrs. A.'s case, she recalled that her father often had given her enemas when she was little. She had had to hold them in until she felt "stretched," and ever after when anything inside her felt stretched, "I had to get it out." Each of her miscarriages had occurred at a time when her pregnancy was sufficiently advanced that she had the sensation of being stretched.

Against such backgrounds of fear and anxiety, there was small wonder that these apparently healthy women could not have children. The reproduction of the human species turns out not to be a mere mechanical or physiological process, but a function of the mind and feelings too. When husband and wife are at peace together, and each without conflict within himself about parenthood, problems of infertility are not likely to arise.

"Half in Love with . . . Birth"

It used to be said by the family doctor that the less a woman knew about her insides the better off she was. And the bridegroom was told to leave the care of the wife's insides to the doctor. These authoritative statements were often confusing to brides and grooms who were left alone, each to adjust his body to the body of the other. This left the field wide open for misinformation and made a heyday for the old wives by creating a curious and frightened audience for their ghost stories. As was indicated in the first section of this chapter, boys and girls are no longer left so much in the dark about sex and parenthood, and are therefore healthier. But they are still left more or less alone to cope with their lingering childhood nightmares about demons and witches, and the misunderstood fragments of conversations between their fathers and their mothers which had not been meant for their ears. Half truths may be rejected or accepted as whole truths, but in any case they create emotional tension and lead to discord inside, or with those nearest to them. It's no fun not to know how to tell the difference between bad dreams, bad oysters, colic and labor pains.

§ 3

Misconceptions about Conception

STERILITY or infertility is one of the most widespread of medical problems in spite of the apparent contradiction of the census figures. America's rising birth rate has given support to a popular belief that any reasonably healthy young couple can have children if they want to. Actually five million of the country's forty million married women have never borne a child, and only a small minority, it is estimated, are childless from choice. The best statistical surveys indicate that one out of ten couples is sterile or infertile. That would mean about four million couples in our present population.

Several years ago Dr. John Rock of Boston, an eminent authority in the treatment of sterility, estimated that modern psychological and physical methods could correct the condition in one case out of five. Today we might be able to place the figure rather higher, thanks to increased understanding of the psychosomatic factors.

It is important that the Fallopian tubes through which the ovum or egg finds its way to the uterus remain open. For a long time it was thought that only an infection or some other injury could close them. It is now known that there are many ways of producing a muscle spasm in these tubes, just as one may temporarily close a rubber hose by stepping on it. An emotional crisis or shock may close these tubes just as it may make one clench one's fist. If this happens at the time of ovulation, which occurs only once a month, the ovum may die before it has made contact with the sperm cell. Conception will be impossible until the next month, and if again and again the same thing happens, the woman may decide that she has blocked tubes and is therefore sterile.

Young Mrs. R. had such spasms. She had married at twenty, and wanted to start a family right away. After three years, she came to her doctor in great distress. She had read that most couples conceive a child within the first year unless they take contraceptive measures. She also had read that many conditions which cause infertility can be corrected if treated early. So she wanted a complete set of tests. The first test, which was to discover whether or not her tubes were open, showed them closed. She was tested again after ovulation had occurred. The tubes were found to be open. The obvious conclusion was that the muscles contracted involuntarily at the time of ovulation.

It developed that Mrs. R. had acquired in girlhood a considerable anxiety over the dangers and discomforts of pregnancy. This is not unusual in circles where a favorite subject of conversation among older women is "the terrible time poor so-and-so had" in delivery. After Mrs. R. grew up and married, she shrugged off her fears—at least she thought so—and assured her doctor, her husband and herself: "There's nothing I want so much as a baby."

Her involuntary nervous system, because of her buried fear,

contradicted her conscious desire. Some women in these circumstances develop a headache or nausea to last for the brief period of ovulation. They thus avoid intercourse during the only time they can conceive, although they keep repeating their desire for children. Other wives suddenly are "too tired." Still others manage to plan a little trip away from home and husband. Sometimes involuntary muscle spasm temporarily seems all that is needed to prevent conception.

Gynecologists have noticed that frequently their patients become pregnant immediately after taking the test which proves whether or not the tubes are open. This seems to happen as often when the report is negative as when it is positive. The explanation would appear to be that the test itself has removed or relieved the emotional tension which caused sterility. It should be added that in other women the test has been found to aggravate the tension.

Sometimes frigid women bear children reluctantly; sometimes frigid women have difficulty in becoming pregnant. But it should be remembered that a great many non-frigid women are as relatively infertile for other reasons.

For many centuries it was believed that sterility was entirely a female disorder. Any man capable of intercourse was supposed by that fact to be fertile. History is full of barren wives who were put aside or killed or perhaps tolerated by their husbands, but it was seldom supposed that the men had any share in the couple's sterility. At the end of the seventeenth century a major political crisis in England was caused by the fact that King William and Queen Mary had no child to inherit the throne. The monarch still had great power in those days, and the growth of Parliament's authority owed much to this couple's childlessness, for the crown passed to Mary's sister, Anne, an invalid without much personality or intelligence who had to rely upon her ministers. During their lifetime, the childlessness of William and Mary was a matter of much concern to all the statesmen of Europe and therefore was widely commented upon. The wife was young, healthy, vigorous. The husband had been asthmatic all his life, racked with digestive disorders, so neurotic that he was described by his admirers as very uncertain in his temper and generally so frail that for thirty years he was supposed to be at death's door. Furthermore, he never had produced a child by any of his mistresses. Yet not even his bitterest enemies—and he had many —suggested seriously that he might be responsible for the couple's sterility.

In recent years it has been found that childlessness is due to defects in the male quite as often as in the female. Dr. Rock, through whose fertility clinic several thousand apparently sterile couples have passed, finds that in about one-third of his cases both partners are infertile.

As attention was turned to the father as a potential factor in the woman's apparent sterility, the age-old problem of impotence was seen in a new light. It has been known for a long time that physiological treatment of impotence is relatively ineffective, but now the effectiveness of emotional difficulties in impotence is coming to be understood. Impotence may have almost the same emotional background as tubal spasm in the female and is readily cured by alleviation of emotional conflict. It has been discovered also that in spite of the spermatozoa nature supplies to be sure of the fertilization of one ovum, the sperm count is an inadequate basis on which to judge the man's capacity to become a father. It is not the number of sperm cells that is important but their quality and motility. These factors can be influenced in many ways, ranging from infection to fatigue. But in the absence of emotional tension and conflict, physical fatigue appears to make little difference.

For example, there are cases on record where, the sterility having been traced to failure of the husband's sperm, rest and a nourishing diet were prescribed only to find that the men were unable to relax sufficiently for the rest to do them any good. It seems that men, too, can have an emotional fear of parenthood, and sometimes that is translated into faulty spermatogenesis.

The role of the emotions in sterility is well indicated by those married couples who, having despaired of ever producing a child, adopt a baby and almost immediately conceive one of their own. This occurs frequently enough to have been greatly exaggerated. But the fact remains that sometimes the tensions and conflicts which have made it impossible for the couple to conceive are eased by the emotional therapy of a decision to adopt. The easing of the tension may relax the Fallopian tubes or otherwise remove the factors leading to sterility in husband or wife, or both.

§ 4

Life and Death in Conflict

OLD WIVES' tales which have been many young people's sole preparation for parenthood frequently scare the would-be-parents half to death. Yet there need not be the suffering they expect to undergo. Their terror can be relieved, for these common fears are not true: First, that delivery has to be one of the most agonizing of human experiences; second, that it is highly dangerous (more women are killed by slipping in the bathtub than by childbirth); third, that life is over when children grow up and marry. As a matter of fact, more women are coming to appreciate this last point; as a result, apparently, more of them are having children easily. This is good for them and for the children, since in general a feeling for living is a good aid to motherhood. Old wives' tales throughout generations have contributed to the tension of parents-to-be. Today more and more women are entering upon motherhood without dread because they know that they can still be active, useful and attractive throughout the childbearing period and even after their offspring have reached maturity.

However, this is far from the whole story of the emotional factors in pregnancy. Mrs. Z., mentioned in the previous section, illustrated some of them; Mrs. Y. illustrates even more.

After three miscarriages in relatively speedy succession, Mrs. Y. consulted a psychiatrist. She and her husband had been trying for a dozen years or more to have a child. Despite tests of both, which showed that they were normally fertile, the first eight

[265]

years had passed without a pregnancy, and then the miscarriages had followed. In each of them, there were adequate medical reasons on the surface, but the succession was rather unusual in the absence of physiological explanations. On the other hand, the emotional factors were suggestive.

As a girl, Mrs. Y. had disliked and despised her mother and been strongly attached to her father. She resented being a girl, and sought to play a man's part in the world. Her intelligence was in some respects offset by her alternating strong aggressive drive and her weak passive helplessness. Her tendency to feel about a given situation or person in exactly opposite ways had developed inner conflicts which could not be readily resolved. In her early twenties she fell in love with a close friend of her father. She was helping to support her parents, and her lover was not sufficiently successful to take on that burden. Before they were married she became pregnant and decided upon an abortion. Her reasons were more than the usual fear of bearing a child out of wedlock or losing her fiancé's affections. He agreed with her that they did not have enough money to support a child, and they were going to have to travel a great deal after their marriage, so that it would be difficult to make a home.

Mrs. Y.'s father, however, was sternly disapproving. He visited his daughter in the hospital after the operation, which seems to have been performed competently enough, and told her:

"This is a terrible thing; now you probably will never be able to have a child."

Because of her strong emotional ties to her father, this condemnation lingered in Mrs. Y.'s mind. After two years, when she and her husband were able to settle down, they decided they wanted children. That was when they began their visits to physicians to seek treatment that would help them. At the end of eight years, Mrs. Y. had decided that she must be sterile. And then her father died. Almost immediately after that she unexpectedly became pregnant.

Her delight was tempered by several emotional circumstances which neither she nor her husband quite understood. They had been living for years in a sort of triangle situation with her father, and after his death they felt for the first time that they "really belonged to each other." Mr. Y., after his long competition with his father-in-law for his wife's affection, was a little concerned that he would have to start it all over again with a child. Both he and Mrs. Y. hoped it would be a girl because then the new triangle would be easier to bear. However, the prospective mother kept thinking of her baby as a re-creation of her father who would carry on her father's life. In the fifth month of her pregnancy she miscarried. The child had been a boy. Her next was a girl, lost in the sixth month while her obstetrician was on vacation; her next a boy, lost in the fourth month. In all these pregnancies, Mrs. Y. had suffered a good deal from colitis, and nausea.

During the last one she had been attended by both a psychiatrist and an obstetrician. She alternated between feeling fine and depressed. One day she could say: "I feel great; I feel reposeful." A little later: "I kept thinking about how long I would go this time—four months, or six, or seven, or when it would happen to me." Then she and her husband went to a show, and with what might be considered characteristic folly selected a farce which relied for humor in its last act on the difficulty of getting a doctor for a pregnant girl.

"It sent me out into the night shuddering," said Mrs. Y. "I could not bear it. I waited outside while my husband saw it through, and I don't think I have felt *such accumulated animosity* to the whole business of being pregnant at any time in the four months as I did in that fifteen minutes. I cursed everybody, you, and my husband, and the obstetrician, and myself, and every damn fool that is involved in this absurd situation. I could see in all its colors, the stupidity which got me into this third pregnancy in two and a half years, unwilling, unready and unconvinced.

"I walked up and down, and by the time my husband came out of the theatre I hated him. He was desperately sorry that we had gone to the show and he wanted me to reassure him that it had not upset me. It *had* upset me badly, and I was damned if I was going to buck him up. . . . I could have screamed at him and at the whole world for what it doesn't know about the enduring of a pregnancy. I felt that if I opened my mouth at all I'd go all to pieces, so I kept my lips buttoned, did my exercises and crawled into bed."

Two weeks later Mrs. Y. went to the hospital for her third miscarriage. Nevertheless, she wanted to try again at once, but was advised against it until her emotional problems had been cleared up a little better. During this time she suddenly achieved a rather spectacular professional success, exceeding any that either her husband or father had ever managed. She reacted to it with an attack of colitis. She wanted to succeed independently of her husband, with whom she had worked in the past, and of the memory of her father, too.

"Don't you see," she said, "it makes me sick to be better than Father, just as it makes me sick to fail like him."

But she had progressed far enough to understand that there was a way out of this apparent dead end. The way out was to become a person who did not need to identify herself with somebody else. Mrs. Y. commented:

"If this really continues to be a success, then I will be free from Father and from my husband [in an emotional sense, not in the sense of wishing to leave him]. I will be an independent person; then I will be able to have a child."

The psychiatrist agreed, although believing that it would take a year or two before it would be possible to say whether the pattern of unsuccessful pregnancy had been changed. Mrs. Y., however, did not wait so long. Before a year elapsed, she undertook another pregnancy, and decided not to see her obstetrician but only the psychiatric consultant who would in return report to the other physician. Mrs. Y. easily went beyond the time within which her miscarriages had taken place, and she was free both from colitis and panic. She had some disturbing dreams, but was completely well. Toward the end she was thinking more about her husband's reactions than her own.

One day during her eighth month she telephoned the consultant and said, "I have very bad pains. I can scarcely get out of

my bed. I think I ate bad oysters last night, or maybe my colitis
has come back." The consultant suggested that she come to the
office anyway in a taxi—it was only a few blocks—which she
did. Brief examination indicated that the pains were not colic
but uterine contractions and that she was going into labor. This
point is of interest only in that a woman after ten years of experience with the kind of contractions that precede miscarriages
thought this time only of colic or bad oysters. The consultant,
after talking to the obstetrician, sent her to the hospital and she
gave birth to a daughter a few hours later. Although the daughter
weighed only three pounds nine ounces, she developed rapidly,
and both parents adjusted well to parenthood, proud of the fact
that after fifteen years they had managed to produce a child.

"I never understood what you meant when you talked about the
involuntary nervous system and conscious control," Mrs. Y. told
the consultant, "but I remembered it during the labor pains. . . .
I feel sure that I shall carry my next baby for nine months."

The confidence and easing of pain which removal of fear can
achieve can create miracles which have their counterpart in the
as yet inadequately realized damage which fear and lack of
assurance can create in a healthy woman. Too long we have
doubted that fear and apprehension in one or both parents seriously decrease a baby's chances to be born. It is now known that
it is not just a miracle that men and women who have been
helped out of their emotional turmoils succeed at long last in
bearing children. Emotional stimuli may make the difference between life and death for the unborn just as they may make the
difference between life and death in a patient suffering from
spasm of the coronary artery.

The dependence of women upon a favorite obstetrician is
natural, and one of the complaints of many of these specialists is
that there is a perversity about nature which seems to intensify
the birth rate whenever they start out on a vacation. Substitu-
tions are often dangerous, since the mother's fear of a new doctor
is often carried to extremes.

One obstetrician a few years ago decided that he would not

accept any patients whose expected dates of delivery fell within the month he had selected for his holiday. Within the next ten days he was visited by five such patients. One agreed to go to another obstetrician. The other four persuaded the hopeful vacationer to accept them on the promise that they would take another physician for the actual delivery if necessary. All four suffered spontaneous abortions within two weeks, and the fifth a little later. Perhaps this proves nothing, but it is certainly suggestive.

Whether or not fear of losing the physician had anything to do with the spontaneous abortions, we would not need these cases to know that the emotions have much to do with the amount and kind of suffering which a pregnant woman may undergo.

[CHAPTER XVI]

The Compleat Patient

§ 1

"KNOWLEDGE is power," people used to say, especially if they were in the business of dispensing knowledge. But the progress of civilization has outmoded the epigram. Science has given us so many tools to work with nowadays that knowledge is change. The change is so rapid that we have not always learned to use the new tools correctly. The penalty is sickness, sickness in the body politic, sickness in the body individual.

Man's inability to handle the powers which science confers upon him is not confined to such awe-inspiring monsters as atomic energy. Man has difficulty in making the best of relatively simple scientific advances. A great many people have difficulty in adjusting themselves to changing environment, especially if the new one is filled with strange pieces of machinery. A great many of them become patients. The rapid pace of scientific change affects these people emotionally long before it catches up with them physically. But the same science fortunately has provided new techniques to enable them to handle their problems. The psychosomatic techniques of modern medicine help guide them toward the achievement of sound minds in sound bodies by recognizing the fact that a human being consists of mind *and* body, now and forever, one and indivisible.

In our national history, the long struggle for unity gave rise to the warning that this nation cannot exist half slave and half free. The same thing is true of individuals. They cannot exist for very long as slaves to fear, doubt or anxiety and still remain free from illness.

Freedom for the individual, as for the nation, has to be earned. Nobody can give it to you. The physician is as powerless to work this miracle as a great statesman is powerless to confer liberty as a boon upon his or any other people. The physician, like the statesman, can help. He can lead. He can point out pitfalls and dangers, safe roads and sensible procedures. He can encourage and inspire and admonish.

The patient, like the nation, must co-operate. He must do his share by looking clearly at the facts and attempting to correct errors which they reveal. He must be willing to follow advice, and also to disclose all the circumstances surrounding his case, since these are essential to intelligent advice. He must make an effort to understand himself and his problems. This co-operation between patient and physician is the essence of psychosomatic techniques. Most of the people I see, however, either want too much help or no help at all.

"Here I am," the first sort of person says. "I put myself in your hands, and all the rest is up to you. Just make me well."

"Here I am," says the second in a rather different tone of voice. "Let's hear what you have to say, but I can take care of myself. I always have, and a little sickness isn't going to change me."

Neither of these is prepared for any co-operation. Very often the first series of treatments has to be devoted to getting such patients to the point where those in the first group are willing to help themselves and those in the second are willing to let the doctor help them. After a while they begin to have fun talking about themselves; then you can get down to business.

The Compleat Patient

This business, the actual application of psychosomatic techniques, seems rather mysterious to a layman. It has its mysteries for a good many physicians, too. One reason for this is that, because of the very nature of his work, the practitioner of this particular science has no audience. The great surgeon demonstrates his skill in an amphitheatre before admiring crowds of his colleagues and medical students, and the patient will be able to display the scar for years to come. The internist can bring in outsiders to thump his patients and pore over charts. X-ray pictures, photographs and diagrams can give a very intimate view of physiological symptoms of assorted kinds.

The physician who is using psychosomatic methods, on the other hand, is alone with his patient. He gives few demonstrations; he can only talk or write about it afterwards.

The danger of attempting anything else in order to help spread knowledge was brought home forcibly to the staff of a large general hospital some years ago. One of the patients had progressed so far on the road to recovery from a particularly stubborn heart condition that it was thought desirable that there should be a demonstration and explanation in the amphitheatre. His improvement was the result of psychosomatic techniques which were new, almost unheard of to the majority of the hospital staff. A living example, it was urged, would be far more valuable to them and more convincing to possible skeptics than any amount of theoretical talk.

The demonstration was quite a success from this point of view, but on the way upstairs after it was over, the patient died. He had been unable to survive the shock of living over again in a few minutes all the experiences which had brought his disease upon him over a period of years.

Psychosomatic mysteries, therefore, cannot be solved through a simple demonstration in the presence of others by those who have learned something about the problem. This is undoubtedly an obstacle to teaching. It is also a handicap in explaining the subject to the general public.

§ 2

What Every Layman Should Know

IN THE course of his everyday life, the average man and woman will do well not to attempt to analyze his and his friends' movements, motives and possible symptoms in accordance with what he believes may be the latest in psychosomatic techniques. That way lies madness—as well as a crop of quarrels, bitterness and frustrations. On the other hand, there are points which it is helpful for anyone to understand. Perhaps they could be discussed in terms of some of the more popular fallacies about the relationships of emotions and bodily functions.

1. *"The less you think about your mind, the better off you will be."* This just is not true. Of course it is a good plan to stop short of obsession when you are thinking about anything at all, but no one ever understood any subject without thinking about it. The mind is a very important matter and intelligent consideration of what it is and how it works will not be wasted. Failure to devote any thought to it turns it over by default to the mercies of the emotions and the involuntary nervous system. They are admirable in their own place, but they can be unsafe guardians of the mind, as the examples cited in this book have shown.

2. *"Some things in your life you can't tell anybody."* That is a very dangerous thought to hold when you are about to approach someone whose advice you think can help you. This is generally recognized as true when the expert is sought as a guide toward success in business, in a career, in a family problem, even in picking out a new hat. Most people will give all the relevant details in such a case, but get tongue-tied when they are asking for the most important advice of all—advice on restoring or safeguarding health. If the trouble can be remedied by psychosomatic treatment, the attitude of modest reserve is highly misplaced.

The practice of hiding facts which are regarded as shameful, silly or irrelevant would be less dangerous if everyone agreed upon the subjects which ought to be taboo. The taboo would be bad for the patient, but at least the doctor would know where to look. We could work out one of those standard formulae, which so far in this field are impossible to devise. Reticence, however, has no uniformity. One of the most stubborn cases of it I ever encountered was in an Englishman who spoke with an ease approaching abandon about the most secret intimacies of his life, once the barriers were down. Although his views and practices in matters of sex, of family relationships, of business, of friendships poured forth freely and in volume, there was one thing that bothered him about which he could not bring himself to talk. The shame of it had bitten too deeply into his soul. It took time, a lot of time, but at last he was brought to the point where he realized that this special worry was a goodly part of his illness and unless he could get it to the surface we could not deal with it. So, one day, he brought himself to make the terrible revelation.

"My great-grandfather," he said, "was a shopkeeper."

To the physician who is looking for the links between emotional disturbances and physical ailments, no secret ever will be any more shameful or disgusting than this one. He will not even find it ridiculous. The physician is trying to be a healer, not a judge. He probably has heard more startling, more dramatic and more complicated stories than most of his patients have ever experienced or could invent. He is proof against shock; he is professionally reluctant and almost constitutionally unable to repeat the secrets of this medical confessional. But he has to know the facts about a patient's anxieties before he can help in relieving them.

Besides, it does anyone good to get these worries off his chest. To the tubercular, for instance, this means literally getting both the worry and the disease off his chest. And the more intelligent priests know that the chief value of confession lies in the relief after unburdening the soul, not in the penance.

3. *"He's a mental case; how frightful!"* The notion that a mental disease is somehow more disgusting than a physiological one is widely held. People who will talk with gusto and a wealth of gruesome detail about their operations and their fevers will shrink

from confiding to anyone a hint that they might be a little sick mentally or emotionally. This same popular prejudice hampered us —and still does—in combating venereal disease. Medical and public health science could have brought gonorrhea and syphilis under control long ago if the public had not believed that decent people should never mention such horrors, let alone fall victim to them.

The same hush-hush attitude keeps our hospitals filled with mental patients, so that they occupy half the beds today. People who come flying to the doctor with a cut thumb or a mild spring cold in the nose will studiously avoid any mention of mental or emotional symptoms out of a deep sense of shame. They will allow their anxieties to go on gnawing away at their health because in their view a weak stomach is a fit subject for parlor conversation, but an irrational anxiety cannot be mentioned to a doctor in the privacy of his office and under the seal of professional silence. This curiously unintelligent attitude is a product of civilization, like many of our diseases.

Most primitive peoples have believed that the mentally unstable were touched by God. Advancing civilization in the Christian era evolved the theory that they were possessed by the devil. Modern science knows that they are simply sick. Nevertheless, far too large a proportion of our population clings to the medieval conception.

The history of medicine is made up of our conquests over prejudice. Surgeons, in the early stages of their progress, battled against a popular superstition that it was somehow impious to open up a fellow creature and remove a piece of diseased tissue. Then they had to overcome objections to the use of anesthetics by people (usually in no pain themselves) who argued that suffering was the lot of man and the will of God.

Our strides in public-health work have been made in the face and over the bitter protests of ignorance, fear and bigotry. The unthinking acceptance of vaccination today is no more than the unconscious tribute which civilization pays to its pioneers. When George Washington became an enthusiast for inoculation against the small pox, which had pitted his own handsome face in youth, he could muster few followers even at the height of his glory. He had to exert all his remarkable forcefulness and prestige and authority to get the practice adopted in the army which he had just finished leading through his most famous victories, the battles of Trenton and Princeton. Even then, some of his critics attributed the defeats of the next fighting season of 1777 to the godlessness of a general who would presume to interfere with afflictions which a benevolent Deity had seen fit to send His children.

Psychosomatic techniques seem doomed to fight against a longer delay in their development than absolute reason would impose because the fear of discussing mental or emotional problems is almost the last of their popular medical prejudices among an otherwise moderately enlightened citizenry.

4. *"He was perfectly all right until that sudden terrible shock knocked him out."* He only seemed all right, but he had been ill for a long time. The way had been prepared by an accumulation of petty troubles. Usually the wear and tear of constant conflict does the damage without the assistance of a major catastrophe, although some spectacular happening may be the match to the fuse. Just as it is less damaging to the brain to be hit over the head than to have water dripping upon the skull hour after hour and day after day, so the major shock can be borne much more easily than the steady perpetual annoyance of trifles.

I frequently see patients who cannot believe that the silly little things which upset them are worth a doctor's time, or are worthy of their own importance in the scheme of things. If they are honest, they will say they feel like a fool; they feel naked and find it more upsetting at first to have the soul laid bare than to have the body laid bare, although they overcome that feeling when assured that everyone has it. When they are less honest, they will proceed to exaggerate their sins and worries so that they will seem to have a good reason to talk about them. The apparent disproportion between their mental troubles and their bodily ailments bothers them. Actually it is not the magnitude of the anxiety but the severity of the emotional conflict which should be studied and remedied.

A severe conflict is seldom the result of any single cause, but nearly always the outcome of a lot of little things which build up one upon another. In his progress through the vicissitudes of life, every patient is a Gulliver among the Lilliputians. He can laugh at the puny little annoyances or anxieties if he sees them one by one. But enough of them, catching him off guard and concentrating their power, can tie him up in very tight knots.

5. *"The more you talk, the better."* That depends upon what you say and to whom. Every physician knows the patient who turns on a ceaseless flow of chatter without apparent effort. Whether the loquacious one knows it or not, he is usually seeking to fulfill Talleyrand's definition of the use of speech—to conceal thought. The babble is simply a cover for the real anxiety. The physician has to know when to cut it short and bring the patient to the point.

Outside the doctor's office, the danger of unlimited conversation is so great that many physicians command their patients to talk to no one else about their symptoms or fears. Some people find the temptation to pour forth their troubles to their friends is almost irresistible. The dangers in this course are more than the risk of losing a friend by boring him to death. He may actually become interested, and then watch out! For he may have an entirely different idea of right and wrong, and confound the talker with a surprising judgment. Or he may get the patient's troubles mixed up with his own, and manage to distort the problem for both. Or he may take sides, and even if he takes the patient's side, he will not be making objective comments.

On the other hand, the voice can serve as a safety valve for perplexed and anxious people. We use about half our energy in inner living and half in outer living. If the inner pressures become strong enough, the safety valve of chatter may offer some relief temporarily because talking about ourselves really makes us forget ourselves. Many people find that a worry leaves them if they have aired it sufficiently. However, if those who habitually run on about themselves and their problems could reach an understanding of why the inner pressure is so strong, they could cut down on their output of words to the relief not only of themselves but also of their associates.

6. *"You can't break away from your early training."* Frequently people can and do. Frequently the fact that they do not is a contributing factor in illness. "I was just born that way; I can't help it," they say over and over again. Rules and customs which were right for one generation can be wrong for the next. The constricting garments of our grandmothers can be no more damaging to our health today than the constricting ideas of our grandfathers. Recognition of this fact might avert a good deal of human trouble.

In big cities especially, the wear and tear of tradition's dead hand is particularly noticeable in the ailments with which citizens become afflicted after years in the metropolis. The changes are more rapid in the cities; the bewildering tools of science more complex. Living and working among people from all over the world and with all sorts of customs, many otherwise quite cosmopolitan individuals cling to the standards which had governed human behavior on the farms or in the villages where they grew up many miles away and a generation ago.

Even though some of these standards may have been given up by the men and women who stayed at home, these emigrants to the city remain tied to the morals and beliefs of their youth. They may not observe all of the old prohibitions very strictly, but every one of their lapses causes them a good deal of mental anguish. But in spite of their excursions into what they were taught is urban wickedness, they seek an assurance of superior morality. They are exaggeratedly conscious of their own rectitude in the face of the sin all around them, and when their anxieties finally manifest themselves in some form of bodily illness, they will say plaintively:

"I don't deserve to have this happen to me."

Actually, of course, they do deserve it in the sense that they have earned it by their own reluctance to progress. The conflict between the impossible standards of a village childhood and the realities of urban life prove too much for their emotional adjustability. Often very gifted men share this state of mind. As they score new successes in their chosen lines of endeavor, they find themselves thrown more and more into a cosmopolitan society where the religious, ethical and cultural patterns of rural America in the early years of the century are out of place. Whether they are better or worse is beside the point. They can lead to anxieties which are productive of disease. However, as soon as these men discover what is making them sick and interfering with their work, they generally succeed in shifting to more tolerant principles and recover.

Cast in much the same mold are those who persist in a certain line of behavior, saying: "I've always done that" or "My whole family was that way" or simply "I'm just eccentric." Rigidity to them takes on a moral value; flexibility is confused with weakness. But rigidity is often brittle, and those who glory in it may find that their defenses against emotional and physical upsets will snap under very little strain.

Illness can stem in part from rigidity about other people's standards as well as one's own. Parents who refuse to recognize the changing *mores* of the times can be made literally sick by the quite harmless antics of their offspring. Perhaps it is poetic justice that children, who often owe a great many of their troubles to the conduct of their parents, have it in their power to retaliate in this way. But poetry is out of place here, and the cause of true justice was seldom served by increasing the number of neurotics in the world.

Our cases show, in short, that if a man sticks to the old rules which are no longer sanctioned or enforced by the society in which he finds himself, he will be in trouble with his emotions. If he flings them aside, but feels guilty about it, he will be in trouble, too. The solution is to maintain a normal human flexibility, to choose a middle way, or even to let the patient find his own way.

§ 3

Can the Layman Treat Himself?

THE MOST perfectly adjusted person in the world can get sick. Illness, therefore, does not need to send its victim into a tizzy of anxiety over possible emotional complications. On the other hand, a knowledge of the fact that emotional conflicts often are a factor in disease is not sufficient training to justify everyone who has that knowledge in undertaking his own treatment or in prescribing for his friends and relatives. A delicate brain operation may sound quite easy when a master explains it. But the possession of a manual showing how he goes about it along with a sharp knife and a steady hand does not qualify the layman to carve other people's heads. The emotional system is as delicate as the brain, and the same rules of professional ability apply to those who would treat it.

This does not mean that the average individual is helpless unless he can get to the nearest physician. Far from it. The healing which has been the work of faith proves what man can do for himself. Indeed, the practice of Christian Science has been confused by many (although not by Christian Scientists) with psychosomatic techniques. For the belief that illness is error has a calming, healing effect upon the individual. It may prevent or remove a disease symptom which stems from emotional conflict. Such faith gives to many the temporary freedom from symptoms which others achieve by understanding the relations of their own mental disturbances to the bodily ailment.

Psychosomatic treatment usually qualifies the patient to help himself afterwards. He has gained experience of his own emotions and conflicts, and of their influence upon his body. He is in a position then to meet without damage the same life experiences which brought on the original illness. He is in somewhat the same condition as an automobile owner who has watched a mechanic adjust the carburetor a few times. The motorist learns to do it himself after a while. But no one is born with an instinctive knowledge of how to adjust a carburetor, and few who have never seen a car could do it merely after reading a book or listening to a lecture on the subject.

The patient who has reached the point of applying a psychosomatic treatment to himself has had more than relief from the bodily symptoms. He has achieved a cure of the whole man; he has become sound both in mind and body. At the same time, the human organism is a delicate as well as a complicated piece of machinery. It is thrown off balance readily by a large variety of shocks. No one is ever so well that his equilibrium cannot be disturbed. So it is impossible to be sure that he will stay well.

We can only be sure that the person who has acquired an understanding of mind and body will be able to take full advantage of the healing elements which exist in every living thing. One of the advantages of life is that it possesses a quality—which no inanimate object can have—that enables the living being to repair its own damage. The human animal has this quality to a higher degree than any other. It is the quality to which the physiologist Cannon gave the name of homeostasis. It is the ability to regain one's equilibrium after being thrown off balance.

Its importance to maintaining the sound mind in the sound body was demonstrated by an experiment several years ago when two groups of men were kept awake for forty-eight hours. One group was composed of neurotics, the other of more stable individuals. At the end of the forty-eight hours, the ordeal of wakefulness had induced exactly the same changes in blood chemistry in every one of them. But afterwards the neurotics all took much longer to get their chemistry back to normal. This variation in homeostasis is an important factor in achieving a cure of any ailment.

Usually such a cure is a protracted business, as for example in the earlier treatment of allergies by psychoanalysis, which sometimes extended over several years. Nevertheless, there are briefer methods of psychotherapy, and the earlier a patient seeks treatment, the briefer that treatment will be.

Today's psychosomatic patient usually has as his first need a sounding board, and this is one role which no man can act satisfactorily for himself. In many instances, the physician has to say very little to such a patient. Often the doctor is rewarded after a series of sessions in which he has been singularly silent by the patient's grateful cry:

"Doctor, you're a wonderful conversationalist!"

Patients, like a great many other people in this frame of mind, really mean "wonderful listener." Without attempting to argue whether there is any essential difference, it can be affirmed that the gentle but difficult art of listening has immense therapeutic value

The Compleat Patient

because the patient, with the help of a sounding board, may obtain an objective picture of himself and his experiences. Contemplating and discussing that picture, he can make his own diagnosis, and after that he needs only a few casual comments as to what he should do about it. The physician is performing the important but not spectacular role of the practice board which a tennis player uses to perfect his strokes. Over and over again, the ball goes up against the wall, and the player gets back just what he hit. Similarly, the patient's words bounce off the doctor, in a sense, and the patient gets in return just what he gives. The tennis player achieves what the psychologists call an objective realization of the wall, the patient an objective realization of his trouble.

Sometimes the greatest contribution a physician can make is to help the patient put into words the things which are puzzling him. Just as a major responsibility of parents is to help a child express his troubles, wishes and needs, so the doctor must sometimes interpret the patient. Nothing can be more uncomfortable than to be bothered by something and not be able to tell what it is. The physician experienced in psychosomatic treatment can guide just because he does not seek to judge. In fact, he gives less advice than his colleagues in any other sphere of medicine. Skill in this course of treatment can be hard for a practitioner who attempts it late in life. Many who try to apply psychosomatic techniques find that they cannot get over the habit of issuing orders, prescribing pills and preaching sermons.

Once a person is able to talk honestly and freely, the important facts in his underlying difficulty stand out in their true perspective. What at first was just a torrent of words becomes a history of illness. Upon the basis of that history, physician and patient together can work out a program of treatment. By that time they are in the position of two friends sitting beside the stream of the patient's life story as he tells it, dipping out the bits of pertinent debris as they float past—with the physician sometimes directing but never interrupting the flow.

This guidance is particularly essential when a disease has progressed to an advanced stage of organic damage. Then the disturbance involved in a recapitulation of life experience may do more harm than good. Sometimes a more gradual approach will be possible, but in every case—and every case will be different—the amount of strain which is permissible must be weighed carefully.

The psychosomatic technique often has been popularly misrepresented as a prodding process, a digging into the unconscious. The physician is regarded as an archaeologist gleefully uncovering the bones, trinkets, treasures and secrets of the past so that he can expose them in all their pitiful shabbiness. This is a very misleading impression. His real task is rather to remove barriers which keep the patient from saying what he means—or even from saying anything at all. It is sometimes necessary to tell the patient himself to stop digging, for he may be trying too hard to find a fact which he considers important or thrilling. At this point the physician has to explain that the treatment is not a contest of wits but a co-operative assembling of facts which the patient supplies.

On the whole, the physician can judge the results of his treatment in this way: If the bodily symptoms are cured, the job has been fair. If the patient's susceptibility to disease has been decreased also, the job has been good. If the patient furthermore has reached the point of understanding himself, the job has been excellent.

For the achievement of this last, there nearly always must be a period of follow-up after treatment has relieved the symptoms. Unless there has been intensive and prolonged therapy, a check-up every month for a time and then every six months for two years is generally required to put the patient in a position to stay well. These are the cases of which we can, when asked the rather common question "Will it last?" answer "Yes."

These patients will have learned to understand the danger signals.

But if they have not followed this regime, they may not in the first couple of years come back for treatment in time if something goes wrong. They need time for their understanding to grow. Sometimes, discharged as cured, they have developed a feeling of gratitude which will take the form of a fear that they are letting the good doctor down if their old trouble returns. They should be warned against this mistake. Much has been said about patients who cannot get along without the doctor, but these are patients who have not become entirely well. They may feel, quite mistakenly, a little shame on their own account, as though they were in some way inadequate because they have not remained in the pink of health. So they may attempt to wrestle with something that is too strong for them and will come to grief doing it, where the thoroughly cured patient will prudently seek help just as he did before.

Sometimes these still insecure patients will use rather pathetic expedients to meet the doctor socially so that they can get back to treatment by indirection and without exposing their secret shame. They will go to a good deal of trouble to get invited to homes where they know the doctor will appear as a guest. Or they will make an elaborate pretense of asking the doctor to dinner as a friend. This beating around the bush and seeking complicated pretexts for a simple visit can be in itself something of a strain. It is far better for both the patients and the physician if they are followed up at infrequent intervals on a purely professional basis.

§ 4

Perils of Mistaken Identity

A MISTAKE often made by those who are just beginning to understand the psychosomatic approach to themselves and others is that one or even five or six traits which are characteristic of certain disease types may be regarded wrongly as conclusive evidence of the existence or the threat of that disease. Quite a few people are fond of their mothers and have a desire to be independent. Not all of them are necessarily susceptible to ulcers. A lot of chubby, intelligent, ambitious fellows with sensitive natures and strict parents will never develop hypertension.

It is the whole personality that matters, not its parts. In diagnosing an illness, the physician has to be careful not to cut off the patient's feet to make him fit some procrustean bed of preconceived ideas. There is danger that an inexperienced layman might lop off a few limbs in the personality, never knowing that they were there, in order to fit himself or a friend into a supposedly healthy pattern of thought.

On the other hand, everyone can learn to recognize a few danger signals. Laymen frequently ask for one which is psychically the equivalent of running a temperature as a somatic danger signal. There is such an easily recognizable warning flag for the approaching emotional collision. Watch for a characteristic in yourself which you do not like. It probably is a symptom of your trouble, and if the trait is one which really bothers you a good deal, it is time to talk to a doctor. A keen dissatisfaction with one part of your personality probably means that it is in conflict with the rest.

In this conflict, the characteristics you like and those you dislike sometimes take on genuinely parental proportions. The ones you like suggest the good parents; the ones you don't suggest the bad parents.

People who come to understand their conditioned reflexes and immature tendencies, as a parent would understand a child, succeed with relative ease in achieving a unified personality. Patients who become irritated with the characteristics which are not in harmony with their ideal of themselves are likely to achieve amputation instead of education of that part of the personality. The way out is to treat yourself the way a good, intelligent modern parent treats a child.

Two men, superficially quite different from each other but as much brothers under the skin as Judy O'Grady and the Colonel's Lady, seem to illustrate this point. For purposes of this comparison they will be called Mr. Alpha and Mr. Omega.

Alpha was middle-aged, bored, spoiled, several times married but only once happily, master of large and varied business enterprises which failed signally to interest him. At one of his first interviews the physician summed him up accurately but perhaps a bit unkindly as "typical thumb-sucking son of the ultra-rich."

The Compleat Patient

Alpha regarded himself as a failure. Even the world-shaking catastrophe of global war had not disturbed the even, dull tenor of his ways, and he felt that he had been something of a slacker while a much envied brother had marched off to war, winning a certain amount of honor and glory by fighting on the Pentagon Front in the Battle of Washington.

Omega on the other hand was a young man who was now unemployed but had become a war hero. He was still in his twenties, proud of the incident which had distinguished him but quite unable to adjust himself emotionally to civilian life. It developed that he had not been very well adjusted to it before he entered the army, either. His childhood and youth had been marred by skin troubles, and he had the emotional history which accompanies that kind of allergy. When he was four years old, his mother had died while away from the family on a vacation, and Omega had never forgiven her for leaving him. He grew into the habit of thinking of her death as a desertion, and had hated all women as a result. His eczema entered his life for the first time that he could remember just after his mother died. He resented being laughed at, but his family—father and two sisters—had ridiculed him a good deal. He had been married recently, but the experiment was a crashing failure almost from the start. Not only were the couple without common interest, but Omega found the girl sexually repulsive to him. They signed a separation agreement less than five months after the wedding.

Neither Alpha nor Omega was suffering from any particular organic disease when they consulted a physician. But each recognized in himself a profound emotional disturbance. Alpha thought that his stemmed from dissatisfaction with his humdrum record while others were fighting a war for him. Omega had no doubts about the quality of his war contribution—he was sure it had been distinguished—but he thought himself emotionally unready to take a job, so he had none.

As the cases were studied, each man was found to be mistaken about himself. Actually Alpha's heroism had been more genuine if less spectacular. He had remained in a dull job which he hated so that the family enterprises could play their part in winning the war and so that his brother could enter the Army. The importance of the work which the business and the brother actually performed is beside the point. Alpha had made a very real sacrifice in sticking to the routine, and he had suffered for it. His resentment rose at times to fury, but he always repressed it, and that was at the root of his bodily discomforts.

Omega's brilliant war achievement became mere folly when it was carefully analyzed. As he explained it at first, he had a mission to perform and he hoped to find a friend who was missing. His men hung back, saying that the ground ahead of them was obviously mined and should be swept before they entered it. Omega brushed these objections aside and led the way. A few minutes later a mine explosion halted the whole party. The mission was not performed; the friend was not found, and Omega lost his left leg.

At his first two interviews with the physician, he calmly denied that he had ever been exposed to any particularly severe shocks. His artificial leg was so well fitted and he used it so expertly that it was not until he was leaving that the physician noticed it at all. Finally, on his third visit, he told the story and admitted that perhaps an amputation is something of a shock. At later sessions he confessed also that the reasons he gave for insisting on the advance over mined territory were only partly true. He always wanted to run his own show his own way and, as he now recognized, was always rushing ahead without much reflection.

So, as their treatment progressed, Alpha discovered that he was not quite the slacker he had supposed, while Omega learned that he had been much less of a hero than many of his associates believed. It is obvious why this should benefit the stay-at-home. To a physician trained in the study of the mind, Omega's relief is equally obvious. The saying that the truth will set you free is not confined to pleasant truths.

Both men were able to deal with their troubles, once they had identified those troubles accurately. Alpha, having talked more than he ever dreamed he could and more than his wife expected that he would, saw his apparently aimless existence in its true light. He was also able to cope with his sexual difficulties to an extent. He could not keep away from the current Mrs. Alpha, but he got sick whenever they were together. Affairs with other women did not offer a satisfactory substitute. The memory of the one wife with whom he had been happy but who had died young could not help his present marriage. In fact the obtrusive way in which he cherished the memory of his beloved—even to the point of keeping her ashes in an urn in the nuptial bedchamber—had led Mrs. Alpha to contemplate divorce.

Treatment enabled the husband to see and correct his mistakes instead of glossing over them. He did not get so far as to regard himself a prince, but he grew to like himself better and so to understand his troubles. For the first time in many months, he was able to report normal and reasonably satisfactory relations with his wife. The divorce idea was abandoned. The Alphas were on their way to the creation of a moderately happy and healthy home life.

Omega, too, began to return to mental and emotional health through understanding that his troubles did not begin with his release from the Army. He realized that even in peacetime he had never been able to submit to the authority of teachers and employers, just as in the Army he could not stand the domination of his colonel. He had been in difficulties whenever he had to work under someone else, yet his men said that when he did run his own show it wound up in disaster, as witness the experience in the mined field. His marriage, a hasty war romance, had been embarked upon with characteristic lack of reflection.

It was also in keeping with the emotional pattern of his kind that when Omega finally took a job, he sought one far below his real capacities, with long hours and a dull routine. Incidentally, his personality and previous history of accidents, all on the left side—broken arm twice, broken foot once, many bruising falls—led the physician to warn him that he was accident-prone. Sure enough, he had one in the machine shop where he was employed. The injury was slight, but Omega said the drill would have gone clean through his hand, he was sure, if the doctor's warning had not made him alert.

When the treatment of these patients is described, it always sounds easy. Anyone can listen, it is said, and most people can talk. But a great deal of training and experience are necessary before a physician can handle the Alphas and Omegas of this world successfully. No two patients are alike. There is no formula for psychosomatic treatment which can be applied. Each case must be treated on its individual merits and needs. The amateur who attempts it will probably do both himself and his victim more harm than good.

§ 5

Sex and the Patient

NEXT TO the reluctance to talk about a mental disease as naturally as a bodily ailment, the chief reticence of most people is sex. When Freud first propounded his theories, the popular outcry against him was based on the prominence he gave to a subject which his critics preferred to pretend did not exist.

We know now that oceans of human misery have been caused by stubborn and stupid silence about one of the most important of human functions. There remains, however, a notion that the psychiatrists and the psychoanalysts place a highly exaggerated value upon the rôle played by sex in illness of all kinds. It may be worth while, therefore, to attempt an objective appraisal of the share which sex actually takes.

The healthy human being, the one with a sound mind in a sound body, is well adjusted in every way. That means he is well adjusted sexually, too. The sick person, whose physical soundness and mental soundness are so often impaired together, obviously is not so well adjusted. It is no more surprising to find that his sexual attitudes and relationships are unsatisfactory than it is to find him running a temperature or having difficulty with his digestive apparatus.

The trouble is that the fever and the upset stomach strike most people as quite normal features of illness, but they think that sex is not. If they were to look upon the sick person's sex problems as equally natural, which of course they are, surprise would vanish. After all, sex is a quite universal quality, as common as appetite or breathing or the circulation of the blood. Emotionally it is even more important, because of the fact that one or more other people are involved, whereas every man is pretty much alone with his digestion or his circulation. These last will have only an indirect even if powerful effect upon others. Society is also concerned in the individual's sex problems in a way which does not hold true of eating or breathing. For better or for worse, society has made rigid rules about sex.

Therefore, when an emotional conflict has reached such an advanced stage that it has helped to bring on an organic disease, the fact that the individual's sexual adjustment is affected does not alarm the physician. In fact if it were otherwise, he would be as suspicious as if he had a patient with malaria who never ran a temperature.

Of course sex is more than a thermometer, more than an indication of something wrong. It is one of the basic human impulses and will have tremendous force as long as the race is to survive. It is perhaps the strongest impulse next to hunger—and there is some argument as to which takes precedence. A patient whose sexual adjustment was unaffected by a psychosomatic disease extending back into his childhood would be one of the wildest freaks of nature.

Almost every generation and every stage of civilization has been amazed by their predecessors' attitudes toward sex. Yet all of them have had one thing in common. The careless promiscuity of animals has always been frowned upon, although you might not think so to hear one moralist talk about the code of another. Primitive peoples generally have been rather frank if somewhat mysterious in their approach to sex. Their simple recognition of its power and their wonder over its consequences led them to make it an important part of their mystical rites and ceremonies. Their practices survived in curious forms and symbols in some newer religions.

In the development of European civilization, periods of outspoken acceptance of sexual impulses have alternated with periods of repression. The Renaissance, for instance, carried a certain amount of sexual freedom with it as it spread slowly over Europe. The freedom consisted largely in recognizing sex as a natural function which might be mentioned without shame. Beginning with the Reformation, a more secretive approach replaced the casual acceptance of sex. For a long time, the standards for the prominent were more tolerant than those for common people. But at last the notion that sex is somehow not nice took firm hold upon the Western world. We are only beginning to get clear of it.

In recent years we have made some strides in the understanding of the medical problems of sex, so that frigidity in women and impotence in men are decreasing. But parents and teachers still all too frequently attempt to hide the realities of sex from children. They act as though they believed that if no one ever mentioned the horrid word, it would somehow go away. Yet even the most primitive bigot who ever tried to bar all forms of sex education from the schools knows that the division of mankind into two sexes is likely to be a permanent arrangement. The very fact that so little is said authoritatively to youth about such an important subject is a factor in the emotional diseases into which so many flounder. Physicians, therefore, must evaluate sex in the proportion that it plays in the make-up of the patient as he exists in his cultural setting.

The cultural factors in sex are clearly seen in the development of what was once regarded as a spontaneous feminine desire to be male. Early psychoanalysts gave this urge the succinct name of "penis envy" and thought that it was one of the things which distinguished one sex from the other. Actually, however, males and females may be equally and similarly shocked by the first discovery of their anatomical differences. Penis envy is unlikely to arise unless the society in which the child lives has set some specific value on possession of the male or female organ.

It would be just as logical to speak of "vagina envy" in those men who have a castration complex because they may want to bear children and would prefer to be mothers rather than fathers. A little boy may develop that complex when he first sees a girl's vagina, especially after an adult has told him that his penis will be cut off if he plays with it or even touches it. The changing values of recent years have been inadequately recognized in psychoanalytical literature, although Freud did before he died. For in fact, penis envy is not a spontaneous reaction. Much more truly spontaneous was the remark of a little girl who, seeing her baby brother in the nude for the first time, said optimistically, "Isn't it lucky that he hasn't got that on his face," or of another girl who said, "Oh, it must hurt very much. Can't we put something on and make it go away?" The girl thought the penis was a boil. Such expressions are a response to anatomic observations which may be good or bad, but the infant is usually unaware of the difference. To the child the difference is an anomaly. Having a penis looks strange and possibly sick to the girls and the opposite is true for the boy. It is the cultural evaluation which then creates the difficulties. "Envy" in either sex is unlikely to start, unless the society in which the child lives, has set some special value upon the possession of the male or female organ.

§ 6

Whither Are We Drifting?

THE DEVELOPMENT of the psychosomatic approach to medical problems is being carried on by specialists of all kinds. The eventual goal is to bridge the gap between scientific knowledge of mind and of body. Construction in the form of research and observation is going on on both sides.

More studies of physical reactions and behavior patterns as they react upon each other, more study of danger signals such as blood pressure bring the bridge ever nearer to the point where medical traffic will be able to move back and forth across it with ease and dispatch. Additional knowledge of blood chemistry may reveal some secrets of emotional effects upon bodily functions.

Another fruitful source of knowledge involves changes which occur in antibodies, those fascinating little friends of man which act as germ killers in the body.

However, today too many patients are still too slow in consulting their physicians and are admitted to hospitals too late. In one general hospital it was observed that one out of every three admitted arrived only in time to die or to be transferred to an institution for chronic invalids; another one of the three was too late for successful treatment. In the same period, nine out of ten patients seen in the clinics recovered completely. It is self-evident that clinic patients are encountered by the doctor at an earlier stage of disease. At least for the time being, the problem is to teach people how to avoid a recurrence of an old illness and to escape falling victim to a new one, and to teach their physicians how to teach them.

The trend of psychosomatic techniques will be toward the prevention of disease. Already it is obvious that early treatment by the methods now known can save a good many patients from becoming chronic invalids, can endow the longer life which science has given us with a proportionate measure of good health.

Once the preventive aspects of the psychosomatic techniques have been established, a more fundamental step can be taken. Some day there will be courses in high school devoted to psychosomatic studies just as today there are courses in physiology and hygiene. Children will be taught how to mind their bodies, and their bodies will learn to mind them—that is, stay well. This is the challenge of preventive medicine today.

When that time comes, the teachers will find that they will have to mingle the new with the old. They will take the concept of the sound mind in the sound body from the Romans. But they will go back even further for some of the ways to achieve it. They will recall that it was Hippocrates who observed that the physician only applies the splint; nature heals the broken bone. They will explain that since the mind and body are one and indivisible, the same principle holds true in healing the breaks in human emotional fabric. They will teach that your mind is your body and vice versa.

And that is the meaning of psychosomatic medicine.

Index

Index

Index

Index